Gender and Archaeology

Gender and Archaeology

Edited by Rita P. Wright

PENN

University of Pennsylvania Press

Philadelphia

Published by
University of Pennsylvania Press
Philadelphia, Pennsylvania   19104–6097

Library of Congress Cataloging-in-Publication Data
Gender and archaeology / Rita P. Wright, editor.
    p.   cm.
    Includes bibliographical references and index.
    ISBN 0-8122-3339-5 (cloth : alk. paper). — ISBN 0-8122-1574-5 (pbk. : alk. paper)
    1. Women, Prehistoric.   2. Women—History.   3. Civilization, Ancient.   4. Gender
identity—Research.   5. Sex role—Research.   6. Feminist archaeology.   I. Wright,
Rita P.
GN799.W66G45   1996
305.4′09′01—dc20   96-25802
                                                                        CIP

Contents

III. Gender and Representation

IV. Gender and Practice

Figures

Tables

Preface

The inspiration for this book was a colloquium and seminar series that I organized at New York University in 1991 which was sponsored by a New York University Curriculum Improvement Grant. It was in the context of that project that I first met several of the contributors to this volume. Since each participant made two presentations, one in a public forum in which she discussed her recent research on gender, and a second that focused on the teaching and practice of archaeology, I heard firsthand the several ways in which gender studies were being integrated into their research and teaching. It was based upon those talks that I began to envision this volume.

Two aspects of the talks and seminars stood out. First, the strong ties between research, teaching, and practice were clearly apparent. They seemed particularly relevant to gender studies, since scholars were exploring all three topics, yet few public forums existed in which the relationships among them were being cultivated. Second, I was impressed by the variability of theoretical and methodological approaches each of the scholars was developing. This variability defied the slotting of any one of them into a single paradigm. Clearly influenced by post-processual critiques, none seemed to fit into the narrowly conceptualized definitions of either "postprocessualism" or "processualism" that had surfaced as a significant point of discussion among archaeologists.

It was with these considerations in mind that I approached the participants and two others about contributing to a volume that would address the research, teaching, and practice of archaeology and in the case of two contributors to discuss the relevance of their gender studies in other fields to archaeology. I am indebted to these authors for enthusiastically embracing the idea and preparing essays specifically earmarked for this book. I also thank them for their good humor and general adherence to deadlines and other logistical matters. Few projects could be more gratifying, from my perspective, since I have learned from each of them.

Many colleagues also shared their expertise with me. Annette Weiner initially suggested that I organize the gender colloquiums. I thank her for her advice and support in that endeavor. Virginia Kerns shared a fund of knowledge and contextualized gender in the history of anthropology for me. Patricia Lynch helped me understand the intricacies of small-scale industries, women's place in global economies, and aspects of the practice side of anthropology. Michelle Marcus and Alison Wylie read the entire manuscript; their generous and incisive critiques were invaluable to me and the other contributors. Two reviewers also provided substantive commentary.

Our editor at the University of Pennsylvania Press, Patricia Smith, was most responsible for the expeditious publication of the book. Her patience and encouragement are gratefully appreciated. My thanks also to Nancy Liebowitz, Christine Kimbrough, and Kim Arndts, who prepared the index.

Many friends and family generously assisted me and offered encouragement. I especially want to thank Lynn deBeer, John Dacey, Jean Freebern, and Bill Potts. Not the least, I thank my parents, Margaret and Joseph Corsi, for their support, and my daughters, Susan Wright and Kara Woods, for their encouragement and interest in my research. That the central topic of this book is gender makes its completion all the more satisfying.

RITA WRIGHT
New York University

Introduction: Gendered Ways of Knowing in Archaeology

Rita P. Wright

> Although the past
> Seems to be level in its place there's room for more
> And the ragged additions polish the previous days.
> —Douglas Crase, *The Revisionist* (8)

It is just over a decade since Margaret Conkey and Janet Spector (1984) called attention to the dearth of systematic work on the study of gender in archaeology. Yet within that short period gender research has profoundly changed the way we think about people in the past, and there now is a sizable and growing literature on the topic.

Part of the impetus for this book—and a goal that draws together the works of the scholars represented here—is to demonstrate the many ways in which feminist scholars are changing archaeological agendas. These agendas include the substantial revision of our understandings of gender-related issues in the past and the introduction of new questions not previously asked of archaeological materials. I suggest that as archaeologists begin to set their "own theoretical and contextually appropriate agenda(s)," as Yoffee and Sherratt have proposed (1993:8), the archaeologies of gender represented in this volume and in the already substantial literature on the topic will be in the forefront of the new agendas archaeologists will embrace.

Archaeologies of Gender

While it is not my intention here to review the history of the last ten years of research on gender in archaeology, since there are many excellent reviews that have documented its progress (see for example, Claassen 1992; Conkey 1993; Conkey and Gero 1991; Wylie 1991, 1993), I raise some points to historically contextualize the contributions in this volume.

Why the interest in gender in archaeology now? Postprocessual critiques have been a strong influence, affecting archaeology in two ways. First, there has been a growing awareness among social scientists of their place in the creation of global histories, through works such as Benedict Anderson's *Imagined Communities* (1991); and in archaeology, more specifically, Mark Leone's (1982) exposure of nationalist tendencies in archaeological interpretation has precipitated a questioning of other subjective aspects of our work. For feminist scholars, this has raised the question "If there is a nationalist bias, then are there other socially informed biases?"

A second way in which postprocessualism has affected the introduction of gender studies in archaeology is a more general willingness among archaeologists today to engage in self-criticism than in the past. As George Cowgill (1993) has pointed out, archaeologists have learned a lot during the past thirty years, and they now stand ready to defend some aspects of processualism while at the same time accepting some "highly appropriate criticisms." Further, he suggests that important concepts have been "neglected by main streams of processual thought that need far more emphasis" and that in certain instances, there have been problematic views that have impeded archaeological research (ibid.: 551).

Although not singled out by Cowgill, gender clearly is one such concept. Archaeologists have made many assumptions about gender that have gone unexamined. These include, but are not limited to, unspoken assumptions about the biological bases for divisions of labor between the sexes, status, and roles, in spite of the availability of substantial research (for example, Fausto-Sterling 1985) that examines these issues. Further, in their assignment of specific tasks to women, archaeologists frequently have ignored productive activities associated with women in our own culture (weaving, cooking, and other "domestic" activities, for example). These "feminine technologies" (see the contribution of Judith McGaw in this volume for an extended definition) have not been subjected to social analysis because archaeologists have thought they were theoretically uninteresting and of no significance to the major transformations in the past.[1] Here, I am not suggesting that today's feminine technologies necessarily were those with which women in the past were engaged, but rather that our modern conceptions about them have affected our research agendas and we have tended to ignore them.

Notwithstanding the historical connection between postprocessual critiques and archaeologies of gender, feminist scholars, or those engaged in gender research in archaeology, should not be "tagged" as postprocessualists. The essays in this volume will show that, while these scholars take postprocessual critiques seriously, they embrace a broad range of theoretical and methodological positions, not encompassed by any single *ism.* They include, for example, structuralists, marxists, reproductive ecologists, and scholars interested in the political economy.

A major premise of the book is that there is no single "archaeology of gender" but many "archaeolog*ies* of gender" (Conkey 1991, 1993). To that end, I have selected authors who employ a variety of theoretical and methodological frameworks to explore this diversity in a single volume. Moreover, as researchers in many geographical and cultural areas, they bring to gender studies a variety of research agendas from their scholarly communities. Since the exploration of gender issues in archaeology has lagged far behind that in related disciplines (for example, history, history of technology, social anthropology, biological anthropology), I believe it is essential that this diversity be explored and nurtured. Highlighting the many theories, methods, data, teachings, and practices that contribute to our knowledge of gender in the past will allow archaeologies of gender to be perceived as central to the archaeological enterprise. In that sense, the diversity represented here is not a distraction but one that contributes to an understanding of the many ways in which an engendered archaeology must be approached. Each aspect of interpretation (teaching, field practice, research) has ramifications on all others.

Each scholar contributes to an expanding body of revisionist scholarship on gender, which, all together, they advance in three important areas of research. First, they integrate gender into the central questions with which archaeologists traditionally have been concerned, rather than conceiving of gender as a separate area of study. Second, they introduce new questions not previously asked of archaeological materials and establish agendas for future research. Third, they consider feminist pedagogy as an essential aspect of an engendered approach in teaching archaeology, mentoring students, and in field practice. Although no one of the essays addresses all of these issues, together they form a comprehensive and mutually reinforcing body of analysis that establishes future directions for an engendered approach to archaeological research.

Gendered Ways of Knowing in Archaeology

The contributors to this volume are established voices in feminist approaches to gender topics. Two, Gillian Bentley, a reproductive ecologist, and Judith McGaw, a historian of technology, are not archaeologists. They are included here to familiarize archaeologists with the varied and thought-provoking literature available to scholars with interests in gender. Indeed, they are relevant even to archaeologists disengaged from gender research. As Alison Wylie has proposed, "the new research on gender in archaeology could have no better model" than the feminist literature on gender in closely aligned fields (Wylie 1993:x). In fact, our failure to include gender as an analytical category in archaeological research has been all the more remarkable given that the major contributions to women's studies and feminist theory have been made by other historians and by our colleagues in other subfields of anthropology. Four contributors, Elizabeth Brumfiel, Cathy Costin, Rosemary Joyce, and I, discuss research topics that focus on the dynamics of state domination and peasant resistance, the practices of leaders in manipulating social identity, the effectiveness of states in the social reproduction of gender differences, and power relations among craft producers in state and nonstate societies. Our principal contributions are in investigating the creation of gender and class differences between men and women and among women. These essays both challenge and affirm more general anthropological discussions, those less well informed by archaeological evidence, on the restructuring of gender relations as key to the centralization and institutionalization of state power. Four other contributors, Margaret Conkey, Joan Gero, Janet Romanowicz (along with me), and Ruth Tringham, work toward rethinking methodological and pedagogical issues in the context of field practices, teaching archaeology, and mentoring students. While the preceding essays explicitly address theoretical and methodological models and attempt to expand our data base, they also establish how the science of archaeology constructs the models and data bases on which it depends. Addressing these issues builds on earlier discussions of androcentrism and bias; here the authors attempt to locate the roots of differences and conceptions about science. In that sense, feminist pedagogies and field practices are about how our knowledge of gender in the past is "made" and transmitted to others.

Taken together, the revisions presented here are positioned at a strategic crossroads of knowledge. The contributions these works make to several major areas of research include the following:

1. New methodological and theoretical issues are introduced from the field of reproductive ecology and the history of technology. Bentley's discussion of reproductive ecology and her considerations of paleodemography and demography bear explicit reference to interpretations of demographic shifts in archaeological contexts.

McGaw's conceptualizations of feminine technologies and society's relationship to them similarly have direct relevance to discussions of technologies in archaeology, where their social aspects have been neglected.

2. The theories, methods, and data bases utilized in five of the chapters focus explicitly on state level societies. At the same time that they contribute to our general understanding of states, they establish models that may be utilized by scholars working in nonstate-level societies as well. Further, while several chapters rely on archaeological and documentary evidence, their "strategies" of inquiry may be applied to cultures in deeper prehistory. The two chapters on gender and production rely on concepts introduced by McGaw, here and elsewhere (for example, McGaw 1989).

3. For many archaeologists, the classroom, the field, and the public media are the first places in which they encounter archaeological evidence. Gero's examination of basic field practices and knowledge production in the context of excavations at a Paleo-Indian site inspects the practice of science and the material circumstances that "underlie the creation of a 'fact.'" Her contribution is complemented by two chapters on the teaching of archaeology. Conkey and Tringham discuss the strengths and weaknesses of an explicitly feminist pedagogy in the context of course offerings in prehistoric art, archaeology of the goddess, and European prehistory. My essay with Romanowicz similarly examines a variety of research topics that can be brought to an engendered perspective in the classroom. Here, our concern is that instructors not simply "add women and stir," but that they engage in self-critical analysis using gender in the past as a focus, while at the same time encouraging students to develop skills with which to evaluate current interpretations of gender both in the classroom and in public presentations. The recording procedures discussed in Gero's essay on field practice and observations by Conkey, Tringham, Romanowicz, and me on feminist pedagogy, the teaching of archaeology, and the mentoring of students in the field and in the classroom should be of relevance to archaeologists with a variety of research interests, academic and nonacademic alike. A central premise is that teaching and fieldwork are knowledge-producing acts that also must be investigated. Finally, these chapters bear a close connection to McGaw's discussion of public perceptions of technologies and her challenge to archaeologists to reexamine their assumptions about both technology and gender since doing so requires a similar self-critical appraisal of the ways we think about and do science.

The book is organized into four parts: "Gender, Reproduction, and Feminine Technologies"; "Gender and Production"; "Gender and Representation"; and "Gender and Practice."

Part I: Gender, Reproduction, and Feminine Technologies

The two chapters in Part I examine gender issues that have received little attention in archaeology in spite of their relevance to major processes in archaeological analyses. Chapter 1, on reproductive ecology, explicitly addresses issues relevant to sexual divisions of labor, changes in population levels, and Malthusian models frequently invoked by archaeologists. Chapter 2, similarly, deals with a topic of long-standing interest to archaeologists, but one that has restricted itself to a narrower view of technology than that proposed by McGaw in the chapter. Here, the social significance of technology is emphasized.

In Chapter 1, "How Did Prehistoric Women Bear 'Man the Hunter'?" Gillian Bentley brings data from reproductive ecology to bear upon questions of fertility reconstruction, demography, and paleodemography. Reproductive ecology is the study of ecological factors that affect fertility, such as diseases, nutritional status, and work load.

In her essay, Bentley adopts a comparative and longitudinal perspective, cautioning archaeologists to look beyond the simple equation of higher fertility rates as causal factors in the interpretation of paleodemographic and demographic trends. To that end, she provides a balanced discussion of the basic biological parameters of fertility and reproduction, including nonenvironmental factors, such as infant and child morbidity and mortality, weaning foods, and nutritional improvements, and she touches upon topics of contraception, abortion, and infanticide.

Bentley presents a broad range of biological data. First, she discusses results of her ethnographic studies of women in foraging and agricultural societies, drawing on data from a variety of cultural groups. Her focus is on reproductive patterns, such as interbirth intervals, lactational practices, nutritional status, energetics, disease load as well as fertility rates, disease factors, and other demographic issues. Second, she proposes ways in which archaeologists may combine skeletal and other analyses to recover similar information in archaeological contexts. Here, she introduces a variety of bioarchaeological, ecological, paleobotanical, and zooarchaeological evidence that complements the results of her ethnographically based data. Finally, she carefully outlines the variables that would affect each factor and systematically introduces forms of evidence that might be utilized.

Bentley's analyses and data provide an important new resource for archaeologists whose research focuses on transitions from mobile to sedentary societies, shifts from horticultural to agricultural societies, or other circumstances in which levels of physical stress on women might affect their reproductive potential. As an archaeologist-turned-biological anthropologist, Bentley is uniquely qualified to adopt the approach taken in her essay.

In Chapter 2, "Reconceiving Technology: Why Feminine Technologies Matter," Judith McGaw, a historian of technology, establishes the critical nature of technologies associated with women. Her central thesis is that studying feminine technology reveals crucial aspects of technology's functions and social significance that are generally missing from traditional technological history, which, as is the case in archaeology, has concentrated on the study of technologies associated with men. Study of feminine technology especially raises questions about the relative importance of technology's knowledge and hardware components, the poor fit between technology and the biological, and the manner in which public/private social distinctions shape technology.

In her chapter, McGaw focuses on several modern, Western technologies: the brassiere, the closet, the white collar (and the laundress who stood behind it), and the toilet (water closet!). First, she demystifies technology by establishing a definition far more inclusive than the machinery/high-tech definitions that skew study toward "masculine" technique. Second, she demonstrates how the study of clothing and household technology reveals the enormous range of women's technological creativity. She also reveals how problematic the whole notion of "progress" becomes when the social aspects of technologies are investigated.

McGaw establishes two points of critical value to archaeologists. In contrast to the standard approach in archaeology, where technology is viewed as an "adaptive" mechanism and a heavy emphasis is placed on its power "over" humans, she treats technology as integral to its social system. She also uses her case studies to reveal many of the cultural assumptions that lead scholars to exclude feminine technologies from consideration, a point directly applicable to archaeology, where technologies such as cooking and weaving have been excluded from the complex of innovations that contributed to human prehistorical development. When technology is conceived as a social phenomenon and is comprehended in gendered terms as McGaw advocates in her essay, archaeologists have a powerful tool with which to understand the relationship between technology and a variety of social phenomena. Her essay complements discussions of technology and the empowerment or disempowerment of women in the following section.

Part II: Gender and Production

The essays in Part II discuss issues related to craft production. One provides an example of the production and use of cloth in a specific historical context. A second examines a variety of methodological issues that pertain to gender attribution in craft production.

In Chapter 3, "Technology, Gender, and Class: Worlds of Difference in Ur III Mesopotamia," I develop some of the issues raised by McGaw using archaeological and documentary sources from the Ur III period in Mesopotamia. Its focus is on the production and use of cloth as a "feminine" technology and cloth as a cultural means of conveying status and role.

In the essay, I concentrate on the social behaviors associated with technologies when people use and create materials and on the effects of state policies on women. My central point is that in Mesopotamia, weaving and cloth were positioned at the center of gender, class, and ethnic differences. These differences were most pronounced, but not limited to, women producers of textiles and those who wore and used high quality cloth. In Chapter 3, I use imagery principally on seals to highlight the symbolic power of cloth in early Mesopotamia, especially when worn by women in occupations associated with temple and palace functions. Their status and role are contrasted to the women producers of cloth who, in spite of (perhaps because of) the importance of cloth in Mesopotamian society, were a relatively impoverished group. In an attempt to reconstruct the circumstances of their existence, I focus on technology as a means of teasing out how labor was organized in the weaver's workshops in which they worked, the production methods used in making cloth and the technical knowledge possessed by women producers, and the various state policies that effectively controlled textile production and women who produced cloth. The ultimate effect of these policies was that, while cloth became a visible carrier of culture, its producers received little recognition and were themselves "invisible."

The essay contributes to the general prehistory of the region by demonstrating the importance of women in the production and use of cloth and textiles. It also establishes the effects of gender, class, and ethnic differences among women and men in one of the first state-level societies in human history.

In Chapter 4, "Exploring the Relationship between Gender and Craft in Complex Societies," Cathy Costin uses archaeological, textual, and ethnographic data in a discussion of methodological and theoretical issues of gender attribution. While she acknowledges that there may be circumstances in which gender attribution is less critical, she argues that in craft production it may be essential to identify gender participation, since certain activities empower or disempower individuals and groups. Costin argues that craft production is an activity in which gender-based differences can lead to gendered differences in social participation, wealth, and legitimization. Specialization, especially in complex societies but in others as well, creates social networks beyond the resident and household groups that are materially and ideologically connected to a variety of power hierarchies.

In her chapter, she assesses the relative strengths and weaknesses of three types of data—archaeological (figurative representation and mortuary data), textual information, and ethnographic—that may be utilized to model and explain the structure of the gendered division of labor in complex societies. A problematic aspect of these data is that they commonly reflect normative or idealized views of gender roles. She suggests that once archaeologists recognize this limitation, they can frame their research questions in ways that explicitly recognize the nature and function of norms and ideals within societies. Costin provides an extensive analysis of ethnographic evidence and pairs that with ethnohistoric data in the context of pre-Inka and Inka state sociopolitics.

Costin illustrates these points by drawing on evidence from a wide spectrum of societies, including Aztec, Maya, Inka, classical Greek, Aegean, and Bronze Age and Neolithic European evidence. In addition, she provides an extensive example of cloth production and gender in the Inka Empire. In her essay, she draws on archaeological evidence from the Upper Mantaro Valley and on complementary ethnographic and ethnohistoric data. Her principal focus is on changes that occurred when the Inka conquered other highland societies and the ways in which gendered divisions of labor were manipulated to conform to prevailing gender ideologies, a theme related to my essay in Chapter 3.

Part III: Gender and Representation

The two chapters in the section on gender and representation illustrate the ways in which the analysis of different types of media may be incorporated into wider questions of social relations between rulers and kinship groups. These topics are central to the traditional concerns of archaeologists. Moreover, the authors' culturally based analyses of art as a representation of images of gender inequality and/or complementarity are a challenge to essentialist interpretations of images as reflections of obesity, sexuality, fertility, or goddess cults.

In Chapter 5, "Figurines and the Aztec State: Testing the Effectiveness of Ideological Domination," Elizabeth Brumfiel discusses epistemological issues that pertain to coercion and ideological dominance in

Late Postclassic central Mexico and the influence of the Aztec state. Brumfiel's central thesis is that peasant or nonelite groups adopt strategies with which to resist state-level intervention and that the existence of different groups of prehistoric social actors, such as peasant, elite, or nonelite groups, can sometimes be identified through the differing images of reality they produce. She examines ceramic figurines depicting women as a medium for understanding the dynamics of state formation and reactions of acquiescence and resistance.

Brumfiel contrasts official and popular imagery of females. The images of women presented by ceramic figurines recovered from peasant households in the Aztec hinterlands differ significantly from the images of women presented in media such as sculpture and manuscript painting, produced in the Aztec capital, Tenochtitlan. The figurines emphasize women's fertility, while the sculptures and painted manuscripts depict mutilated or androgynous women, or emphasize women as producers of cloth and food. Thus, the portrayal of women in different social contexts can be contrasted. These differences, then, reflect the existence of potentially opposing gender ideologies held by different groups of social actors within Aztec society.

The existence of a distinctive image of women in Aztec peasant households indicates that peasant groups in Aztec society were able to maintain their own definition of reality, despite efforts by the ruling elite to dominate ideology. These distinctive images suggest that ideological domination had not occurred and that coercion was the key to Aztec dominance. Thus Brumfiel challenges previous views of Aztec peasant groups and the roles played by women in resisting state domination and contributes to a more general understanding of state-level dominance and development.

In Chapter 6, "The Construction of Gender in Classic Maya Monuments," Rosemary Joyce examines images on Maya monuments and the strategies employed by elites as a cultural means of responding to and shaping the conditions of social existence in some Classic Maya polities. Her central thesis is that Maya elites actively used imagery on monuments to define gender identity. The depictions of male and female costumes and spatial placement established symbolic codes that emphasized the political importance of women as members of significant genealogical groups and in specific productive activities. These activities were performed in collaboration with important men (husbands or sons). Thus the images served an ideology in which male and female identities in ritual action were complementary in establishing genealogical relationships and claims to leadership and ritual power.

In her chapter, Joyce establishes a symbolic vocabulary in which sequences of action are viewed in the representation of a single moment.

Taking this diachronic perspective, she outlines the multiplicity of texts that can be conveyed by establishing these metonymic links. Together, they embody the interplay of elite status, genealogical relations, productive activities, and dimensions of social differentiation. It is Joyce's contention that the actions, objects, and costumes represented are the embodiment of culturally defined forms. She directly challenges essentialist views of gender status, role, and power by problematizing them in the context of specific historical moments.

Part IV: Gender and Practice

The essays in the section on gender and practice discuss teaching engendered courses, feminist pedagogy, and field practices. Each raises provocative questions about knowledge production in archaeology and reflects back on some of the research discussed in preceding chapters.[2]

In Chapter 7, "Gendered Perspectives in the Classroom," Janet Romanowicz and I discuss some practical considerations in the implementation of courses in which gender issues are either a central focus or one aspect of broader course content.

Two types of courses are discussed. One provides suggestions for including gender issues at introductory levels; a second is an upper-division/graduate course dedicated to gender issues in archaeology. In addition, we discuss ways in which courses on gender issues in archaeology can be incorporated into departmental and college or university-wide curricula. We draw on the essays in this book, discussions with other archaeologists, several of whom are contributors to this volume, and materials from published sources. Our major premise is that archaeologists must transmit a more balanced view of the role of gender in early human societies, ideologies, economic systems, and political structures in their reconstructions of the past and in their classrooms. By communicating this knowledge in programs designed for undergraduates, as well as in upper-division and graduate courses, archaeologists can help students develop critical skills with which to evaluate presentations of gender (and by extension, other forms of social difference) in the past and in contemporary popular media.

In Chapter 8, "Cultivating Thinking/Challenging Authority," Margaret Conkey and Ruth Tringham discuss and define a concept of feminist pedagogy in archaeology. Drawing on recent works by Jane Tompkins and others, they examine the attributes of a feminist pedagogy based on their experiences teaching several courses in which they implemented new approaches, formats, and styles. Although their examples are designed for the teaching of archaeology, they are of general relevance to all interpretations of gender in the past.

Conkey and Tringham are concerned with two aspects of feminist pedagogy. First, they discuss how to implement a feminist pedagogy in the teaching of archaeology, whether the course is one of the standard offerings, such as "European Prehistory," or a topic that is somewhat experimental, such as "Archaeology and the Goddess." They argue for a "coaching" model of teaching that is more participatory than a "performance" model, and they discuss some of the specific aspects of archaeology that render it a challenge and yet particularly amenable to a feminist approach. They present specific examples of different formats, organizations, and requirements in four of their courses: "Archaeology and the Goddess," "Archaeology and Prehistory of Europe," "Mediterranean Archaeology," and "Prehistoric Art."

This chapter establishes an important area of concern to a gendered way of knowing in archaeology. Work relationships, specializations, and divisions of labor frequently are the basis on which women and feminist archaeology are excluded from domains of research. Their success in implementing the coaching model demonstrates the wider implications of a feminist archaeology.

In Chapter 9, "Archaeological Practice and Gendered Encounters with Field Data," Joan Gero addresses work relationships, specializations, and divisions of labor within the context of a broader critique of archaeological methods and the cultural politics of knowledge accumulation. Her central thesis is that values of the scholarly community are reflected in how archaeological work is carried out, what work is carried out, and ways in which its results are interpreted. Further, knowledge of the past is entrenched in everyday, unquestioned practices; in the accepted use of specific instruments; and in the carefully inculcated technical abilities taught and expected of practitioners.

To demonstrate how cultural politics works "on the ground," Gero provides an example from her observations of field practice at the Paleo-Indian site of Arroyo Seco in Argentina. In it, she focuses on "gender in practice," especially the acquisition of skills and validation of research styles.

Beyond the specific issues addressed in these chapters, there are a number of themes that crosscut individual contributions. These themes have an impact on several methodological and theoretical issues and provide a rich resource for archaeologists with interests in gender and in more general applications.

Crosscutting Themes

The authors introduce a rich array of textual, ethnographic, ethnohistoric, and biological data and forge new ways in which to employy them in conjunction with archaeological evidence. In the case of ethno-graphic data, each author establishes plausible methodologies by intro-ducing innovative ways in which to utilize either specific ethnographies or cross-cultural analyses in archaeological contexts. These include the use of ethnographic data combined with concepts from reproductive ecology (Bentley) for assessments of work-load stress and fertility in ar-chaeological contexts, cross-cultural data from the Human Relations Area Files (HRAF) for questions of gender attribution and craft produc-tion (Costin), regionally based evidence to document shared concepts of gender complementarity (Joyce) over broadly defined cultural areas, and an ethnographic account (Gero) of archaeological field practices. Other critiques of ethnography underlie the course content in the chap-ters by Conkey and Tringham and Romanowicz and Wright.

The use of textual sources, either as translated from cultural docu-ments or ethnohistorical accounts, also are examined and utilized in conjunction with archaeological data. In some cases they are combined with ethnographic materials. Documentary sources are crucial to the research of Brumfiel, Costin, Joyce, McGaw, and Wright, but each em-ploys them in different ways. Brumfiel's approach is regional and "tests" diverging interpretations of ethnohistoric accounts against archaeologi-cal evidence, while Costin examines diachronic shifts in divisions of labor and craft production in the context of sociopolitical change. Joyce utilizes texts in conjunction with image in an examination of Maya monuments to demonstrate important tensions between the messages conveyed through each medium, while I combine an analysis of images on seals with archival data from a single period in early Mesopotamian history. McGaw's contribution, especially her discussion of closets and cupboards is diachronic. She traces the development of the "technology of filing" and demonstrates the variety of ways in which historical in-ventories, linguistic history, and material culture can be effectively com-bined. Janet Romanowicz and I also provide examples of ways in which documentary and archaeological evidence can be used as complemen-tary forms of evidence in classroom contexts.

A second theme is the intertwined nature of women's bodies, repro-duction, and cultural constructs. These factors are either explicitly ad-dressed or underlie the analyses of many of the chapters. Bentley, for example, examines women's unique biological potential as contrasted with social imperatives such as contraception, abortion, or infanticide. Brumfiel, Costin, and Wright address the close relationship between human reproduction and state policies. The exploration of feminine technologies, especially McGaw's discussion of the brassiere, graphically demonstrates the wide range of creativity and social choice exercised by women in their encounters with technologies associated with their bodies. At the same time, McGaw demonstrates how cultural concepts can become biological givens. Still, women are not the only recipients of culture's claims, since concepts of female and femininity rely on their polar opposites, male and masculinity. Two of the chapters (Costin, Wright) explore how states come to have a stake in manipulating prevailing ideas about appropriate masculine behavior.

At the same time that women's bodies and reproduction represent natural phenomena, these attributes, when represented in art and craft, are imbued with cultural meanings and are subject to social conventions. While in twentieth-century contexts breasts are contoured to follow changes in fashion (McGaw), it is the bare breast that is most prominent in the representations of women known in many prehistoric contexts. Women's images, modeled in stone or clay, are known throughout human history, but in prehistoric contexts, figurine imagery are a dominant mode of expression that has survived the archaeological record and they provide an important resource in gender studies. Brumfiel's use of popular and official Aztec images in figurine and sculptural depictions of women as contrastive devices demonstrates differences between the gender ideology of elites and commoners. Conkey and Tringham challenge the "goddess literature" in their courses by examining the faulty logic and absence of evidence behind essentialist arguments that pair women with nature (or the natural) and ancient matriarchies.

But the human body is subject to adornment, and, in the process, the imagery of women's bodies becomes "humanized" so that their bodily characteristics may be suppressed or enhanced to represent or encode natural and essential human behavior. Cloth figures prominently in these chapters. Rosemary Joyce and I view cloth as a potential signifier of status and role that conveys important concepts about gender and kinship (Joyce).

A third theme that crosscuts several of the chapters is a critique of science. McGaw addresses the faulty assumptions behind interpretive frameworks with respect to technology, while in a different vein Gero questions the basic practices behind data acquisition and recording in archaeology. Similar issues underlie Conkey and Tringham's discussion of feminist pedagogy and the structuring of the panels they propose for teaching a variety of courses, especially their focus on the role of speculation in archaeology and the evaluation of inferences from existing archaeological interpretations.

Closely related to a feminist pedagogy and the critique of science is style of discourse. Conkey and Tringham raise important questions about the types of dialogue that traditionally are used in classrooms and in scholarship. Even the very act of discussing teaching methodology as Conkey and Tringham and Romanowicz and I have done breaks new ground. Their experimentation with different formats for teaching are at "the intersection of feminist thinking, archaeology, and pedagogy" (Conkey and Tringham). Although the courses they propose cover very different ground and are taught in different formats, these scholars advocate the use of mediative styles of discourse, rather than the "straw man" or more contentious form common to most classrooms. This viewpoint is very much in line with Gero's suggestion that field methodologies should implement more inclusive and embracing cognitive values. Although styles of discourse are not discussed by the other authors, their essays illustrate a kind of "respectful engagement" (Wylie, personal communication) with their data and the interpretations of other archaeologists, which is no less incisive in its critique of other works than a more contentious approach. Thus one aspect of a feminist agenda in archaeology, exemplified by the essays in this volume, is a more open-ended and relational style of discourse that promotes productive and fruitful exchange. None of the authors is suggesting that the styles of discourse implied by a feminist pedagogy are possessed exclusively by females; quite the opposite, feminist pedagogy argues against built-in, innate, natural states of gender constructs.

From a theoretical perspective, the essays here make important contributions to both gender and general anthropological theory. Several of them draw on feminist theory in anthropology. While these theories provide a framework for analysis, they are reconceptualized to follow agendas in archaeological research and evidence from specific historical contexts. Thus, the theoretical constructs are stretched and elaborated upon. A very strong influence in several of the essays (Brumfiel, Costin, Joyce, Wright) are the works of Christine Ward Gailey (1987), Rayna Rapp (1978), and Irene Silverblatt (1987), and the proposition that state or elite policies are central to gender constructs. Still, these authors explore the plasticity of gender constructs in different domains, especially as developed out of elite administrative needs and those of nonelites. For example, Brumfiel demonstrates that gender parallelism prevailed outside of administrative structures, even though Aztec state ideology disparaged female gender. Joyce, Costin, and I similarly emphasize the internal differentiation of gender (and class) and the establishment of gender hierarchy either through the direct control of women producers (Costin and Wright), elite women in ritual display (Joyce and Wright), and women in high ranking kinship groups (Joyce). In sum, the authors contribute to feminist theory in anthropology by providing more fine-grained accounts that reveal the social, political, economic, and ideological complexity involved in the institutionalization of gender differences.

A significant contribution to theory is based upon drawing on scholarship from outside of anthropology. The contribution of McGaw, a historian of technology, provides one example of the important theoretical sources that have gone largely untapped in archaeology. She speaks directly to archaeologists, since technology has been at the forefront of archaeological research programs from its inception. The utility of rethinking technology as a social phenomenon and as intertwined with gender is demonstrated in my contribution on gender and cloth in Mesopotamia and in Costin's on the Inka. Similarly, Joyce draws from outside of archaeology on the works of Barthes (1977a, b, c) as a model for examining the multiplicity of narratives in imagery and text in Maya monumental sculpture. Bentley's discussion of reproductive ecology, also from fields outside of archaeology, adds a new and untapped dimension for archaeologists to employ in their future research, especially where skeletal remains are present.

Conclusion

Three decades ago archaeologists, under the influence of cultural ecology and general systems theory, drew on a range of interdisciplinary techniques with which to reconstruct the environment and subsistence systems, and in this book, contributors similarly have cast a wide net. In a variety of ways, they represent a kind of watershed in gender studies. Both in the data they discuss and the reformulation of basic theoretical premises, they have established new ways of approaching standard topics and materials, either by drawing on knowledge developed in other fields or rethinking basic assumptions. Using gender as a central focus, these new approaches include the potential use of data from the field of reproductive ecology, rethinking of conceptions about technology, implementation of cross-cultural analysis and complementary data sets, examination of relationships between states and women's production and social identities, feminist pedagogies, and the field practices behind our knowledge base.

Together, the contributors provide an enriched and seasoned approach to the archaeologies of gender. Through the investigation of either a specific prehistoric/historic time and place or the practices that contribute to the accumulation of data and their interpretation, each focuses on gender as a central problematic in understanding human societies. The questions they ask are fundamental to any reasonable social analysis and they establish a strong voice both for revisions within archaeology and for the wider field of feminist scholarship.

Notes

1. Rosaldo and Lamphere (1974) made a similar point over two decades ago for anthropology, more generally. A review of the literature on women and gender relations should alleviate any uncertainty about the importance of considering gender in social analyses (for example, Rogers 1978; Sacks 1979; Weiner 1976; Kerns and Brown 1992; Leacock 1983; Silverblatt 1988; Sutton 1993, to name a few).

2. The essays in Part IV complement articles in three recent publications on gender and archaeological practices: Claassen 1994; du Cros and Smith 1993; and Nelson, Nelson, and Wylie 1994).

References

Anderson, Benedict
    1991   *Imagined Communities: Reflections on the Origin and Spread of Nationalism.* New York: Verso.
Barthes, Roland
    1977a   "Diderot, Brecht, Eisenstein." In *Image-Music-Text,* translated by S. Heath, 69–78. New York: Noonday Press.
    1977b   "Introduction to the Structural Analysis of Narratives." In *Image-Music-Text,* translated by S. Heath, 79–124. New York: Noonday Press.
    1977c   "Rhetoric of the Image." In *Image-Music-Text,* translated by S. Heath, 32–51. New York: Noonday Press.
Claassen, Cheryl, ed.
    1992   *Exploring Gender through Archaeology: Selected Papers from the 1991 Boone Conference.* Madison, Wis.: Prehistory Press.
    1994   *Women in Archaeology.* Philadelphia: University of Pennsylvania Press.
Conkey, Margaret W.
    1991   "Does It Make a Difference? Feminist Thinking and Archaeologies of Gender." In *The Archaeology of Gender,* edited by Dale Walde and Noreen D. Willows, 24–33. Calgary: Archaeological Association of the University of Calgary.
    1993   "Making the Connections: Feminist Theory and Archaeologies of Gender." In *Women in Archaeology: A Feminist Critique,* edited by H. du Cros and L. Smith, 3–15. Canberra: Australian National University.
Conkey, Margaret W., and J. M. Gero
    1991   "Tensions, Pluralities, and Engendering Archaeology: An Introduction to Women and Prehistory." In *Engendering Archaeology: Women and Prehistory,* edited by Joan M. Gero and Margaret W. Conkey, 3–30. Oxford: Basil Blackwell.
Conkey, Margaret W., and Janet D. Spector
    1984   "Archaeology and the Study of Gender." In *Advances in Archaeological Method and Theory,* edited by M. Schiffer, 7:1–38. New York: Academic Press.
Cowgill, George
    1993   "Distinguished Lecture in Archaeology: Beyond Criticizing New Archaeology." *American Anthropologist* 95 (September): 551–73.
Crase, Douglas
    1971   *The Revisionist.* Boston: Little, Brown.

du Cros, Hilary, and Laurajane Smith, eds.
  1993   *Women in Archaeology: A Feminist Critique.* Canberra: Australian National University.
Fausto-Sterling, Anne
  1985   *Myths of Gender: Biological Theories about Women and Men.* New York: Basic Books.
Gailey, Christine Ward
  1987   *Kinship to Kingship: Gender Hierarchy and State Formation in the Tongan Islands.* Austin: University of Texas Press.
Kerns, Virginia, and Judith K. Brown
  1992   *In Her Prime: New Views of Middle-Aged Women.* Urbana: University of Illinois Press.
Leacock, Eleanor
  1983   "Interpreting the Origins of Gender Inequality: Conceptual and Historical Problems." *Dialectical Anthropology* 7:263:284.
Leone, Mark P.
  1982   "Some Opinions about Reconstructing Mind." *American Antiquity* 47 (1): 742–60.
McGaw, Judith
  1989   "No Passive Victims, No Separate Spheres: A Feminist Perspective on Technology's History." In *History and the History of Technology: Essays in Honor of Melvin Kranzberg,* edited by Stephen N. Cutliffe and Robert C. Post, 172–91. Bethlehem, Pa.: Lehigh University Press.
Nelson, Margaret C., S. M. Nelson, and A. Wylie
  1994   *Equity Issues for Women in Archeology.* Washington, D.C.: Archeological Papers of the American Anthropological Association, no. 5.
Rapp, Rayna
  1978   "The Search for Origins: Unraveling the Threads of Gender Hierarchy." *Critique of Anthropology* 3:5–24.
Rogers, Susan C.
  1978   "Women's Place: A Critical Review of Anthropological Theory." *Comparative Studies in Society and History* 20 (1): 123–62.
Rosaldo, Michelle Zimbalist, and Louise Lamphere, eds.
  1974   *Woman, Culture and Society.* Stanford, Calif.: Stanford University Press.
Sacks, Karen
  1979   "State Bias and Women's Status." *American Anthropologist* 78 (3): 565–69.
Silverblatt, Irene
  1987   *Moon, Sun and Witches: Gender Ideologies and Class in Inca and Colonial Peru.* Princeton, N.J.: Princeton University Press.
  1988   "Women in States." *Annual Review of Anthropology* 17: 427–60.
Sutton, Constance, ed.
  1993   *From Labrador to Samoa: The Theory and Practice of Eleanor Burke Leacock.* Washington, D.C.: Feminist Anthropology and American Anthropological Association.
Weiner, Annette
  1976   *Women of Value, Men of Renown: New Perspectives in Trobriand Exchange.* Austin: University of Texas Press.
  1989   "Why Cloth? Wealth, Gender and Power in Oceania." In *Cloth and Human Experience,* edited by A. B. Weiner and J. Schneider, 33–72. Washington, D.C.: Smithsonian Institution Press.

Wylie, Alison
    1991   "Gender Theory and the Archaeological Record: Why Is There No Archaeology of Gender?" In *Engendering Archaeology: Women and Prehistory,* edited by Joan M. Gero and Margaret W. Conkey, 31–54. Oxford: Basil Blackwell.
    1993   "Gender Archaeology/Feminist Archaeology." In *A Gendered Past,* edited by W. A. Bacus et al. University of Michigan, Technical Report No. 25: vii–xiii.
Yoffee, Norman, and A. Sherratt
    1993   *Archaeological Theory: Who Sets the Agenda?* Cambridge: Cambridge University Press.

Part I
Gender, Reproduction, and Feminine Technologies

Chapter 1
How Did Prehistoric Women Bear "Man the Hunter"? Reconstructing Fertility from the Archaeological Record

Gillian R. Bentley

Introduction

While there has been a growing literature in the archaeology of gender in recent years, little has been written on the topic of women and
reproduction in prehistory.[1] There are, perhaps, three reasons for this
lacuna. First, reconstructing fertility from the archaeological record is
a difficult endeavor,[2] one which we admittedly will never be able to
achieve with any certainty. This caveat, however, applies to many other
well-researched areas in archaeology. Second, a full consideration of
fertility requires a degree of biological knowledge that may be difficult
for archaeologists to acquire in addition to their own specialties. Third,
archaeological studies of gender (many of which have been explicitly
feminist in orientation) have shied away from what might be considered the more traditional domain of women—reproduction—to focus
instead on the productive elements of womens' lives (see essays in Claassen 1992; Gero and Conkey 1991). We should not deny, however, that
the reproductive roles and responsibilities of women have been both
critical and, in most cases I suspect, unavoidable; that is before the advent of effective contraceptives and the social acceptance of women as
viable contributors outside the domestic domain.

Furthermore, in ignoring reproductive aspects of women's lives, I
believe we continue the pervasive paradigm dominant in our own culture, as well as in many others, that devalues women in spite of, and
sometimes because of, their critical reproductive roles in childbearing
and nurturing. (Ironically, Conkey and Gero [1991] have pointed out

how women's labor [or *production*] has been systematically devalued or ignored in archaeological and other literatures). Rather, by drawing more attention to reproduction and particularly those biological aspects that are solely feminine, we acknowledge the unique roles that women play without degrading them in comparison to males.

The study of reproduction within archaeology is, moreover, crucial if we are to understand aspects of women's lives that are inextricably tied to this function, as well as other social characteristics of archaeological communities. The following outlines just some of the areas that can be affected by differential reproduction and fertility.

1. The sexual division of labor is often dependent on a woman's reproductive status. For example, it is argued that in most hunting and gathering groups, with the exception of the Agta (Estioko-Griffin and Griffin 1981) and Tiwi (Goodale 1971), women do not hunt because this activity is incompatible with childbearing and child rearing (Brown 1970; Watson and Kennedy 1991). Possibly then, many technologies associated with prehistoric groups that are accessible to archaeological study—such as the manufacture of hunting tools—may in most cases be correctly interpreted as the exclusive domain of males (see Conkey 1991:76; Gero 1991).
2. In many societies, females that are either premenarcheal or postmenopausal are able to participate in social activities and enter social spaces otherwise denied to women of reproductive age (e.g., Kerns and Brown 1992). Such distinctions could affect archaeological interpretations of how spaces may have been used.
3. Family size, which is dependent on female fertility among other aspects, may also determine household structure and architectural design, both of which are accessible for archaeological reconstruction. High status families, which can be identified in the archaeological record through differential house sizes and residential areas, as well as household and burial contents, are often characterized by high fertility (Betzig 1986; Irons 1979). This may be due to several reasons: there may be multiple wives, or multiple caretakers that promote higher fertility for individual women, there may also be better nutrition and health that enhance fertility and fecundity, and lower infant and child morbidity and mortality.

It is clear from these examples that, if we have more details about levels of fertility in specific archaeological communities, we can have a much more informed basis from which to draw inferences in related social domains. The study of reproduction is also important from the macroperspective, particularly in relation to changes in population levels. Such changes are caused by one of three demographic variables: fertility, mortality, or migration. Given the preponderance of burial data at archaeological sites, as well as the numerous indicators of population movements (such as changes in various artifacts and styles), it is not surprising that archaeologists have tended to focus on the latter two variables. They have, however, routinely discussed whether fertility may have changed during subsistence transitions such as the development of agriculture, and what fertility levels may have been like for foraging versus agricultural groups. Yet, in all this, a specific discussion of women's roles in reproduction has been missing.

Some of the problems that have been traditionally associated with archaeological reconstructions of fertility may now be aided by emerging fields in anthropology, as well as by combining a variety of existing archaeological approaches. One of the most instructive developing fields in anthropology is reproductive ecology, which examines ecological factors affecting fertility such as diseases, nutritional status, and work loads (Ellison 1991). This field also allows one to focus more on *individual* fertility. Using this approach, several recent studies of reproduction have been made among noncontracepting, contemporary foraging, horticultural, and agricultural groups that can be used instructively for comparison with prehistoric groups. Such comparisons do require, however, a parallel knowledge of the health and nutritional status of the latter. Concerning the combination of existing archaeological approaches, bioarchaeology offers the best possibility for reconstructing prehistoric fertility accurately. All these approaches are discussed in further detail below.

In this essay then, I begin with a brief historical overview of how archaeologists have traditionally approached reproduction from the macroperspective, and how this underwent change through the 1970s and 1980s. I then move on to discuss how we might, in contrast, obtain a more detailed *micro*perspective on fertility in the archaeological record by employing a variety of methods drawn from demography and paleodemography. In the next section, I outline the specific utility of reproductive ecology for the archaeological reconstruction of prehistoric fertility, and how this might be used in conjunction with bioarchaeological methodologies. Finally, I briefly discuss the contentious issues of abortion, contraception, and infanticide, in as much as these are important and possibly archaeologically invisible checks on reproduction that have been discussed in many relevant publications. My goal in these endeavors, as stated above, is to introduce ways through which female fertility may be reconstructed in archaeological settings, with the understanding that such reconstructions illuminate many other social aspects of prehistoric groups. In addition, given the title, this essay is biased toward discussing fertility among hunting and gathering groups, and how this might be contrasted with agricultural societies.

Historical Perspectives on Fertility Reconstructions

Archaeological thinking about fertility has generally focused on periods of cultural change. In particular, the relationship between population change and crucial technological transitions, such as those between the major subsistence life-styles of foraging, horticulture, and agriculture, have attracted a great deal of attention. While there were some dissenting voices (e.g., Denham 1974; Nag 1968), until the 1980s paleodemography was based on Malthusian assumptions; namely, prehistoric populations were thought to be characterized by high levels of fertility and mortality (e.g., Birdsell 1968; Carr-Saunders 1922; Divale 1972; Dumond 1975; Hayden 1972; Krzywicki 1934; Polgar 1972).[3] Where natural checks on fertility were too low, it was generally believed that population levels were controlled by cultural practices such as infanticide and abortion. These were considered to be especially important among hunting and gathering populations since this subsistence mode and the carrying capacity of the environment dictated low population numbers. For example, Birdsell (1968) suggested a 15 to 50 percent rate of infanticide among Pleistocene foraging groups based on genealogical data from Australian aborigines and early postcontact ethnological observations. In general, however, the fertility patterns of different subsistence groups in prehistory were thought to be similar—both foragers and farmers had high (and uncontrolled) fertility. What limited population growth, however, were mortality checks. Agriculturalists, with their ability to produce and store food, were considered able to support higher densities of populations (Dumond 1975; Hassan 1973), leading to a relaxation of Malthusian checks on fertility with subsequent increases in population numbers (e.g., Acsádi and Nemeskéri 1970:215).

These models began to undergo radical changes in the 1970s with the publication of ethnographic and demographic data for the Dobe !Kung San of the Kalahari Desert. The data for this foraging group were more detailed and interdisciplinary than those produced for almost any other anthropological population (e.g., Lee and DeVore 1976; Lee 1979; Howell 1979). Rather than supporting the established high fertility/mortality paradigm, what emerged from the Harvard Kalahari project was a picture of a hunting and gathering group with low fertility and mortality characterized by a total fertility rate (TFR)[4] of only 4.7, and negligible rates of abortion and infanticide (Howell 1979). The high quality of research undertaken with the !Kung resulted in a very compelling demographic picture. They were a foraging society in which women's gathered produce provided most of the caloric intake (70 percent) for the group, particularly from the nutritious mongongo nut, but at the expense of an arduous gathering routine. Lee (1979:310–12) estimated that !Kung women walked an average 2,400 kilometers each year, including gathering trips and camp moves. During such travels, many !Kung women were also burdened with an infant or child.

There have been many explanations about how low fertility among the !Kung was achieved, including their prolonged periods of lactation (up to four years) producing extended interbirth periods (Howell 1979; Lee 1979), the poor nutritional status of !Kung women (Howell 1979; Wilmsen 1986), their high energy output (Bentley 1985), and more recently, the historical prevalence of venereal diseases in Botswana (Pennington and Harpending 1993). The reproductive period for !Kung women also appeared shorter than that typical for healthy Western women. The !Kung experienced menarche (first menstruation) at close to seventeen years of age, and they may also have ceased reproducing earlier than Western women by about five years on the average (Howell 1979). This early age at last birth may have been affected, however, by exposure to venereal diseases (Pennington and Harpending 1993).

There were also a variety of biosocial explanations suggesting that !Kung reproductive patterns were adaptive given the harsh environment of the Kalahari Desert. For example, long interbirth intervals meant that children could walk by themselves when their siblings were born. A !Kung mother could therefore conserve her long-term energies while foraging by carrying just one infant at a time (Blurton-Jones 1986, 1987; Blurton-Jones and Sibly 1978). Long birth spacing also meant better care for each child, with an extended period of reliance on breastfeeding in an environment where suitable early weaning foods were not readily available. Moreover, low fertility in itself was seen to be a physiological adaptation to harsh living conditions (Bentley 1985). These biosocial concerns also shifted attention away from strictly cultural factors like abortion and infanticide.

The paradigm change from a high fertility/mortality profile also meant a shift in paleodemographic reconstructions associated with the advent of agriculture. Archaeological data consistently indicated an increase in population numbers with this technological transition (Cohen 1977; Hassan 1981; Spooner 1972). During the 1970s, archaeologists became preoccupied with this association, partly as a result of Ester Boserup's (1965) notable publication on the conditions of agricultural growth (e.g., Ammerman, Cavalli-Sforza, and Wagener 1976; Bronson 1975; Cohen 1977; Cowgill 1975; Hassan 1981; Spooner 1972). Contrary to the Malthusian perspective where population growth was considered dependent on mortality checks, Boserup viewed population as a far more elastic variable that could stimulate technological development, particularly among agricultural groups. This, is turn, allowed for the continued support of greater numbers of people. So, at approximately the same time that the !Kung data were available, there were also theoretical developments by economists that supported a non-Malthusian view of population regulation. Many archaeologists came to believe then that the development of agriculture was stimulated, if not made inevitable, by increasing population pressure (e.g., Cohen 1977). But, if population growth at that time was not due to a relaxation of mortality measures on high fertility populations as the Malthusians had supposed, could it be due to a change from a previously low fertility pattern?

A variety of osteological data published during the 1980s appeared to support this latter scenario (e.g., Cohen and Armelagos 1984). These data pointed to an increase in human morbidity and mortality at the transition to agriculture, rather than the opposite as had once been supposed. In addition, a number of scholars have pointed out that, in nonstationary populations, changes in life expectancies or the mean age-at-death calculated from paleodemographic data may reflect changes in fertility rather than changes in mortality (Corrucini, Brandon, and Handler 1989; Milner, Humpf, and Harpending 1989; Sattenspiel and Harpending 1983; Wood et al. 1992). Although not explicitly espoused by these authors, their findings would appear to support the idea that changes in fertility, not mortality, led to population increase.

But, is this necessarily the case? To begin with, in recent years, reproductive ecologists and biosocial anthropologists have been collecting data from traditional foraging and horticultural societies other than the !Kung, and discovering that the extremely low fertility pattern typical for the !Kung is not replicated among other groups. In other words, prehistoric hunting and gathering groups may not uniformly have been characterized by low fertility. These other subsistence societies include the Ache of Paraguay (Hill and Hurtado 1995; Hill et al. 1984, 1985; Hurtado et al. 1985), the Hiwi of Venezuela (Hurtado and Hill 1987, 1990), the Hadza of Tanzania (Blurton-Jones et al. 1992), and the Agta of the Philippines (Griffin and Estioko-Griffin 1985). For example, the Ache have a TFR that is almost twice that of the !Kung, at 7.2, while the Agta and the Hiwi are somewhat intermediate at 6.5 and 5.1, respectively (see Bentley, Goldberg, and Jasieńska 1993; Campbell and Wood 1988). There are also ecological contrasts between the groups. The Ache live in a neotropical, evergreen forest habitat compared to the desert environment of the !Kung, and their foraging pattern is almost the reverse of the !Kung. Ache women contribute only 13 percent of total calories to the diet, due mainly to a heavy reliance on meat hunted by Ache men. Their diet is also higher in calories, averaging about 3,800 a day for each Ache woman compared to 2,350 for the !Kung (Hill and Hurtado 1994; Lee 1979).

At the same time, in a recent study using a cross-cultural comparison of fifty-seven different traditional societies, Bentley, Goldberg, and Jasienska (1993; Bentley, Jasieńska, and Goldberg 1993; cf. Campbell and Wood 1988) found that mean TFRs did vary significantly between groups with contrasting subsistence practices. Specifically, nonagricultural groups, comprising both foragers and shifting horticulturalists, had significantly lower fertility (TFR = 5.5) than agricultural groups (TFR = 6.6). This may be due to a variety of causes among agriculturalists, such as a desire for larger family sizes to undertake field labor, the availability of suitable weaning foods that could shorten postpartum periods of lactation, a higher nutritional intake due to the ability to store foods, or a reduction in energy expenditure by women whose work loads altered with agricultural technology. Even if these differences in TFRs can be retrojected to prehistoric times, it does not necessarily follow that higher fertility rates were responsible for population increase. For example, among agricultural groups the availability of good weaning foods, as well as potential improvements in nutrition, could have led to higher fertility. However, if shorter birth intervals accompanied higher fertility, there could also be an increase in infant or child morbidity and mortality. Given this scenario then, population levels theoretically might have been lowered. Such a pattern has, for example, been documented among nomadic compared to settled Turkana women in Kenya (Brainard 1991). Moreover, Pennington (1996; cf. Handwerker 1983) has recently demonstrated that decreases in childhood mortality alone could have produced significant population increase in prehistory, although this also causes increases in adult mortality statistics.

In addition, there appears to be a relatively broad range of fertility rates associated with traditional, noncontracepting societies that results from a variety of environmental and cultural effects (see Bentley, Goldberg, and Jasieńska 1993, Appendix 1; Bentley, Jasieńska, and Goldberg 1993; Campbell and Wood 1988). This realization has led to a research focus on some of the parameters that underlie the range of patterns in fertility, such as nutritional status, lactational practices, and energy output, that might help us to understand the different fertility levels observed, and that might also help with an archaeological understanding of population shifts in prehistory. This change in focus is reflected in the relatively new anthropological subfield of reproductive ecology, which may be defined as the study of various ecological influences on reproduction, including nutritional status, energetics, and disease load (Ellison 1990, 1991; Ellison et al. 1993). These factors will be discussed further below.

Demographic and Paleodemographic Contributions to Prehistoric Fertility

Judging from the above section, one of the problems clearly associated with ethnographic analogy for the reconstruction of prehistoric fertility is the very diverse set of TFRs associated with different groups despite similarities in subsistence mode. This problem would seem to contradict the possibility of being able to draw any generalized conclusions about fertility rates in prehistory. There are certain common features, however, underlying the reproductive patterns among even different groups of foragers and agriculturalists that are amenable to analysis, and that may also be accessible for archaeological study. One means of examining such fertility patterns is to look at what demographers call the proximate or intermediate determinants of fertility—those mechanisms through which all outside influences must express themselves in order to translate into achieved fertility (Bongaarts 1978; Bongaarts and Potter 1983). For example, while higher education among women is associated with lower fertility, this is usually achieved through a later age at marriage and greater use of contraceptives, both of which are considered intermediate variables. The first list of proximate determinants was developed in 1956 by Kingsley Davis and Judith Blake and has undergone various refinements since then (e.g., Bongaarts 1978; Bongaarts and Potter 1983). I will discuss here a recent list that includes more biological factors than the original construction (Wood 1994). These are divided into what are called exposure factors and susceptibility factors (Table 1.1).

Most of the susceptibility factors would be impossible to reconstruct from the archaeological record, although there have been some intriguing discoveries relating to menstruation in recent excavations (Krzywinski, Fjelldal, and Soltvedt 1983). One can be much more optimistic about the exposure factors. How important these are for the determination of fertility can be seen by a comparison of some relevant factors for various contemporary foraging societies discussed earlier (Table 1.2). The Hutterites are included for comparison since they are one of the best examples of a noncontracepting, well-nourished, healthy Western population that also has one of the highest recorded TFRs. There is sufficient variation in the proximate determinants listed for the foraging groups such that the reproductive life span, as well as the length of fecund intervals, of women among these groups is very different and contributes to the range in TFRs. How could we ever reconstruct these important factors in archaeology? This is admittedly a difficult area. Skeletal material offers the best, albeit imperfect, approach to questions of this sort. I will thus give an outline here of the kinds of analyses that

TABLE 1.1. The proximate determinants of fertility.

I. Exposure Factors
  A. Age at marriage or first intercourse
  B. Age at menarche (first menstruation)
  C. Age at menopause (last menstruation)
  D. Age at development of pathological sterility (if earlier than menopause)
II. Susceptibility Factors
  A. Duration of lactational infecundability (i.e., loss of fecundity due to lactation)
  B. Duration of the fecund waiting time to conception, determined by the following:
    1. Frequency of insemination
    2. Length of ovarian (menstrual) cycles
    3. Proportion of ovulatory cycles
    4. Duration of the fertile period following ovulation (time during which sperm and egg are still viable)
    5. Probability of conception from a single insemination during the fertile period
  C. Probability of fetal loss
  D. Length of infertile (nonsusceptible) period following a fetal loss
  E. Length of gestation

After Wood (1994).

TABLE 1.2. Some proximate determinants for foraging groups.

Proximate Determinants (years)	!Kung	Ache	Agta	Hutterites
Age at menarche	16.6	14.3	17.1	[12–13]
Adolescent subfecundity	2.2	4.2	3.0	?
Age at first intercourse	16.9	13.6	?	20.7
Age at first birth	18.8	18.5	20.1	22.2
Length of lactation	3.7	[3.0]	[2.0]	[2.0]
Interbirth interval	3.7	3.2	2.4	2.1
Age at last birth	34.4	41.5	?	40.9
Age at menopause	?	?	43.9	?
Reproductive life span	15.6	23.0	23.8	20.2
Total fertility rate	4.7	7.8	6.5	9.7

Data from Howell (1979) (!Kung); Hill and Hurtado (1995) (Ache); Goodman, Estioko-Griffin, and Grove (1985) (Agta); Eaton and Mayer (1953) (Hutterites). Data in brackets are approximate.

might be undertaken in terms of reconstructing aspects of prehistoric fertility, as well as current prognoses for the degree of reliability that may be associated with these methods. Many of these fall under the domain of paleodemography.

Given the often fragmentary nature of the biological data available to archaeologists, as well as disputes over appropriate statistical methodologies, there have been a number of controversies surrounding the utility of paleodemography (Bocquet-Appel and Masset 1982; Buikstra and Konigsberg 1985; Jackes 1992; Roth 1992; Van Gerven and Armelagos 1983; Wood et al. 1992). It is true that there is no reliable means, as yet, to calculate fertility rates from individual female skeletons.[5] Nor is there any effective means to date for obtaining *absolute* levels of fertility at any one time from osteological or paleodemographic data. However, it is possible to infer *changes* in fertility from skeletal series using changes in the mean ages-at-death or life expectancies that derive from nonstationary populations (Corrucini, Brandon, and Handler 1989; Sattenspiel and Harpending 1983).

Skeletal material can also inform us about the occurrence of certain venereal diseases that affect fertility, like syphilis, although there are associated caveats (Jacobi et al. 1992; Ortner and Putschar 1985; Steinbock 1976). For example, skeletal lesions only appear when the disease reaches an advanced state and, therefore, would not appear in other infected individuals. Other venereal diseases that can have devastating effects on fertility, like gonorrhea and chlamydia, unfortunately do not affect the skeleton and would remain undetected by osteologists.

There are other areas of osteological analysis, however, that are potentially invaluable for reconstructing fertility, given sufficiently large sample sizes for accurate statistical reconstruction. For example, osteological material could be used to indicate mean ages of menarche and menopause in a population. Since age at menarche and skeletal age are highly correlated (Ellison 1981, 1982; Tanner 1989), it is possible to estimate approximately when the former might have occurred in a skeletal population by comparing long bone length and bi-iliac diameter against ages independently derived from dental eruption sequences. It is not clearly known how different growth indices may vary at the inter- and intra-population level, thus complicating the reliability of such measurements (Eveleth and Tanner 1990:175). At the other end of the reproductive span, one might be able to infer a mean age at menopause by plotting the age at onset of osteoporosis since, even in well-nourished populations, postmenopausal women are significantly more at risk for suffering from this pathology (Ortner and Putschar 1985; Stini 1990).

We may also be able to calculate the length of the interbirth interval in prehistoric populations by obtaining information on lactation and weaning ages from skeletal remains. Indeed, the length of interbirth intervals is one of the single most important variables determining a woman's completed fertility (Wood 1994), while the length of lactation is one of the most important determinants of the interbirth interval in noncontracepting populations. Lactation can suppress menstrual function for up to two years, resulting in birth intervals as long as forty-four months—the average for !Kung women (Howell 1979). In traditional societies, where infants are kept in close contact with their mothers even during the night, nursing is frequent and periods of lactational subfecundity are long. For example, Konner and Worthman (1980; Stern et al. 1986) showed that !Kung mothers nursed their infants about four times an hour for approximately two minutes each time, with as little as thirteen minutes between each nursing bout. This nursing pattern contributes to the exceptionally long !Kung interbirth intervals. Similarly, among the Gainj—a horticulturalist society in highland New Guinea—Wood et al. (1985) documented a mean interbirth interval of forty-two months. The pattern of Gainj suckling is also very frequent, with nursing intervals as short as twenty-four minutes in newborns to eighty minutes in children three years of age.

It would seem that reconstructing information about the length of lactation and/or the interbirth interval for prehistoric women would be the most difficult area of all in determining prehistoric fertility parameters. But, in fact, this is an area where bioarchaeologists have been able to shed the most light using a variety of data. There are a number of paleopathological indicators that have been used to infer ages at weaning or the length of lactation for skeletal individuals. For example, bone chemistry analyses and paleopathological indicators provide two archaeological areas that can illuminate weaning patterns and presumed interbirth intervals among prehistoric populations. In addition to bone chemistry analysis, the integration of paleobotany, zooarchaeology, and palynology as archaeological subspecialties has also made it possible to reconstruct prehistoric diets.

Since bone composition (comprising several elements and isotopes) partly reflects an individual's nutritional status, various isotopes and trace elements can be used to reconstruct the dietary makeup of prehistoric individuals and groups, as well as diachronic changes in these diets (e.g., Bumsted 1985; Hastorf 1991; Katzenberg 1992; Price 1989; Price, Schoeninger, and Armelagos 1985; Sandford 1992). Andrew Sillen and Maureen Kavanagh (1982; Sillen 1988) noted that there are higher levels of circulating strontium in pregnant and lactating laboratory animals, which finding could be used to develop a method for examining fertility in skeletal samples. This technique may be useful for estimating numbers of lactating and pregnant women in archaeological skeletal samples, and possibly for verifying the length of the reproductive life span. Following this work, Michael Blakely (1989) more recently suggested that higher strontium/calcium ratios among prehistoric female skeletons from northwest Georgia are indeed related to changes in adult bone composition during pregnancy and lactation. It may also be possible to look for pulses of elevated strontium/calcium ratios in cementum or secondary dentine from human female dentitions that might correlate with pregnancy and lactation sequences (Sillen, personal communication). Such a technique would have to be verified using samples with known fertility histories.

Variation in nitrogen isotope values between individuals can also be used to deduce whether infants were still being breast-fed or had been weaned in a skeletal sample. Differences in such values can be used to infer variation in trophic levels since breast-fed infants feed at a higher trophic level (directly from their mothers) compared to older individuals with a more varied omnivorous diet. Such findings have been used to infer weaning ages in historical populations in Canada (e.g., Katzenberg 1993). Of course, the ages at weaning that are identified for infants in skeletal samples may actually be biased toward earlier weaning since lactation confers many nutritional and immunological benefits. This would lead to better survival rates among infants and children who are breast-fed for longer durations.

Enamel hypoplasias have also been used in several cases to reconstruct age at weaning among skeletal populations (Goodman and Armelagos 1989; Goodman and Rose 1990; Huss-Ashmore, Goodman, and Armelagos 1982; Lanphear 1990). These disruptions in normal enamel formation occur during the long period of dental development and, thus, if measured precisely, can be correlated against ages when presumably the specific developmental disturbance occurred. Enamel hypoplasias are usually measured on adult skeletons, individuals who must have survived the specific stress during childhood in order to be able to exhibit these dental disturbances. For example, in a recent study using skeletons from nineteenth-century Italy, researchers observed a clear increase in the number of enamel defects when individuals were one and a half to two years of age, and a peak at around two and a half to three years (Moggi-Cecchi, Pacciani, and Pinto-Cisternas 1994). They attribute these defects to weaning stress. The authors suggest that the long period of stress and the pattern of hypoplasias are associated with the gradual introduction of supplementary foods, with complete weaning occurring at around two and a half to three years. This supposition is supported by historical demographic data for the length of lactation among Italian women of lower socioeconomic status.

There are, however, problems in using enamel hypoplasias for reconstructing weaning ages. First, hypoplasias are indicative of generalized stress whether from nutritional, disease-related, or other disruptions in enamel formation. These could occur in young children independently of weaning stress. Secondly, there is controversy over which teeth are optimal for accurately measuring stress episodes since it appears that different tooth sectors might have different susceptibilities to stress during development (Goodman and Armelagos 1985; Blakey, Leslie, and Reidy 1994).

Another bioarchaeological example for reconstructing interbirth intervals and lactational practices is from the prehistoric American Midwest.[6] Here, mortuary and settlement evidence point to a steady rise in population through the Middle and Late Woodland periods, that is from about 150 B.C. onward, when subsistence patterns had already changed from foraging toward the use of high carbohydrate starchy seeds. Higher fertility is also marked between the Middle and Late Woodland periods coincident with the apparent use of these carbohydrate food sources (Buikstra, Konigsberg, and Bullington 1986). Moreover, beginning in the fifth century A.D., large, thin-walled ceramic vessels, characterized by increased thermal conductivity and resistance to thermal stress, appear in the archaeological record. Pots made with these new technological features were probably used to prepare gruel from the starchy seeds, which would have provided excellent weaning foods for young infants (Buikstra, Konigsberg, and Bullington 1986). These ceramic data are supported by osteological evidence; Buikstra, Konigsberg, and Bullington point to the earlier occurrence of dental caries in Late Woodland juveniles which is consistent with an earlier and increased consumption of soft, palatable high carbohydrate weaning foods.

The Utility of Reproductive Ecology for Paleodemographic Reconstructions

The reconstruction of nutritional stress from skeletal samples introduces another aspect of fertility that can be potentially reconstructed for prehistoric groups. I mentioned earlier that most of the susceptibility factors are not amenable to archaeological analysis. However, many of these factors are influenced by variables that are accessible to reconstruction. For example, the length of the menstrual cycle as well as the proportion of ovulatory cycles are influenced by the environmental conditions in which women live. Nutritional stress is known to impact women's ovulatory patterns both among Western (Bates 1985; Cumming, Wheeler, and Harber 1994; Green, Weiss, and Daling 1988; Warren 1983) and more traditional societies (Ellison, Peacock, and Lager 1989; Panter-Brick, Lotstein, and Ellison 1993). For example, caloric insufficiencies are known to alter menstrual patterns, hormonal levels and may, in extreme cases, cause amenorrhea or loss of menstrual function.

Among traditional societies, seasonal nutritional stress has been linked to seasonal changes in ovarian function as well as seasonality of conceptions and births (e.g., Bailey et al. 1992).

Osteological data offers an exciting possibility for estimating energy balance among prehistoric women—a crucial aspect of their potential fecundity. Many studies have documented apparent nutritional stress among prehistoric populations, particularly with the advent of agriculture (e.g., Cohen and Armelagos 1984; Gilbert 1985; Goodman and Armelagos 1989; Schoeninger 1981), raising the question of whether female fecundity may have been altered at this crucial subsistence transition. Several bioarchaeologists have suggested that there was a loss of dietary diversity with agricultural development, leading to, among other conditions, the increase of iron deficient anemias, at least in North America where maize became a staple crop (Cohen and Armelagos 1984). This would certainly have had an impact on pregnant and lactating women. In addition, even straightforward analysis of changes in stature from skeletal populations, for example, at different time periods have suggested early agriculture entailed significant physiological hardships for many human societies (e.g., Kates 1994). On the other hand, agricultural production together with increased sedentism also makes it possible to produce significant food surpluses. These surpluses coupled with the appropriate storage technology probably provided a buffer against nutritional stress, particularly in seasonal environments. The archaeological record documents numbers of storage facilities springing up in large Neolithic settlements that could support denser populations (Rindos 1984; Struever 1971). Under these conditions we can speculate that the nutrition of reproductive women could have potentially improved provided caloric sufficiency was also accompanied by adequate dietary composition.

Nutritional stress is determined by the balance between energy input and output. Therefore, the amount of exercise that a woman performs is another, independent factor that can suppress ovarian function (Cumming, Wheeler, and Harber 1994; Ellison et al. 1993; Rosetta 1993). There are a number of clinical studies demonstrating that chronic aerobic exercise (such as running, gymnastics, rowing, and ballet dancing) affects ovarian function and can lead to what has been called athletic amenorrhea (Bullen et al. 1985; Prior 1985; Rosetta 1993; Warren 1980). Even moderate exercise can apparently affect ovarian function adversely among healthy Western women (Ellison and Lager 1986).

We can make an analogy between the kinds of work that women undertake in contemporary ethnographic societies and these aerobic activities recorded among Western groups (Bentley 1985). In most foraging and horticultural societies, women are heavily, sometimes exclusively involved in food production, activities which are frequently aerobic in nature. In most horticultural societies women do the bulk of the garden labor, including planting and weeding, as well as most of the daily domestic chores of preparing food, cooking, fetching water and firewood. In both horticultural and foraging groups, many women may also have to walk long distances to carry out their subsistence-related activities. With the advent of intensive agriculture, however, women may have found that their work loads changed and, in some cases, may have been reduced (Ember 1983; Goody 1976).

Again, osteological studies offer us some of the best data for reconstructing women's labor in prehistory. These data appear to confirm that work requirements for women changed and, in most cases, probably became more arduous with the beginnings of garden cultivation or horticulture. For example, Robert Pickering (1984) has interpreted changes in the cervical vertebrae of Mississippian and Late Woodland females as evidence for their greater participation in subsistence-related chores such as food processing. Similarly, Patricia Bridges (1982, 1985a, 1985b, 1989) has shown that Mississippian women from northern Alabama were characterized by greater long bone size and strength compared to Archaic foraging females. She relates these significant skeletal changes to the activities required of Mississippian horticulturalist women, including their garden labor, food preparation and cooking, hauling of firewood and water, ceramic and leather manufacture, and a variety of other miscellaneous tasks. Among these, the pounding of corn using pestles and mortars was a particularly onerous task. In contrast, Clark Larsen and Christopher Ruff found that, in populations from the coast of Georgia, there was probably a decrease in energy output among both males and females with the advent of agriculture (Larsen 1981; Ruff 1987). Both long bone dimensions and cases of osteoarthritis decreased in these skeletal groups. Each of these examples are relevant since we can use these data to reconstruct the kinds of work-load stresses experienced by prehistoric women that could affect their fertility.

Contraception, Abortion, and Infanticide

Finally, this essay would not be complete without some discussion of how prehistoric women may have coped with the contentious issue of un-wanted births since methods for controlling this in prehistory are likely to remain invisible to archaeologists. It is highly unlikely that we will ever be able to answer the question of whether, and how, women might have contracepted or aborted in prehistory, but it is important that we acknowledge that they may have done so. Although many researchers have denigrated the possibility that women in contemporary and past traditional societies have had any effective contraceptives available to them, recent research by historians has suggested that certain herbal remedies are more efficacious than was previously supposed (Riddle and Estes 1992; Riddle, Estes, and Russell 1994; Riddle 1992). This makes it difficult, of course, to assume that childbearing was an inevitable consequence for sexually active women in prehistoric *and* historic societies.[7] It is possible that paleobotanists could find the remains of efficacious contraceptive plants at archaeological sites, judging by extensive use by the Greeks of the now extinct *silphion* as a contraceptive (Riddle, Estes, and Russell 1994). But this remains speculative for the present.

The ethnographic record also contains many examples of women aborting unwanted fetuses through a variety of means (e.g., Devereux 1976; Early and Peters 1990) that could equally have been available to prehistoric women. Most such occurrences appear to be due to illicit liaisons, or when adequate postpartum support of an infant is in question. It is also unlikely that abortion would have much impact on fertility, since a woman would quickly return to a fecund state unless there were physiological problems associated with the abortion itself. It would also be impossible to detect abortions in the archaeological record, unless a woman died during the attempt and remains of the fetus were preserved in the pelvic cavity of her skeleton.

Infanticide is, strictly speaking, an issue of mortality control. But we have far more success in documenting cases of infanticide at archaeological sites. Most instances of which I am aware are fairly dramatic and are often supported by historical data. For example, one of the most compelling and disturbing examples of mass infanticide that can be reconstructed by archaeologists is from the ancient site of Carthage (Stager 1980; Stager and Wolff 1984). Here, a vast cemetery called the Tophet, dating from around 700–146 B.C. was filled with a number of urn burials. In most cases, these urns contained the charred remains of infants or young children, comprising hundreds of individuals sacrificed to the Phoenician gods over a period of 550 years. The excavators estimated that over twenty thousand urns were deposited during the period of 400 to 200 B.C. alone. Given the associated historical data, the deposits appear to have been made by the wealthy Carthaginian community as an expression of religious piety, since these infants were sacrificed to the Phoenician gods in religious ceremonies and documented on stone stelae at the site. Lawrence Stager (1980; Stager and Wolff 1984) has suggested, however, that these sacrifices functioned on a more practical level to reduce the number of potential heirs to large estates, given that the Phoenician system of land succession was based on partible inheritance.

Another archaeological example of fairly systematic infanticide comes from the Late Roman-Early Byzantine period at the site of Ashkelon in Israel (Smith and Kahila 1992). Here the remains of one hundred neonates were found in the sewer system suggesting the hasty and unceremonial disposal of infant bodies. Analysis of the tooth buds from these infants showed that many of them were stained with pigment from iron oxide deposits. This phenomenon is known to occur during asphyxiation when blood is forced into the dentine. It is possible, however, that these remains represent infants that were stillborn as opposed to pedocide victims. In addition, iron oxide staining may result from taphonomic conditions alone.

Infanticide that occurred immediately postpartum would have much the same impact on fertility (or lack of) as abortion, in that women would quickly return to a fecund state. It is likely to have involved fewer physiological complications for a mother than abortion, which, in the absence of adequate medical technology, can be a highly dangerous procedure. In the Carthaginian example cited above, however, young children of age two or thereabouts were sometimes sacrificed. This would have a greater impact on a woman's interbirth intervals provided she also breast-fed her infant postpartum, and did not use a wet nurse.

Conclusion

In this essay I have presented a range of issues that relate to prehistoric fertility, drawing on the most recent data from studies in demography, osteology, and reproductive ecology. Although the use of these data in archaeological contexts is complicated, I have suggested a number of instances where analyses are very promising. On the whole, the best interpretive results rely on skeletal material and interdisciplinary approaches. Future successful studies of prehistoric fertility will, therefore, incorporate a variety of data with which to tackle this issue, embracing ethnography, paleodemography, reproductive ecology, and other subdisciplines within anthropology.

Perhaps most significantly, archaeologists have hitherto ignored the crucial issue of women's role in reproduction. Although the complex social issues surrounding women's reproductive roles have not been discussed, we can at least begin to document the basic biological parameters of fertility and reproductive constraints in prehistory. While there continue to be several methodological problems surrounding analyses of this topic in archaeology, the examples given here should provide archaeologists with sufficient information to construct problem-oriented research designs through which data collection and analyses can be undertaken. For too long, women have been invisible actresses in prehistory despite their crucial role in the perpetuation of our species.

Acknowledgments

I would like to thank Rita Wright for stimulating me to write this essay following a lecture on this topic at New York University and for her vision in producing this book. I am also grateful to Robert Aunger, Mary Lucas Powell, George Milner, Andrew Sillen, and Catherine Smith for their very helpful comments on earlier versions of this essay. During its completion, I learned firsthand how women have struggled with the dual tasks of production and reproduction with the appearance of my son, Justin Aunger. Nothing could be more rewarding!

Notes

1. This statement does not include the several publications dealing with so-called fertility figurines, which have, for the most part, dealt more with technological or ritual aspects of prehistoric societies rather than the physiological aspects of fertility and birth (e.g., Bolger 1992). Other exceptions include Bolen 1992 and Willows 1991.

2. Fertility refers to live births experienced by a woman during her reproductive life span, in contrast to *fecundity*, which is the biological capacity to conceive.

3. This perspective also drew on demographic transition theory where demographers argued that populations were routinely characterized by high fertility and mortality prior to modernization (Notestein 1953).

4. The total fertility rate refers to the total number of children born to a woman during her reproductive career.

5. At one time, there was hope that one could accurately estimate the number of children ever born to a woman through analyzing female pubic bones (Angel 1969). Osteologists had observed that the pubic bones of women often demonstrated particular lesions—which came to be called parturition scars—that were thought to result from childbirth. It was also speculated that the number of scars was correlated to the number of children that a woman had ever born. However, subsequent work with autopsy specimens with known reproductive histories showed that we simply cannot use these scars as accurate indicators of a woman's parity (Holt 1978; Suchey et al., 1979).

6. This example has not been without criticism, however (Corrucini, Brandon, and Handler 1989; Holland 1989; see reply by Konigsberg, Buikstra, and Bullington 1989).

7. Recent research among contemporary African groups where modern contraceptives have become available suggests that, where child mortality remains relatively high, women use contraceptives mostly as a spacing device to ensure adequate nutrition and childcare for previously born infants, and not as devices to limit the total number of births (Bledsoe et al. 1994). We should not ignore the fact, though, that total fertility would be reduced by the resulting increase in birth interval length.

References

Acsádi, György, and János Nemeskéri
    1970   *History of Human Lifespan and Mortality.* Budapest: Akademiai Kiado.

Ammerman, Albert J., Luigi Luca Cavalli-Sforza, and Diane K. Wagener
1976   "Toward the Estimation of Population Growth in Old World Prehistory." In *Demographic Anthropology: Quantitative Approaches,* edited by Ezra B. W. Zubrow, 27–61. Albuquerque, N.M.: University of New Mexico Press.

Angel, J. Lawrence
1969   "The Bases of Palaeodemography." *American Journal of Physical Anthropology* 30:427–37.

Bailey, Robert C., Mark R. Jenike, Peter T. Ellison, Gillian R. Bentley, Alisa M. Harrigan, and Nadine R. Peacock
1992   "The Ecology of Birth Seasonality among Agriculturalists in Central Africa." *Journal of Biosocial Science* 24:393–412.

Bates, G. William
1985   "Body Weight Control Practice as a Cause of Infertility." *Clinical Obstetrics and Gynecology* 28:632–44.

Bentley, Gillian R.
1985   "Hunter-Gatherer Energetics and Fertility: A Reassessment of the !Kung San." *Human Ecology* 13:79–109.

Bentley, Gillian R., Tony Goldberg, and Grażyna Jasieńska
1993   "The Fertility of Agricultural and Non-agricultural Traditional Societies." *Population Studies* 47:269–81.

Bentley, Gillian R., Grażyna Jasieńska, and Tony Goldberg
1993   "Is the Fertility of Agriculturalists Higher Than That of Non-agriculturalists?" *Current Anthropology* 778–85.

Betzig, Laura L.
1986   *Despotism and Differential Reproduction: A Darwinian View of History.* New York: Aldine.

Birdsell, Joseph B.
1968   "Some Predictions for the Pleistocene Based on Equilibrium Systems among Recent Hunter-Gatherers." In *Man the Hunter,* edited by R. B. Lee and I. DeVore, 229–40. New York: Aldine.

Blakely, Robert L.
1989   "Bone Strontium in Pregnant and Lactating Females from Archaeological Samples." *American Journal of Physical Anthropology* 80:173–85.

Blakey, Michael L., Teresa E. Leslie, and Joseph P. Reidy
1994   "Frequency and Chronological Distribution of Dental Enamel Hypoplasia in Enslaved African Americans: A Test of the Weaning Hypothesis." *American Journal of Physical Anthropology* 95:371–83.

Bledsoe, Caroline B., Allan G. Hill, Umberto D'Alessandro, and Patricia Langerock
1994   "Constructing Natural Fertility: The Use of Western Contraceptive Technologies in Rural Gambia." *Population and Development Review* 20:81–113.

Blurton-Jones, Nicholas G.
1986   "Bushman Birth Spacing: A Test for Optimal Birth Intervals." *Ethology and Sociobiology* 7:91–105.
1987   "Bushman Birth Spacing: Direct Tests of Some Simple Predictions." *Ethology and Sociobiology* 8:183–203.

Blurton-Jones, Nicholas G., and Richard M. Sibly
1978   "Testing Adaptiveness of Culturally Determined Behaviour: Do

Bushman Women Maximise Their Reproductive Success by Spacing Births Widely and Foraging Seldom?" In *Human Behaviour and Adaptation*, edited by N. Blurton-Jones and V. Reynolds, 135–58. Society for the Study of Human Biology Symposia, No. 18. London: Taylor and Francis.

Blurton-Jones, Nicholas G., Lars C. Smith, James F. O'Connell, Kristen Hawkes, and Chrys L. Kamuzora
  1992   "Demography of the Hadza, an Increasing and High Density Population of Savanna Foragers." *American Journal of Physical Anthropology* 89:159–81.

Bocquet-Appel, Jean-Pierre, and Claude Masset
  1982   "Farewell to Palaeodemography." *Journal of Human Evolution* 11:321–33.

Bolen, Kathleen M.
  1992   "Prehistoric Construction of Mothering." In *Exploring Gender through Archaeology: Selected Papers from the 1991 Boone Conference*, edited by Cheryl Claassen, 49–62. Monographs in World Archaeology, No. 11. Madison, Wis.: Prehistoric Press.

Bolger, Diane L.
  1992   "The Archaeology of Fertility and Birth: A Ritual Deposit from Chalcolithic Cyprus." *Journal of Anthropological Research* 48:145–64.

Bongaarts, John
  1978   "A Framework for Analyzing the Proximate Determinants of Fertility." *Population and Development Review* 4:105–32.

Bongaarts, John, and Robert G. Potter
  1983   *Fertility, Biology, and Behavior: An Analysis of the Proximate Determinants.* New York: Academic Press.

Boserup, Ester
  1965   *The Conditions of Agricultural Growth: The Economics of Agrarian Change under Population Pressure.* Chicago: Aldine.

Brainard, Jean M.
  1991   *Health and Development in a Rural Kenyan Community.* New York: Peter Lang.

Bridges, Patricia S.
  1982   "Postcranial Size in Prehistoric Northern Alabama: Implications for Prehistoric Nutrition and Behavior." *American Journal of Physical Anthropology* 57:172–73.
  1985a   "Changes in Long Bone Structure with the Transition to Agriculture: Implications for Prehistoric Activities." Ph.D. dissertation. Ann Arbor, Mich.: University Microfilms International.
  1985b   "Structural Changes of the Arms Associated with Habitual Grinding of Corn." *American Journal of Physical Anthropology* 66:149–50.
  1989   "Changes in Activities with the Shift to Agriculture in the Southeastern United States." *Current Anthropology* 30:385–94.

Bronson, Bennet
  1975   "The Earliest Farming: Demography as Cause and Consequence." In *Population, Ecology and Social Evolution*, edited by S. Polgar, 53–78. The Hague: Mouton Publishers.

Brown, Judith K.
  1970   "A Note on the Division of Labor by Sex." *American Anthropologist* 72:1073–78.

Buikstra, Jane E., and Lyle W. Konigsberg
  1985   "Palaeodemography: Critiques and Controversies." *American Anthropologist* 87:316–33.
Buikstra, Jane E., Lyle W. Konigsberg, and Jill Bullington
  1986   "Fertility and the Development of Agriculture in the Prehistoric Midwest." *American Antiquity* 51:528–46.
Bullen, Beverly A., Gary S. Skrinar, Inese Z. Beitins, Gretchen von Mering, Barry A. Turnbull, and Janet W. McArthur
  1985   "Induction of Menstrual Disorders by Strenuous Exercise in Untrained Women." *New England Journal of Medicine* 312:1349–53.
Bumsted, M. Pamela
  1985   "Past Human Behavior from Bone Chemical Analysis—Respects and Prospects." *Journal of Human Evolution* 14:539–51.
Campbell, Kenneth L., and James W. Wood
  1988   "Fertility in Traditional Societies." In *Natural Human Fertility: Social and Biological Mechanisms*, edited by P. Diggory, S. Teper, and M. Potts, 39–69. London: Macmillan.
Carr-Saunders, Alexander M.
  1922   *The Population Problem.* Oxford: Clarendon Press.
Claassen, Cheryl
  1992   *Exploring Gender through Archaeology: Selected Papers from the 1991 Boone Conference.* Monographs in World Archaeology, No. 11. Madison, Wis.: Prehistory Press.
Coale, Ansley J.
  1974   "The History of the Human Population." *Scientific American* 231:40–51.
Cohen, Mark N.
  1977   *The Food Crisis in Prehistory.* New Haven, Conn.: Yale University Press.
  1980   "Speculations on the Evolution of Density Measurement and Population Regulation in Homo Sapiens." In *Biosocial Mechanisms of Population Regulation*, edited by M. N. Cohen, R. S. Malpass, and H. G. Klein, 275–303. New Haven, Conn.: Yale University Press.
Cohen, Mark N., and George J. Armelagos
  1984   *Paleopathology at the Origins of Agriculture.* New York: Academic Press.
Conkey, Margaret W.
  1991   "Contexts of Action, Contexts for Power: Material Culture and Gender in the Magdalenian." In *Engendering Archaeology: Women and Prehistory*, edited by J. M. Gero and M. W. Conkey, 57–92. Oxford: Basil Blackwell.
Conkey, Margaret W., and Joan M. Gero
  1991   "Tensions, Pluralities, and Engendering Archaeology: An Introduction to Women and Prehistory." In *Engendering Archaeology: Women and Prehistory*, edited by J. M. Gero and M. W. Conkey, 3–30. Oxford: Basil Blackwell.
Corruccini, Robert S., Elizabeth M. Brandon, and Jerome S. Handler
  1989   "Inferring Fertility from Relative Mortality in Historically Controlled Cemetery Remains from Barbados." *American Antiquity* 54:609–14.
Cowgill, George L.
  1975   "Of Causes and Consequences of Ancient and Modern Population Changes." *American Anthropologist* 77:505–25.

Cumming, David C., Garry D. Wheeler, and Vicki J. Harber
1994   "Physical Activity, Nutrition, and Reproduction." *Annals of the New York Academy of Sciences* 709:55–76.

Davis, Kingsley, and Judith Blake
1956   "Social Structure and Fertility: An Analytic Framework." *Economic Development and Cultural Change* 4:211–35.

Denham, Woodrow W.
1974   "Population Structure, Infant Transport, and Infanticide among Pleistocene and Modern Hunter-Gatherers." *Journal of Anthropological Research* 30:191–98.

Devereux, George
1976   *A Study of Abortion in Primitive Societies.* Revised edition. New York: International Universities Press.

Divale, William T.
1972   "Systematic Population Control in the Middle and Upper Palaeolithic: Inferences Based on Contemporary Hunter-Gatherers." *World Archaeology* 4:222–37.

Dumond, Don E.
1975   "The Limitation of Human Population: A Natural History." *Science* 187:713–21.

Early, John D., and John F. Peters
1990   *The Population Dynamics of the Mucajai Yanomama.* New York: Academic Press.

Eaton, Joseph W., and Albert J. Mayer
1953   "The Social Biology of Very High Fertility among the Hutterites: The Demography of a Unique Population." *Human Biology* 25:206–64.

Ellison, Peter T.
1981   "Prediction of Age at Menarche from Annual Height Increments." *American Journal of Physical Anthropology* 56:71–75.
1982   "Skeletal Growth, Fatness, and Menarcheal Age: A Comparison of Two Hypotheses." *Human Biology* 54:269–81.
1990   "Human Ovarian Function and Reproductive Ecology: New Hypotheses." *American Anthropologist* 92:933–52.
1991   "Reproductive Ecology and Human Fertility." In *Biological Anthropology and Human Affairs*, edited by G. Lasker and N. Mascie-Taylor, 14–54. Cambridge, England: Cambridge University Press.

Ellison, Peter T., and Catherine Lager
1986   "Moderate Recreational Running Is Associated with Lowered Salivary Progesterone Profiles among College Undergraduate Women." *American Journal of Obstetrics and Gynecology* 154:1000–1003.

Ellison, Peter T., Catherine Panter-Brick, Susan F. Lipson, and Mary O'Rourke
1993   "The Ecological Context of Human Ovarian Function." *Human Reproduction* 8:2248–58.

Ellison, Peter, Nadine Peacock, and Catherine Lager
1989   "Ecology and Ovarian Function among Lese Women of the Ituri Forest, Zaire." *American Journal of Physical Anthropology* 78:519–26.

Ember, Carol R.
1983   "The Relative Decline in Women's Contribution to Agriculture with Intensification." *American Anthropologist* 85:285–304.

Engelbrecht, William
  1987   "Factors Maintaining Low Population Density among the Prehistoric New York Iroquois." *American Antiquity* 52:13–27.
Estioko-Griffin, Agnes, and P. Bion Griffin
  1981   "Woman the Hunter: The Agta." In *Woman the Gatherer*, edited by F. Dahlberg, 121–51. New Haven, Conn.: Yale University Press.
Eveleth, Phyllis B., and James M. Tanner
  1990   *Worldwide Variation in Human Growth.* 2d edition. New York: Cambridge University Press.
Gero, Joan M.
  1991   "Genderlithics: Women's Roles in Stone Tool Production." In *Engendering Archaeology: Women and Prehistory*, edited by Joan M. Gero and Margaret W. Conkey, 163–93. Oxford: Basil Blackwell.
Gero, Joan M., and Margaret W. Conkey, eds.
  1991   *Engendering Archaeology: Women and Prehistory.* Oxford: Basil Blackwell.
Gilbert, Robert
  1985   "Stress, Paleonutrition, and Trace Elements." In *The Analysis of Prehistoric Diets*, edited by R. Gilbert, and J. Mielke, 339–58. New York: Academic Press.
Goodale, Jane C.
  1971   *Tiwi Wives: A Study of the Women of Melville Island, North Australia.* Seattle: University of Washington Press.
Goodman, Alan H., and George J. Armelagos
  1985   "Factors Affecting the Distribution of Hypoplasias within the Human Permanent Dentition." *American Journal of Physical Anthropology* 68:479–93.
  1989   "Infant and Childhood Morbidity and Mortality Risks in Archaeological Populations." *World Archaeology* 21:225–43.
Goodman, Alan, and Jerome Rose
  1990   "Assessment of Systemic Physiological Perturbations from Dental Enamel Hypoplasias and Associated Histological Structures." *Yearbook of Physical Anthropology* 33:59–110.
Goodman, Madeleine J., Agnes Estioko-Griffin, and John S. Grove
  1985   "Menarche, Pregnancy, Birth Spacing and Menopause among the Agta Women of Northeastern Luzon, the Philippines." In *The Agta of Northeastern Luzon: Recent Studies*, edited by P. B. Griffin and Agnes Estioko-Griffin, 147–56. Cebu City, Philippines: University of San Carlos.
Goody, Jack
  1976   *Production and Reproduction: A Comparative Study of the Domestic Domain.* Cambridge, England: Cambridge University Press.
Green, Beverly, Noel Weiss, and Janet R. Daling
  1988   "Risk of Ovulatory Infertility in Relation to Body Weight." *Fertility and Sterility* 50:721–26.
Griffin, P. Bion, and Agnes Estioko-Griffin
  1985   *The Agta of Northeastern Luzon: Recent Studies.* Cebu City, Philippines: University of San Carlos.
Handwerker, W. Penn
  1983   "The First Demographic Transition: An Analysis of Subsistence

Choices and Reproductive Consequences." *American Anthropologist* 85:5–27.

Harpending, Henry, and Patricia Draper
1990   "Estimating Parity of Parents: Application to the History of Infertility among the !Kung of Southern Africa." *Human Biology* 62:195–203.

Hassan, Fekri A.
1973   "On Mechanisms of Population Growth during the Neolithic." *Current Anthropology* 14:535–40.
1980   "The Growth and Regulation of Human Population in Prehistoric Times." In *Biosocial Mechanisms of Population Regulation*, edited by M. N. Cohen, R. S. Malpass, and H. G. Klein, 305–19. New Haven, Conn.: Yale University Press.
1981   *Demographic Archaeology*. New York: Academic Press.

Hastorf, Christine A.
1991   "Gender, Space and Food in Prehistory." In *Engendering Archaeology: Women and Prehistory*, edited by Joan M. Gero and Margaret W. Conkey, 132–62. Oxford: Basil Blackwell.

Hayden, Brian
1972   "Population Control among Hunter/Gatherers." *World Archaeology* 4:205–21.

Hill, Kim, Kristen Hawkes, A. Magdalena Hurtado, and Hillard Kaplan
1984   "Seasonal Variance in the Diet of Ache Hunter-Gatherers in Eastern Paraguay." *Human Ecology* 12:101–35.

Hill, Kim, and A. Magdalena Hurtado
1995   *Ache Life History: The Ecology and Demography of a Foraging People*. Chicago: Aldine.

Hill, Kim, Hillard Kaplan, Kristen Hawkes, and A. Magdalena Hurtado
1985   "Men's Time Allocation to Subsistence Work among the Ache of Eastern Paraguay." *Human Ecology* 13:29–47.

Holland, Thomas D.
1989   "Fertility in the Prehistoric Midwest: A Critique of Unifactorial Models." *American Antiquity* 54:614–25.

Holt, C. Adams
1978   "A Re-examination of Parturition Scars on the Human Female Pelvis." *American Journal of Physical Anthropology* 49:91–94.

Howell, Nancy
1979   *Demography of the Dobe !Kung*. New York: Academic Press.

Hurtado, A. Magdalena, Kristen Hawkes, Kim Hill, and Hillard Kaplan
1985   "Female Subsistence Strategies among Ache Hunter-Gatherers of Eastern Paraguay." *Human Ecology* 13:1–28.

Hurtado, A. Magdalena, and Kim R. Hill
1987   "Early Dry Season Subsistence Ecology of Cuiva (Hiwi) Foragers of Venezuela." *Human Ecology* 15:163–87.
1990   "Seasonality in a Foraging Society: Variation in Diet, Work Effort, Fertility, and Sexual Division of Labor among the Hiwi of Venezuela." *Journal of Anthropological Research* 46:293–346.

Huss-Ashmore, Rebecca, Alan Goodman, and George Armelagos
1982   "Nutritional Inferences from Palaeopathology." *Advances in Archaeological Method and Theory* 5:395–474.

Irons, William
1979   "Cultural and Biological Success." In *Evolutionary Biology and Human*

Social Behavior: An Anthropological Perspective, edited by N. A. Chagnon and W. Irons, 257–72. North Scituate, Mass.: Duxbury Press.

Jackes, Mary
1992   "Paleodemography: Problems and Techniques." In *Skeletal Biology of Past Peoples: Research Methods,* edited by S. R. Saunders and M. A. Katzenberg, 189–224. New York: John Wiley and Sons.

Jacobi, Keith P., Della C. Cook, Robert S. Corruccini, and Jerome S. Handler
1992   "Congenital Syphilis in the Past: Slaves at Newton Plantation, Barbados, West Indies." *American Journal of Physical Anthropology* 89:145–58.

Kates, Robert W.
1994   "Sustaining Life on Earth." *Scientific American* 271:114–22.

Katzenberg, M. Anne
1992   "Advances in Stable Isotope Analysis of Prehistoric Bones." In *Skeletal Biology of Past Peoples: Research Methods,* edited by S. R. Saunders and M. A. Katzenberg, 105–19. New York: John Wiley and Sons.
1993   "Age Differences and Population Variation in Stable Isotope Values from Ontario, Canada." In *Prehistoric Human Bone: Archaeology at the Molecular Level,* edited by J. B. Lambert and G. Grupe, 39–62. New York: Springer-Verlag.

Kerns, Virginia, and Judith K. Brown
1992   *In Her Prime: New Views of Middle-Aged Women.* 2d edition. Urbana: University of Illinois Press.

Konigsberg, Lyle W., Jane E. Buikstra, and Jill Bullington
1989   "Palaeodemographic Correlates of Fertility: A Reply to Corrucini, Brandon, and Handler and to Holland." *American Antiquity* 54:626–36.

Konner, Melvin, and Worthman, Carol
1980   "Nursing Frequency, Gonadal Function, and Birth Spacing among !Kung Hunter-Gatherers." *Science* 207:788–91.

Krzywicki, Ludwik
1934   *Primitive Society and Its Vital Statistics.* London: Macmillan.

Krzywinski, Knur, Sissel Fjelldal, and Eli-Christine Soltvedt
1983   "Recent Palaeoethnobotanical Work at the Mediaeval Excavations at Bryggen, Bergen, Norway." In *Site, Environment and Economy,* edited by B. Proudfoot, 153–63. B.A.R. International Series, No. 173.

Lanphear, Kim
1990   "Frequency and Distribution of Enamel Hypoplasias in a Historic Skeletal Sample." *American Journal of Physical Anthropology* 81:35–42.

Larsen, Clark S.
1981   "Skeletal and Dental Adaptations to the Shift to Agriculture on the Georgia Coast." *Current Anthropology* 22:4.

Lee, Richard B.
1979   *The !Kung San: Men, Women, and Work in a Foraging Society.* New York: Cambridge University Press.

Lee, Richard B., and Irven DeVore
1976   *Kalahari Hunter-Gatherers: Studies of the !Kung San and Their Neighbors.* Cambridge, Mass.: Harvard University Press.

Leonard, Robert
1989   "Resource Specialization, Population Growth, and Agricultural Production in the American Southwest." *American Antiquity* 54:491–503.

Milner, George R., Dorothy A. Humpf, and Henry C. Harpending
   1989   "Pattern Matching of Age-at-Death Distributions in Paleodemo-
            graphic Analysis." *American Journal of Physical Anthropology* 80:49–58.
Moggi-Cecchi, Jacopo, Elsa Pacciani, and Juan Pinto-Cisternas
   1994   "Enamel Hypoplasia and Age at Weaning in Nineteenth-Century
            Florence, Italy." *American Journal of Physical Anthropology* 93:299–306.
Nag, Moni
   1968   *Factors Affecting Human Fertility in Nonindustrial Societies: A Cross-
            Cultural Study.* New Haven, Conn.: Human Relations Area Files Press.
Notestein, Frank.
   1953   "Economic Problems of Population Change." In *Proceedings of the
            Eighth International Conference of Agricultural Economists,* 13–31. Lon-
            don: Oxford University Press.
Ortner, Donald, and Walter Putschar
   1985   *Identification of Pathological Conditions in Human Skeletal Remains.* Wash-
            ington, D.C.: Smithsonian Institution Press.
Panter-Brick, Catherine, Deborah Lotstein, and Peter T. Ellison
   1993   "Seasonality of Reproductive Function and Weight Loss in Rural
            Nepali Women." *Human Reproduction* 8:684–90.
Pennington, Renee L.
   1996   "Causes of Early Human Population Growth." *American Journal of
            Physical Anthropology* 99:259–74.
Pennington, Renee, and Henry Harpending
   1993   *The Structure of an African Pastoralist Community: Demography, History,
            and Ecology of the Ngamiland Herero.* New York: Oxford University
            Press.
Pickering, Robert B.
   1984   "Patterns of Degenerative Joint Disease in Middle Woodland, Late
            Woodland, and Mississippian Skeletal Series from the Lower Illinois
            Valley." Ph.D. dissertation. Ann Arbor, Mich.: University Microfilms
            International.
Polgar, Steven
   1972   "Population History and Population Policies from an Anthropologi-
            cal Perspective." *Current Anthropology* 13:203–11.
Price, T. Douglas
   1989   *The Chemistry of Prehistoric Human Bone.* New York: Cambridge Uni-
            versity Press.
Price, T. Douglas, Margaret J. Schoeninger, and George J. Armelagos
   1985   "Bone Chemistry and Past Behavior: An Overview." *Journal of Human
            Evolution* 14:419–47.
Prior, Jerilynn
   1985   "Luteal Phase Defects and Anovulation: Adaptive Alterations Occur-
            ring with Conditioning Exercise." *Seminars in Reproductive Endocrin-
            ology* 3:27–33.
Riddle, John M.
   1992   *Contraception and Abortion from the Ancient World to the Renaissance.*
            Cambridge, Mass.: Harvard University Press.
Riddle, John M., and J. Worth Estes
   1992   "Oral Contraceptives in Ancient and Medieval Times." *American Sci-
            entist* 80:226–33.

Riddle, John M., J. Worth Estes, and Josiah C. Russell
    1994   "Ever Since Eve . . . Birth Control in the Ancient World." *Archaeology*
           (March/April): 29–35.
Rindos, David
    1984   *The Origins of Agriculture: An Evolutionary Perspective.* New York: Aca-
           demic Press.
Rosetta, Lyliane
    1993   "Female Reproductive Dysfunction and Intense Physical Training."
           Oxford Reviews of Reproductive Biology 15:114–41.
Roth, Eric A.
    1992   "Application of Demographic Models to Paleodemography." In *Skele-
           tal Biology of Past Peoples: Research Methods*, edited by S. R. Saunders
           and M. A. Katzenberg, 175–88. New York: John Wiley and Sons.
Ruff, Christopher B.
    1987   "Postcranial Adaptations to Subsistence Changes on the Georgia
           Coast." *American Journal of Physical Anthropology* 72:248.
Sandford, Mary K.
    1992   "A Reconsideration of Trace Element Analysis in Prehistoric Bone."
           In *Skeletal Biology of Past Peoples: Research Methods*, edited by S. R.
           Saunders and M. A. Katzenberg, 79–103. New York: John Wiley
           and Sons.
Sattenspiel, Lisa, and Henry Harpending
    1983   "Stable Populations and Skeletal Age." *American Antiquity* 48:489–98.
Saunders, Shelley R., and M. Anne Katzenberg
    1992   *Skeletal Biology of Past Peoples: Research Methods.* New York: John Wiley
           and Sons.
Schoeninger, Margaret J.
    1981   "The Agricultural 'Revolution': Its Effect on Human Diet in Prehis-
           toric Iran and Israel." *Paléorient* 7:73–92.
Sillen, Andrew
    1988   "Elemental and Isotopic Analyses of Mammalian Fauna from South-
           ern Africa and Their Implications for Paleodietary Research." *Ameri-
           can Journal of Physical Anthropology* 76:49–60.
Sillen, Andrew, and Maureen Kavanagh
    1982   "Strontium and Paleodietary Research: A Review." *Yearbook of Physi-
           cal Anthropology* 25:67–90.
Sillen, Andrew, and Patricia Smith
    1984   "Sr/Ca Ratios in Juvenile Skeletons Portray Weaning Practices in a
           Medieval Arab Population." *Journal of Archaeological Science* 11:237–
           45.
Smith, Patricia, and Gila Kahila
    1992   "Identification of Infanticide in Archaeological Sites: A Case Study
           from the Late Roman-Early Byzantine Periods at Ashkelon, Israel."
           Journal of Archaeological Science 19:667–75.
Spooner, Brian
    1972   *Population Growth: Anthropological Implications.* Cambridge, Mass.: MIT
           Press.
Stager, Lawrence A.
    1980   "The Rite of Child Sacrifice at Carthage." In *New Light on Ancient
           Carthage*, edited by J. G. Pedley, 1–11. Ann Arbor: University of Michi-
           gan Press.

Stager, Lawrence E., and Samuel R. Wolff
    1984   "Child Sacrifice at Carthage—Religious Rite or Population Control?" *Biblical Archaeology Review* 10:31–51.
Steinbock, R. Ted
    1976   *Paleopathological Diagnosis and Interpretation.* Springfield, Ill.: C. C. Thomas.
Stern, Judith M., Melvin Konner, Talia N. Herman, and Seymour Reichlin
    1986   "Nursing Behaviour, Prolactin and Postpartum Amenorrhoea during Prolonged Lactation in American and !Kung Women." *Clinical Endocrinology* 25:247–58.
Stini, William A.
    1990   "'Osteoporosis': Etiologies, Prevention and Treatment." *Yearbook of Physical Anthropology* 33:151–94.
Stott, Denis H.
    1969   "Cultural and Natural Checks on Population Growth." In *Environment and Cultural Behavior: Ecological Study in Cultural Anthropology,* edited by A. P. Vayda, 90–120. Austin: University of Texas Press.
Struever, Stuart
    1971   *Prehistoric Agriculture.* Garden City, N.Y.: Natural History Press.
Suchey, Judy, Dean Wiseley, Richard F. Green, and Thomas Noguchi
    1979   "Analysis of Dorsal Pitting in the *Os Pubis* in an Extensive Sample of Modern American Females." *American Journal of Physical Anthropology* 51:517–39.
Tanner, James M.
    1989   *Foetus into Man: Physical Growth from Conception to Maturity.* 2d edition. Ware, England: Castlemead Publications.
Van Gerven, Dennis P., and George Armelagos
    1983   "'Farewell to Palaeodemography?' Rumors of Its Death Have Been Greatly Exaggerated." *Journal of Human Evolution* 12:353–60.
Warren, Michelle
    1980   "The Effects of Exercise on Pubertal Progression and Reproductive Function in Girls." *Journal of Clinical Endocrinology and Metabolism* 51.
    1983   "Effects of Undernutrition on Reproductive Function in the Human." *Endocrine Reviews* 4:363–77.
Watson, Patty Jo, and Mary C. Kennedy
    1991   "The Development of Horticulture in the Eastern Woodlands of North America: Women's Role." In *Engendering Archaeology: Women and Prehistory,* edited by J. M. Gero and M. W. Conkey, 255–75. Oxford: Basil Blackwell.
Willows, Noreen D.
    1991   "Hominid Fertility Parameters during the Plio-Pleistocene." In *The Archaeology of Gender,* edited by D. Walde and N. Willows, 53–63. Calgary: Archaeological Association of the University of Calgary.
Wilmsen, Edwin N.
    1986   "Biological Determinants of Fecundity and Fecundability: An Application of Bongaarts' Model to Forager Fertility." In *Culture and Reproduction: An Anthropological Critique of Demographic Transition Theory,* edited by W. P. Handwerker, 59–89. Boulder, Colo.: Westview Press.
Wood, James W.
    1994   *Dynamics of Human Reproduction: Biology, Biometry, Demography.* Hawthorne, N.Y.: Aldine de Gruyter.

Wood, James W., Daina Lai, Patricia L. Johnson, Kenneth L. Campbell, and Ila A. Maslar
  1985   "Lactation and Birth Spacing in Highland New Guinea." *Journal of Biosocial Science,* Supplement 9:159–73.
Wood, James W., George R. Milner, Henry C. Harpending, and Kenneth M. Weiss
  1992   "The Osteological Paradox: Problems of Inferring Prehistoric Health from Skeletal Samples." *Current Anthropology* 33:343–70.

Chapter 2
Reconceiving Technology: Why Feminine Technologies Matter

Judith A. McGaw

What can we learn about gender and technology by subjecting contemporary artifacts to the close material and cultural scrutiny we generally reserve for prehistoric and precapitalist objects? Can the gender-conscious study of modern, Western technology offer archaeologists analyzing gender and technology in earlier eras a salutary comparative perspective? This essay demonstrates the utility of such an approach. It carefully examines several objects—the brassiere, the closet, the white collar, and the bathroom—selected to represent what I call "feminine technologies." I argue that unearthing the cultural context and artifactual precursors of such feminine technologies exposes pervasive aspects of our society's relationship to technology—aspects that as scholars and as citizens we ignore at our peril.

Although informed by perspectives drawn from historic and industrial archaeology and physical and cultural anthropology,[1] what follows is the work of a historian of technology rather than an archaeologist. It also differs from this volume's other essays in presenting for archaeologists' consumption the results of research designed with broad interdisciplinary and nonscholarly audiences in mind. These differences give it special relevance for readers of this collection. Archaeologists face the perennial challenge of being sufficiently self-critical to avoid reading personal cultural conditioning into the artifacts of other times and places. Turning to a new area of concern—the archaeological study of gender and technology—creates a new responsibility to become aware of the intertwined assumptions about gender and technology that inform our modern, Western perspective. Ideally, the historical study of recent technology promotes such cultural awareness. And research such as mine—shaped by the desire to address general public concerns—is especially suited to provoke personal reflection among Americans who are also archaeologists.

My concern to reach an audience that includes the literate lay public also raises issues germane to this volume's emphasis on teaching about technology and gender. Like most Americans, our students often feel disenfranchised in the realm of technological decision-making because they lack the requisite expertise. In fact, my commitment to research and write so as to communicate with a broader audience stems from my growing conviction that, in asserting their claims to expertise as befits a rapidly professionalizing group of scholars, historians of technology merely deepen the central dilemma of modern technology—the pervasive conviction that most of us do not know enough to participate in technological decision-making; that we have to trust technology to the experts.

My guess is that, like most of us, when it comes to understanding technology and gender, archaeologists and their students know too much rather than too little. For example, one of my principal arguments is that when we consider modern American technology, we are most constrained by our narrow preconceptions of technology. We start off on the wrong foot because we hear the word "technology" and immediately envision complex mechanisms, sophisticated electronics, or mysterious molecular combinations. In any event, our initial image is of technology as hardware. We may, as historians of technology generally do, notice the "-ology" in technology and concede that it includes knowledge as well as tools, but, again, we tend to imagine most of that knowledge as the purview of engineers and their corporate and government managers.[2] Hence my title: "Reconceiving Technology." My largest contention is that we will continue in the squirrel-wheel of current technological thinking as long as we construe technology so narrowly.

My subtitle—"Why Feminine Technologies Matter"—is meant to point the way toward a broader outlook. There are, of course, lots of reasons why the technologies associated with women should matter to scholars and citizens. Feminist scholars have already articulated many of them (Cowan 1979; McGaw 1982, 1989). At the very least, a full picture of technology has to include the tools, skills, and knowledge associated with the female majority. Moreover, in societies such as ours in which women do most child rearing and tending, our subconscious, unarticulated technological convictions must derive principally from our early preverbal experience around technologies selected and manipulated by women. It is also true that until we began to study women and technological change, we were able to remain unaware and ignorant of technology's masculine dimensions—we studied inventors, engineers, and entrepreneurs as though they were simply "people," oblivious to the ramifications of the overwhelming masculine predominance, both numerically and politically, in the so-called technological professions.

Thus, there is an abundance of good reasons to study women and technology. In what follows I emphasize yet another reason: looking at feminine technologies makes visible precisely those aspects of technology that we need to examine if we seek alternatives to a modern, Western technology that appears to be self-destructive, self-justifying, and self-perpetuating. By feminine technologies, I mean those technologies associated with women by virtue of their biology: tampons, brassieres, and IUD's, for example. And I mean those technologies that almost all American women use by virtue of their social roles: kitchen utensils, household cleaning products, and sewing needles, for example. Beginning with a look at such items, I hope to suggest a broader view of feminine technologies as well.

Archaeologists, anthropologists, and historians of non-Western technology might readily argue that studies of prehistoric and non-Western technologies serve equally well to make visible aspects of technology that we fail to see when examining more familiar examples. Although this is certainly the case, archaeologists also recognize how inextricably intertwined are technologies and their cultures. Indeed, many have learned from their own experiences how formidable is the challenge of disentangling their personal cultural sense of technology from the assumptions they deploy when associating prehistoric or non-Western technology with its culture. For Westerners generally and for archaeologists who are also Westerners, then, the more idiosyncratic features of our technological beliefs and practices may best be observed by working with Western examples. Feminine technologies have the advantage of already being domesticated, in both senses of the word: they are Western, but outside the masculine mainstream.[3]

Moreover, an accessible study of feminine technologies promises an immediate practical payoff. It can help to persuade the people in our society most convinced that they lack technological expertise—namely women—that, to the contrary, they know more than enough to contribute intelligently to any discussion of technology policy. Simultaneously, it can challenge archaeologists and other scholars with an interest in gender to recognize unexamined and unsupported assumptions about the sexual division of technological expertise in the past.

In what follows, I discuss briefly several of the case studies that form the backbone of my current work. In so doing I will delineate some of those neglected aspects of technology that we suddenly see clearly when we look at feminine technology. In general, by calling our attention to the technological knowledge associated with the selection and use of products, the study of women's technologies reveals technological choice and technological knowledge to be pervasive, not confined to a corps of experts. It shows that neither tools nor professional technologists determine the ultimate form of a technological activity: purchasers and users do.

Looking at feminine technologies also means looking especially at the relations of technology and biology. In the process, it suggests how extensively modern technology has been driven by the impulse to obscure the reality that we are animals as well as intellects. And, because feminine technologies are often the technologies of the private sphere, bringing them to light exposes how interwoven with modern technologies are novel conceptions of privacy, conceptions very much at issue in current political debates. At the same time, examining women's technological activities helps expose the deep and obscure ties between public and private, linkages that ultimately make the distinction problematic, linkages encapsulated in such an oxymoron as the "right to privacy."

Finally, and perhaps most importantly for archaeologists and other students of the past, studies of feminine technology give us a novel perspective on that most troublesome of notions in technological history: progress. Although historians of technology have made a major commitment to eradicating this value-laden concept, what they have mostly done is to reveal technology's social construction (Staudenmaier 1985).[4] They have demonstrated, that is, that technology has no inherent logic of its own, but embodies the perspective of its creators: that it gets "better" only in the sense that it better serves the interests of those empowered to make technological decisions. This is a long and laudable step away from the "march of progress" story that historians generally made of technology several decades ago. Nonetheless, it leaves untouched the notion that there is such a thing as a "better" technology: one that would materialize if only a better social system governed technology's development.

Mechanizing the Biological: The Brassiere as High-Tech

Close scrutiny of feminine technologies reveals that our whole notion of "better" may be specious. Consider, for example, the brassiere. The brassiere is one of the many feminine technologies about which technological history tells us virtually nothing. Yet in other respects—other than being used by women, that is—the brassiere falls into precisely those categories that scholars have deemed most worthy of study. Judging from the word *brassiere*'s initial appearance in our language—1911 according to the OED supplement—this undergarment is a thoroughly modern invention (Burchfield 1987).[5] Like many of the technologies historians of technology have deemed especially worth studying—automobiles, industrial research labs, and electric light and power systems, for example—it evidently originated during the late nineteenth and early twentieth centuries, the era often designated the Second Industrial Revolution. As clothing goes, the brassiere qualifies as "high tech," incorporating relatively early on such sophisticated products of the chemical industries as rubber and synthetic fiber. And its inclusion of such components as wires to stabilize it and adjustable straps and fasteners to modify it make it visibly more complex than we expect of mere clothing (Hawthorne 1992; Cunnington and Cunnington 1992; Craik 1994:129). Indeed, early brassieres frequently list patent numbers on attached labels, underscoring their technological character.

Those of us who lived through the early years of the contemporary women's movement, when feminists were often dismissed as "bra burners,"[6] will immediately recognize one way in which the history of the brassiere renders progress a profoundly dubious notion. The avowed purpose of the brassiere is to support the breast tissue, yet there is no convincing evidence that breasts need support. Even breasts so large that they quickly droop in the absence of support cannot be said to "need" support; at best we are discussing a preference. Clearly, the brassiere serves essentially cosmetic purposes; changes in it are closely associated with changes in fashion, changing definitions of feminine beauty, and changing prescriptions for feminine behavior.

Our first impulse, then, might be to dismiss brassieres as not "real" technology, like such functional technologies as automobiles, industrial research labs, and electric light and power systems, for example. Yet if we are willing to take this feminine technology seriously we may be pushed to ask important neglected questions about "real" technologies. How much, for example, do automobiles serve a cosmetic purpose, especially a purpose associated historically with enhanced masculinity? Do they in fact provide the freedom and speed of travel often considered as their function, or merely the illusion of freedom and speed? Likewise, how much of the role of industrial research labs is "real" and how much part of projecting the image that DuPont wants us to experience "better living through chemistry" and that GE devotes itself to bringing "good things to light"? For that matter, although anyone who knows the history of industrial fires or of domestic cleaning can recognize important safety and labor-reducing functions of electric light and power systems, how much of their early and continuing output has gone to uses best described as decorative, cosmetic? How bright do our homes and offices "need" to be, for example?

Looking at the brassiere more closely makes the notion of technological progress problematic at yet another level. The heart of my study of this technology has involved talking with women, focusing on a single question: How do you know that your bra fits? When women's answers are combined with the accounts of saleswomen and gynecologists, and with prescriptive literature on the subject, articles in girls' and women's magazines, for example, one large conclusion emerges: it doesn't. No one's bra fits. When asked, women talk in terms of making the best of a limited array of choices or of finding something less unsatisfactory than their previous choice. They may even wax enthusiastic about the latest innovation: a more comfortable fabric, less irritating strap width, more accommodating cup size, less inconvenient fastener. But although no one says it directly, it is implicit in everyone's responses: brassieres don't fit. At best the real experts in this field—individual consumers and saleswomen—learn to know what brands come closest in particular cases.

The central problem with this feminine technology goes beyond issues of capitalist exploitation of the consumer or patriarchal disregard for women's concerns, arguments to which analysis through social construction readily leads. The central problem is that you cannot make a bra that fits. You cannot because breasts are living things, not standardized commodities. Any given woman's two breasts are never exactly the same size and shape. And the size and shape of any given woman's breasts change continuously—as she ages, as she gains or loses weight, as she goes through pregnancies, as she experiences her monthly hormonal cycles. Added to the underlying problem with all ready-to-wear clothing—that people do not come in standard sizes—these considerations make the brassiere an especially stark example of modern technology's inherent inadequacy in the area to which it has increasingly turned its attention: standardizing the biological (Brownmiller 1984:40; Ayalah and Weinstock 1979).[7]

Myths of technological expertise to the contrary notwithstanding, ordinary women are the great experts in this area. They make the compromises and create the knowledge that permits a deeply flawed system to work. In the case of brassieres they begin in adolescence to build and maintain a highly personalized body of information (technology as knowledge) that serves to adjust a standard system to individual difference. Thus far, I have found little evidence that women have ever gained much of this expertise from their mothers, probably because adolescence—the time when a woman would be most likely to need it—is, in this culture, a time when communication between the generations is especially difficult—and nowhere more so than in decisions about personal appearance. Peer exchanges and individual experimentation serve as the principal sources of technological development, with professional expertise—either from saleswomen or from written materials—playing a distinctly minor role.[8] The resulting body of knowledge about the best brands and styles for the individual, the necessary adjustments, including structural modifications and additions, and the variations that suit particular overgarments and activities needs continuous modification because the options available for purchase change frequently. And, as women who want or need to avoid synthetic fabrics make especially clear, there is little to suggest that, even within the inherent limitations of the technology, brassieres exhibit technological progress.

Brassieres are only one of many technologies intended to suit the mechanical to the biological. And women's knowledge plays a crucial role by compensating for the inadequacies of many of these technologies. Women do a disproportionate share of the society's clothes shopping and clothing modification, an area in which their labor is economically and socially invisible and is further obscured by jokes about their propensity to shop (Benson 1986). Likewise, women work hard to offset the deficiencies of the various foods suited to mechanical harvesting and long-term storage, devising ways to create flavorful meals while relying on products such as canned vegetables, iceberg lettuce, and Delicious apples, to name but the most obvious examples, and acquiring the continuously changing knowledge of how to assess food's probable freshness, potential longevity, and possible safety (Cowan 1983). And they have developed the skill that has modified several generations worth of new and standardized diapering products to variously shaped and rapidly changing infants and toddlers.

Thus, beginning with a simple technology like a bra and asking a simple question like, "How do you know it fits?" leads us rather quickly to some important reconceptualizations of technology. First, we find that, although we usually associate technology with utility, its actual role is often decorative or cosmetic. Its kinship to the visual arts, heretofore recognized mostly in studies of inventors (Hindle 1981a), may turn out to be its most important relationship. Second, we recognize that, where living things and people are concerned, apparently functional technology is inherently flawed; that the services which the producers of goods apparently render actually serve us only because goods are made serviceable through women's invisible bodies of knowledge—the technology of consumption and modification. In sum, these observations reveal technology to be far less solid, substantial, and straightforward than we commonly assume in our discussions of technological progress or technology policy. Assessing whether technology is "better" seems a pretty dubious enterprise once we see how much of it is smoke and mirrors, how illusive are its boundaries and intentions.

Inside the White Box: Closets, Cupboards, and the Technology of Filing

Feminine technology proves equally provocative when we turn to an older, simpler, and more clearly utilitarian example: the closet. For those acquainted with early modern Anglo-American material culture, the story of closets begins as a familiar one. In fact, its history offers an abbreviated account of technological development from the late medieval and early modern era through the Industrial Revolution. Judging from surviving structures, house plans, inventories, and the linguistic history of terms such as "closet," "cupboard," "dresser," "bureau," "pantry," "larder," and "cabinet," closets and other storage spaces were comparatively rare until the century or so just before the onset of the British and American Industrial Revolutions (McGaw 1994b; Furnivall et al. 1933; Upton and Vlach 1986).[9] Earlier usage of terms denoting the technologies of storage expresses that closets and other built-in or wooden containers were limited to the dwellings of the extremely affluent or privileged: royalty, the church, and those with plate, jewelry, or similar goods requiring specialized storage.

Beginning in the seventeenth century, this situation began to change. Words such as closet and cupboard came increasingly to be used in their modern sense, as storage spaces for utensils, provisions, and other, more common goods. Inventories confirm that storage furniture such as cabinets and dressers grew more pervasive. They also reveal that storage technology had developed at least in part because more and more people had more and more goods to store. Thus, the growing commonness of closets and cabinets highlights something histories of industrial technology too often ignore: the Industrial Revolution was, in the first instance, a response to rising consumption—to a growing market among people of the middling sort for goods such as ceramics, woodenware, textiles, and iron implements. Consumer initiative directed the activity of those who came to invent, develop, and invest in the new manufacturing technology (Shammas 1980; McKendrick, Brewer, and Plumb 1982; Campbell 1987).[10]

By the early nineteenth century the Industrial Revolution was in full swing, lowering substantially the real cost of most of the items people had come to store in closets. Not surprisingly, closets proliferated. Indeed, the abundance of closets—built-in storage spaces—is one key technological change evident in Victorian house plans (Clark 1986; McMurry 1988).[11] Building technology abetted this innovation. By the nineteenth century, Americans generally employed balloon-frame construction, a system using light two-by-fours and nails in lieu of heavier timbers of irregular dimensions that had been specially notched and pegged together. The new system dramatically reduced building costs, permitting house purchasers not only to have more rooms, but also to have more ells, bay windows, closets, and similar small nooks set apart within larger rooms.

Linguistic clues show that, within the new context of abundance, storage technology was also transformed—we might even say reinvented. Historically the various sorts of storage spaces had been highly specialized. The "-ology" part of the technology—the rules governing use of closets, larders, and pantries—had circumscribed their contents. Thus, larders, as the word echoes, originally housed pork products in particular and came to serve as meat storehouses. Pantries, as the word's French derivative might signal, were bread rooms, a use broadened to include other foodstuffs by the seventeenth century. Cupboards originally held cups and other vessels, as one might guess from looking at the word. Cabinets, historically meaning "little cabins," were repositories with locks for storing valuables such as jewels or documents.

By the eighteenth century these distinctions were clearly breaking down. Cupboards had come to hold meat, money, bread, and books; larders stored food of all sorts; and pantries might contain plate and linen, as well as provisions generally. Nineteenth-century usage suggests even more overlap in function. Nor was the reinvention of storage technology confined to its software: the rules governing what might be stored where. At the close of the eighteenth century, that mistress of precise word use, Jane Austen, wrote of "A closet full of shelves . . . it should therefore be called a cupboard rather than a closet" (Furnivall et al. 1933:440). Her attempt to reassert traditional usage signals its decline. Clearly, closets—separate tiny rooms—now sometimes contained shelves, whereas formerly shelf storage had characterized cupboards, pieces of furniture often placed in a room's corner or recess.

The most pervasive change in the hardware of storage was the shift from open display to total enclosure. Originally the cupboard was a board or table on which plate and ceramics were displayed. Likewise, "dresser" designated the kitchen table on which food was dressed and the hall or dining room table from which dishes were served and on which empty dishes were arrayed. Both word usage and surviving artifacts show dressers and cupboards becoming more cabinet-like, more enclosed. Simultaneously, the terms "closet" and "cabinet," originally signifying separate rooms, increasingly referred to mere storage enclosures.

Although the axiom "necessity is the mother of invention" might explain the proliferation of storage spaces, the abundance of new things to be stored did not necessitate their enclosure, much less their increasingly promiscuous arrangement. Indeed, one might more easily imagine that having more things to keep track of would encourage people to place them where they could be seen and to array them in specialized containers.

Making sense of the new storage technology begins by remembering who performed the work of storage. In late medieval and early modern England, where larders and cupboards and closets were confined to palaces and monasteries, specialized servants supervised and manipulated the technology of storage. Terms such as "butler's pantry" or "housemaid's pantry" indicate the linkage of specialized technology with specialized laborer. By contrast, as household goods grew more numerous in common people's homes on the eve of industrialization and, later, as they gradually filled the residences of the new industrial middle class, a single, unspecialized worker—the housewife—supervised disposition of the entire array and performed much of the manual labor of storage and retrieval as well (Cowan 1983).

Housewives, because of their multiple concerns, brought new considerations to decisions about how to array goods. For example, eighteenth- and nineteenth-century housewives could expect to spend a substantial part of their careers supervising small children while performing their work. Storing goods so as to keep them away from infants and toddlers must have been important to such women, whereas the butlers of the noble or affluent could expect nursemaids to keep children away from ceramics, foodstuffs, and linen.

Similarly, as unspecialized domestic workers, housewives performed cleaning as well as storage tasks. Storing goods in enclosed spaces greatly reduced the work of cleaning by separating linen and utensils from the soot and ash pervasive in houses containing the innumerable fires necessitated by eighteenth- and nineteenth-century cooking, heating, and lighting technologies. Indeed, as Ruth Schwartz Cowan has observed (1983:162–63), modern notions of household cleanliness are only conceivable where most items are no longer left on the table, but have separate places where they can be stored. Only where goods and implements can be moved to cupboards or closets can table and counter surfaces be kept free from food debris and dust.

So much for the hardware of the closet, what of the software? Why wouldn't it still make sense to keep the contents of closets homogeneous? Judging from household inventories, the answer, once again, lies in the fact that closets had become women's technologies. And what housewives needed most from their storage technologies was to find the implements of their work proximate to their workplaces. Food, cooking implements, and serving dishes belonged together in the kitchen pantry or dresser. Dining linen was handiest when placed with china and glassware, whereas bed linen was most accessible if stored in bed chamber closets alongside the clothing and personal goods of the chamber's occupant. Whatever their original uses, broken goods, obsolete tools, and worn-out items could be consigned to attics or spare rooms.

This new technology of filing did not emerge overnight. Household inventories from the eighteenth century suggest a diversity of arrangements although, as Robert St. George has noted, rules of appropriate order become increasingly evident (St. George 1986). By the mid-nineteenth century, the process was sufficiently complete, at least in the mid-Atlantic states, that inventory takers could merely list "Sundries in the Kitchen," "Sundries in the Pantry," and "Sundries in the Chamber" in the certainty that people knew roughly what items belonged where.

But only the housewife knew *precisely* what belonged where. As with all filing systems, the knowledge part of the technology had to be idiosyncratic to function successfully. No two households had the same array of goods, users, or storage spaces, or the same chronology of acquisition. So only the housewife knew where to find and where to replace all of the family's diverse and growing inventory of possessions. By the late nineteenth century virtually all middle-class girls must have received domestic training in this sort of filing. Thus, it is hardly surprising that, once government and corporate bureaucracies came to require extensive filing systems, they could find an abundant supply of female employees to perform the labor skillfully, yet at low pay,[12] just as manufacturers had experienced little trouble finding cheap female labor to perform supposedly unskilled sewing tasks.

Ironically, then, like the complex household appliances of the twentieth century, the eighteenth- and nineteenth-century closet began by promising to be labor-saving—to reduce cleaning, that is—but ended up creating more work (Cowan 1983). Anyone who has kept house knows how much time is spent in picking things up and putting them away. And, like most twentieth-century household appliances, the work of nineteenth-century storage technology came to be used not to reduce cleaning, but to permit higher standards of cleanliness.

Anyone who has performed housework also knows how hard it is to delegate tasks, such as cooking, to someone who does not know where to find the tools and ingredients, or tasks, such as laundry, to someone who does not know where to put things away. In other words, comic strips and sitcoms featuring the inept husband dependent on his wife to find necessary items of dress or grooming point to real skills housewives need to have. The extensiveness and social invisibility of these household filing skills helps explain why housework has remained so resistant to the division of labor, even where husbands and wives have attempted more equitable arrangements (Vanek 1974).

White Collar: On Cleanliness and Class

Since women's work often employs apparently simple technology, such as closets, that actually entail extremely complex bodies of knowledge, such as filing, study of feminine technology makes us especially aware that much resistance to technological change derives from our investment in the invisible software that is generally the largest aspect of technology and the aspect we most frequently miss when attempting to comprehend technology. Not only does the knowledge and skill part of technology help account for the persistent gendered division of labor that remains inexplicable in terms of economic rationality, it also helps explain many other apparently irrational aspects of technological choice. Why, for example, has the desire for greater cleanliness inspired extensive innovation in household technology and household labor for more than two centuries? The answer to that question is multifaceted and largely beyond the scope of this essay. A full answer will certainly require that we examine the profound influence of evangelical Protestantism in our avowedly secular culture. It is no coincidence, for example, that the belief that "cleanliness is next to godliness" was first articulated on the eve of industrialization. And it is no surprise that the originator of the axiom was John Wesley, writing in a tract entitled "On Dress" that was especially directed to women.

Understanding the driving force of cleanliness also involves tracing the association of cleanliness and class, especially in America where geographic mobility and ethnic diversity made external markers more essential than in most other Western societies.[13] Ruth Cowan's work conveys with particular clarity the dynamic linkages between class, cleanliness, and twentieth-century household technology (1983:152–219). My window on the process is a single artifact—the white collar—whose history encapsulates central themes in the history of women's domestic work.

Although specific features of the white collar's history differ from anything archaeological evidence is likely to reveal, at least two aspects of its history are germane to interpreting archaeological evidence. First, the case of the white collar directs our attention to a prerequisite for technology's adoption and diffusion that scholars rarely consider: maintenance. The diffusion of the white collar—a clothing technology employed to signify class—cannot be understood without comprehending the nature of laundry technology—the maintenance tools and procedures that assured the white collar's social utility. Second, study of the white collar indicates that we cannot simply write off changes in a garment's form as superficial matters of fashion. As in this instance, fluctuations in form may be firmly linked to a garment's shifting social function. Thus, where archaeologists have reason to suspect the presence of social hierarchy, engendering archaeology may call for close attention to technology's possible symbolic functions. Or it may require imaginative reconstruction of maintenance procedures that were the work of very different people from those who deployed the technology.[14]

The history of the white collar may be recounted briefly. Among early modern English people and colonial Americans, almost no one wore collars, or anything we would consider white. The starched white ruff or collar band had long symbolized gentility, because, unlike the rest of the shirt, its quality and condition were visible.[15] Keeping a collar starched and white required considerable labor, despite the general practice of making ruffs and collars detachable, a practice that at least limited the laundress's most heroic efforts to collars alone.[16] A white collar signified that someone, usually a female servant supervised by the mistress of the house, had performed the following tasks: making soap, hauling water, filling and emptying washtubs a number of times, building a fire and heating the water, soaking the clothes, rubbing the clothes against a washboard, wringing them out several times, soaping dirty spots several times, boiling the clothes, rinsing them, making starch, dipping collars and other parts to be stiffened in the starch, hanging the clothes to dry, dampening them, heating irons on the hearth, testing the irons, and ironing the garments.

During the late eighteenth and early nineteenth century when industrial and political revolutions were transforming Anglo-American class structures, the white collar reflected that social instability in its exceedingly diverse forms. Among the elite, the collar was now generally attached to the shirt, underscoring the owner's ability to pay someone to render the whole garment white. Its size varied considerably. In the early nineteenth century, fashionable men's collars might be so large that before folding they hid the face entirely. Contemporaries clearly recognized what large white collars represented in women's work. One early nineteenth-century periodical commented that when Beau Brummell first sported the new fashion "dandies were struck dumb with envy and washerwomen miscarried" (quoted in Cunnington and Cunnington 1992:100). At the same time, many men eschewed the display of the collar as undemocratic, wearing neckcloths that hid it completely. This was also the era when the "dickey" or false shirtfront with attached collar appeared to accommodate those who couldn't afford to launder entire shirts. Although out of favor among the genteel, detachable collars also persisted. In sum, during an era of enormous social change and unrest, collars reveal the guardians of gentility struggling to maintain "the thin white line which cut the community in two, separating the gentleman of leisure from the manual worker" (Cunnington and Cunnington 1992:99).

Part of the difficulty, of course, was the proliferation of ambiguous jobs whose occupants were neither leisured nor manual laborers: professionals, factory owners, and, especially, clerks and salesmen of various sorts—people who came to be designated white-collar workers. By mid-century the vast majority of those sporting white collars fell into the latter category. What distinguished white-collar workers was that, despite their modest incomes, their work entailed close proximity to employers or customers who required assurance of their social respectability. White collars continued to testify that the wearer could afford their maintenance, which remained considerable. The technical aspects of keeping white collars white had changed little by the mid-nineteenth century save that women now often purchased ready-made soap and they increasingly used cast iron stoves to heat their water and irons. They also generally subjected white garments to an extra rinse in water containing bluing, requiring an extra wringing as well. In general, then, wearing a white collar showed that a man paid a laundress, but also supported a full-time housewife who supervised the labor. In other words, white collars signaled adherence to the basic tenets of Victorian middle-class life.

As the nineteenth century wore on, the tenuous hold many white-collar workers had on middle-class status was recognized by the increased acceptability of detachable collars, although the existence of disposable paper collars reveals that maintaining white-collar respectability remained a struggle for many. It also remained a struggle for their wives, although by the late nineteenth and early twentieth centuries increasing numbers of women had indoor running water, eliminating the heaviest washday chore. At the same time, however, burgeoning white-collar demand made good servants harder to find. One response was to send at least some laundry, especially the breadwinner's valuable white collars and cuffs, to one of a growing number of commercial establishments (Strasser 1982:104–24; Cowan 1983).

Only in the post–World War I era did detachable shirt collars disappear, meaning that someone had to keep the whole garment white. Initially that someone was likely to be a woman tending a machine in a commercial laundry; men's shirts were the one item even hard-pressed white-collar households managed to send out. After commercial establishments had underwritten the development of a washing machine technology that could be modified and marketed to middle-class households, however, the someone in question was increasingly the housewife who washed, starched, and ironed the family's shirts, using new electrical appliances to compensate for the dearth of domestic servants, appliances whose cost discouraged white-collar families from sending any laundry outside the home. We all know the end of the story. By the 1960s and 1970s, household technology and clothing technology made ironing and starching relatively unnecessary. Instead, housewives laundered many more shirts and blouses in an increasingly diverse array of fabrics and hues, requiring more extensive software in the form of washing procedures and chemical agent selection. The progressive extension of standards of cleanliness is nicely summarized in our ability to concern ourselves with the hidden rings inside our collars.

For me, the persistent extension of the white collar and its associated technological and labor system nicely captures the powerful, largely unexamined role of women's maintenance labor in defining who qualifies for white-collar work. Perhaps part of our current preoccupation with "the decline of the family" stems from our inability to rely on such external evidence to assess and avoid those whose family structures we deplore. After all, we cannot really see inside people's collars. Like the mass-produced calicoes that made it possible for early nineteenth-century working girls to dress like ladies—a phenomenon their contemporaries found simultaneously attractive and unnerving—modern household technology had rendered traditional markers of class increasingly obsolete. Although our culture generally applauds cleanliness, we are made uneasy by its pervasiveness. How can we tell whose homes our children can safely visit? Who can we trust in front of our classrooms? Is there a way to use data bases and electronic technology to screen potential life partners? [17]

From Closet to Water Closet: The Technology of Privacy

To comprehend more fully this aspect of technology, let us return to the closet. Or, to be more precise, let us consider what returning to the closet has come to signify. Clearly, in modern parlance, the notion of people being in closets conveys the sense of something amiss. People are being forced to hide something, usually their sexuality, that should not need to be hidden and, thus, in a real sense, to hide themselves. The very choice of the phrase announces that, among the many acceptable uses of closets, the housing of people is not one.

Originally, by contrast, that is precisely what closets were meant to do—assure people privacy. All of the early uses of the word refer to small enclosed spaces where people performed acts that early modern English people deemed best carried out in private: sleeping, dressing, praying and meditating, studying and speculating. Indeed, so strongly were closets associated with privacy that in the seventeenth century "closet" served as an adjectival synonym for "private," in the full and positive sense of that word. "Cabinet," the other general term for an enclosed storage space, has a similar history. Only in the seventeenth century, on the eve of industrialization, that is, did closets and cabinets become places for things rather than for people. And part of the software of enclosed spaces that was transposed from people to things was the emphasis on privacy, a linkage succinctly conveyed in one of the industrial era's favorite phrases: "private property."

Neither the limits of the essay form nor the state of my researches permits an attempt to explain how the shifts in who and what deserved privacy played out. One thing is clear: the increased relegation of women to the private sphere was only one of several redefinitions of privacy's role that coincided with the great technological revolutions of the eighteenth and nineteenth centuries. Again, paying attention to feminine technologies matters because the association of women and privacy has been so visible, and because women have often been especially associated, rhetorically at least, with other increasingly private aspects of life.

One especially arresting embodiment of the technology of privacy, and one of more than passing interest to archaeologists, is the bathroom. The bathroom ranks as a truly remarkable technological development because of the rapidity with which this utterly new room assumed its standard modern form—a process completed within a few decades in the late nineteenth and early twentieth centuries (Gideon 1948:682–711; Strasser 1982:96–103). The invention of the bathroom meant more than just privatizing excretion by moving it inside the house. It also meant use of a new piece of hardware, generally denominated a "water closet," a term that also applied to the room in which the toilet, to use more modern parlance, was housed. After a few decades in which closets had been deemed appropriate receptacles mostly for things, new standards of privacy made it appropriate to return at least some human activities to the closet.

Moreover, the original hardware of the bathroom makes clear that all excretion—sweating and menstruation as well as urination and defecation—grew increasingly private. The growing social value assigned to hot water baths to remove sweat and sebaceous excretion was the other principal motive for creating the new room, a motive embodied in the sink and bathtub installed together with the toilet in the standard American bathroom. Simultaneously, the early development of disposable menstrual products permitted the gradual confinement of menstrual blood to the water closet rather than permitting it in the laundry.

The other significant cultural function of the water closet was to "eliminate waste," a phrase worth paying attention to. Environmentally, of course, there was nothing particularly novel about Americans' using the continent's abundant pure water to carry away waste; early

American factories were situated on rivers as much for their utility in removing industrial byproducts as for their water power. What was remarkable about the bathroom was the growing conviction that humans could be rendered immaculate, divorced from the aromas and physical evidence of their status as animals. It is both ironic and unsurprising that a people intent on denying their biology created a system of waste removal that helps to threaten our survival as animals, both through its excessive use of and its extensive pollution of water.

Nor is it coincidence, I think, that the era in which Americans committed themselves to eliminating evidence that humans excrete ushered in the era in which engineers became obsessed with eliminating industrial waste. What they meant, unfortunately, was not the elimination of industrial pollution, but the reduction of production workers to automatons through time-motion studies, and the elimination of white-collar and managerial discretion through the wholesale introduction of new record-keeping forms and quantitative assessment techniques. As in the bathroom, so also in scientific management, eliminating waste meant denying the full range of human behavior.

Here, as elsewhere, feminine technology matters, because the technology of women's work made both odor-free bathrooms and paper-filled offices possible. In the process, of course, women, at least, remained fully cognizant that family members excreted and that proliferating forms did not make bosses scientific. Of course, women were creatures of the private sphere—schooled through the decades to launder, rather than air, the dirty linen. It seemed safe to trust them with the secrets.

No wonder women's growing unwillingness to stay in the private sphere or keep the customary secrets has created such a backlash. Far more is at stake here than who changes dirty diapers, although this act, too, has wider technological, social, and environmental implications. What is at stake is an entire economic, technological, cultural system— in essence, the society erected through the Industrial Revolution. That revolution has been widely touted as a great miracle: creating abundance, leisure, longevity, and a host of other good things. Certainly, critics have noted the inequity of the system, but by confining their focus to masculine, public technology they have tended to limit their critique as well. They have mostly been concerned with who runs the machines versus who manages, and with how the spoils are divided. They have generally missed such important and central issues as the qualitative inadequacy of the system's products—such as brassieres or iceberg lettuce; the inherent tendency of the system to create more work—such as putting everything away in closets or rendering whole garments spotlessly clean; or the frightening prospect that a system so divorced from biological reality inevitably threatens the biological—as do water closets and scientifically managed factories. Feminine technologies matter because they disclose the system's fatal flaws: it threatens and reduces natural abundance, necessitates increased labor, and promises longevity at best only to the current occupants of the planet.

For archaeologists, I expect that the lessons of these cases will be as diverse as their researches. Certainly many will find my concern with distinctive feminine attire, storage technology, class-specific household labor, and technological activities shrouded in privacy directly applicable to the era and culture they study; they are certainly technological features common to many times and places. Certain themes that surface in my research also seem broadly relevant.

First, because software, the knowledge component of technology, predominates in our society's feminine technologies, it requires a special effort to make the nature and implications of that technology visible. It is especially easy to dismiss women's technological knowledge—filing items in closets and cupboards or selecting and modifying garments, for example. Although it is certainly possible to recognize in other cultures what we fail to see in our own, our tendency will be to miss precisely those aspects of the past that we miss in the present. Given the nature of artifactual evidence, seeing the software will always require greater commitment than seeing the hardware. Gender bias can only exacerbate our blindness.

Second, because the public/private dichotomy in our society is pervasive and emotionally charged, and because technology is culturally associated with public, masculine endeavor, it takes an extra effort to identify as technological those artifacts associated with the private, feminine aspects of culture. Neither the brassiere nor the closet comes to anyone's lips when asked to list some technologies. Rather, we put up a bit of a struggle before conceding their relevance to the topic. Given the nature of the archaeological enterprise, this challenges us to avoid reading such associations into the remote past. Even where we recognize the irrelevance of our culture's public/private dichotomy, we may still tend to see activities currently denoted private as inherently less technological.

Third, the persistent association of Western, feminine technology with human biological functions also tends to render these technologies less visible—to naturalize them in a sense. Whereas we know that we don't need automobiles, industrial research labs, and electric light and power systems, for example, we assume some level of need for food, clothing, shelter, and hygiene and we inadvertently extend the aura of necessity to the technologies that serve those functions. We are less likely, that is, to view human creativity and social choice as just as free ranging when it comes to producing technologies tailored to biological needs. We reason as though the need dictated the shape of the technology. Coming from a Western perspective this may make us especially blind when a culture gives low priority to technologies closely linked to the body, especially the female body.

Finally, if, as I think they do, these case studies of feminine technologies raise fundamental and troubling questions about the entire modern, Western technological enterprise—questions very different from those raised by the technologies we usually study—the lesson for archaeologists and other students of technology seems especially clear. Paying attention to technologies associated with women can neither be dismissed as a luxury nor written off as a concession to political correctness. Some might argue that neglecting feminine technology means telling only half of the technological story. I submit that it means missing the most important parts.

Acknowledgments

I wish to thank Ruth Schwartz Cowan, Mary Kelley, Patrick Malone, Jean Silver-Isenstadt, Fredrika Teute, and Rita Wright for reading and commenting on earlier versions of this essay. I am also grateful to Kristina Haugland, assistant curator of costume and textiles at the Philadelphia Museum of Art, for sharing her expertise in the history of underwear and for showing me a collection of historic brassieres.

Notes

1. Like many social historians of women, in framing my early research I depended on scholarship in physical and cultural anthropology, guided by my then colleague Jane Lancaster (Brown 1970, 1976; Lancaster 1976; Rosaldo and Lamphere 1974; Tanner and Zihlman 1976; Zihlman 1978; Frisch 1978). Many of these are the same works Gero and Conkey (1991) cite as current resources for the construction of an engendered archaeology. My training and practice of the history of technology has also consistently emphasized the importance of the artifact, relying on scholarship in historic and industrial archaeology, and material culture (for example, Deetz 1977; Quimby 1978; Hindle 1981b; Gordon and Malone 1994; McGaw 1996).

2. This "high-tech" bias is evident in the history of technology as well as in popular thought (McGaw 1994a:2–7; see also Staudenmaier 1985). Needless to say, an emphasis on technology as the purview of engineers and managers means telling a story with an overwhelmingly male cast of characters.

3. Here and hereinafter, in the interest of brevity, I use the term "feminine technology" to mean "modern, Western, predominantly American, feminine technology."

4. The popularity of the rhetoric of social construction becomes apparent from even a cursory reading of recent volumes of *Technology and Culture*, the

journal of the Society for the History of Technology. For an outstanding example of such scholarship see MacKenzie (1990).

5. Feminine technology throws into high relief the gradual, incremental nature of most technologies' development, and, hence, the relative meaninglessness of precise dates of origin. Here and in what follows I will often rely on word origins to supply a good rough chronology. The virtue of this approach is that word use signals the time by which a technology not only was in existence but also had sufficient cultural visibility to warrant linguistic innovation to permit discussion of it. By contrast, other frequently used measures such as patenting or initial production do not guarantee that anyone other than the patentee or the manufacturer had any awareness of the technology.

6. Although it is beyond the scope of this discussion, one of the more fascinating aspects of this technology is the mythology that has grown up surrounding it. That feminists burned bras is one such myth. Virtually everyone I discuss my research with knows that feminists burned bras in protest. Indeed, I also knew it. Nonetheless, there is no evidence that anyone in the women's movement ever burned a bra. The power of this image, probably "coined by some feature writer searching for a clever phrase" (Brownmiller 1984:45–46; but see also Faludi 1991:75), says volumes about gender and technology in America. Of course, brassieres are not unique among technologies in the elaborate mythology surrounding and partially obscuring them, an aspect of technological history that has attracted little serious scholarly attention.

7. In the history of technology, most scholarship on this topic treats agricultural technology (Fitzgerald 1991; Hightower 1972).

8. As with mother-daughter exchanges of information, young women's distrust of older women as a source of information about dress and appearance makes them unlikely to seek advice from saleswomen or to accept advice when it is proffered. It is easy to see how American culture helps young women develop their suspicion. To take but one example, "wardrobe engineer" John T. Malloy, in his first *Dress for Success* book offered only a few comments on women's dress, under the heading "How to Set Dress Codes for Women Employees." After noting that men's and women's perceptions of what is good and beautiful in clothing are "diametrically opposed," Malloy adds, "By the way, fifty-five-year-old female executives are no better or only slightly better qualified to choose the clothing for young female employees than are their male counterparts" (Malloy 1975).

9. As archaeologists certainly know, storage technology has a long history and prehistory. Thus, it is important to note that my phrasing here is not meant to assert the novelty and/or rarity of storage technology generally. Certainly many early modern houses had attics or cellars where an array of items was stored and they held barrels, ceramic containers, and other items used to store food in particular. My focus here is on a particular type of storage technology that consisted either of a separate small room built into the living areas of the house or of substantial pieces of furniture that fulfilled similar functions. In the interest of succinct exposition, I will sometimes refer to this particular class of items by the more general terms "storage technology" or "storage spaces."

Here and in what follows I draw on the rich and growing body of literature derived from probate inventories, described more fully in my own study of such materials (1994b:340n. 20). I also draw on several decades worth of visits to historic structures, principally in New England, the mid-Atlantic states, and Virginia. Sources cited here form the basis for many of the observations that follow.

10. Here, let me note in passing that most new consumer goods raised people's living standards only after domestic processing. Yard goods, for example, had to be sewn into clothing and linen. Many of the newly emphasized processing tasks—laundering and baking, for example—combined to comprise a new form of labor—an activity for which a new word, "housework," was coined (Cowan 1983: esp. 16–18).

11. Despite its increasing evidence in the floor plans illustrating most histories of American family houses, the closet has evoked virtually no comment from historians of American building. The word is, for example, absent from all of the indexes I consulted, offering additional testimony to the relative invisibility of technologies associated with women's work.

12. It is still true, as I noted more than a decade ago (McGaw 1982:811), that we lack a history of filing as a technology. The overwhelming predominance of software over hardware, combined with its feminization, readily explain its neglect.

13. This is an especially challenging question to answer for *American* domestic technology. Whenever I talk about the history of domestic technology for an audience that includes Europeans, someone invariably asks about the apparent American obsession with cleanliness, submitting their personal experience as evidence.

14. On the importance of imaginative reenvisioning to an engendered archaeology see Gero and Conkey (1991: esp. 20–21).

15. Historically the shirt was a male undergarment, so displaying the whole garment was not customary. Attitudes informed by the shirt's history still clearly undergird rules of male business and formal attire (Cunnington and Cunnington 1992).

16. In general, my account here and below of changes in shirt form relies on Cunnington and Cunnington (1992), modified to take account of American variation as necessary.

Given the considerable gulf between early modern behavior and our own, it is probably worth stating that there was no need to keep the shirt body particularly clean. It was not visible and any odors that permeated it would hardly be perceptible since no one bathed very often. Indeed, the practical function of the shirt was to protect the outer garments from bodily filth.

17. Here and elsewhere, my research reflects my conviction that the historian's task is to look to the past for insight on contemporary social, political, or cultural concerns; that history is never merely about the past; antiquarianism is. Although not peculiar to feminists, this is an approach especially suited to feminist scholarship because of our commitment to the relevance of personal experience. At least some archaeologists committed to the study of gender share my perspective (Gero and Conkey 1991: esp. 22–23).

References

Ayalah, Daphna, and Isaac J. Weinstock
    1979   *Breasts: Women Speak about Their Breasts and Their Lives.* New York: Summit Books.
Benson, Susan Porter
    1986   *Counter Cultures: Saleswomen, Managers, and Customers in American Department Stores, 1890–1940.* Urbana: University of Illinois Press.

Brown, Judith K.
1970 "A Note on the Division of Labor by Sex." *American Anthropologist* 72:1073–78.
1976 "An Anthropological Perspective on Sex Roles and Subsistence." In *Sex Differences: Social and Biological Perspectives,* edited by Michael S. Teitelbaum. New York: Anchor Books.
Brownmiller, Susan
1984 *Femininity.* New York: Ballantine Books.
Burchfield, R. W., ed.
1987 *The Compact Edition of the Oxford English Dictionary: Volume III, A Supplement to the Oxford English Dictionary, Volumes I–IV.* Oxford: Clarendon Press.
Campbell, Colin
1987 *The Romantic Ethic and the Spirit of Modern Consumerism.* Oxford: Basil Blackwell.
Clark, Clifford Edward, Jr.
1986 *The American Family Home.* Chapel Hill: University of North Carolina Press.
Cowan, Ruth Schwartz
1979 "From Virginia Dare to Virginia Slims: Women and Technology in American Life." *Technology and Culture* 20:51–63.
1983 *More Work for Mother: The Ironies of Household Technology from the Open Hearth to the Microwave.* New York: Basic Books.
Craik, Jennifer
1994 *The Face of Fashion: Cultural Studies in Fashion.* London: Routledge.
Cunnington, C. Willett, and Phillis Cunnington
1992 *The History of Underclothes.* New York: Dover Publications.
Deetz, James
1977 *In Small Things Forgotten: The Archaeology of Early American Life.* New York: Anchor Books.
Faludi, Susan
1991 *Backlash: The Undeclared War against American Women.* New York: Anchor Books.
Fitzgerald, Deborah
1991 "Beyond Tractors: The History of Technology in American Agriculture." *Technology and Culture* 32:114–26.
Frisch, Rose E.
1978 "Population, Food Intake, and Fertility." *Science* 199:22–30.
Furnivall, F. J., et al.
1933 *The Compact Edition of the Oxford English Dictionary.* Oxford: Oxford University Press.
Gero, Joan M., and Margaret W. Conkey
1991 "Tensions, Pluralities, and Engendering Archaeology: An Introduction to Women and Prehistory." In *Engendering Archaeology: Women and Prehistory,* edited by Joan M. Gero and Margaret W. Conkey. Oxford: Basil Blackwell.
Gideon, Siegfried
1948 *Mechanization Takes Command: A Contribution to Anonymous History.* New York: W. W. Norton and Company.

Gordon, Robert B., and Patrick M. Malone
 1994   *The Texture of Industry: An Archaeological View of the Industrialization of North America.* New York: Oxford University Press.
Hawthorne, Rosemary
 1992   *Bras: A Private View.* London: Souvenir Press.
Hightower, Jim
 1972   *Hard Tomatoes, Hard Times.* Cambridge, Mass.: Schenkman.
Hindle, Brooke, ed.
 1981a   *Emulation and Invention.* New York: W. W. Norton and Company.
 1981b   *Material Culture of the Wooden Age.* Tarrytown, N.Y.: Sleepy Hollow Press.
Lancaster, Jane Beckman
 1976   "Sex Roles in Primate Societies." In *Sex Differences: Social and Biological Perspectives,* edited by Michael S. Teitelbaum. New York: Anchor Books.
MacKenzie, Donald
 1990   *Inventing Accuracy: A Historical Sociology of Nuclear Missile Guidance.* Cambridge, Mass.: MIT Press.
Malloy, John T.
 1975   *Dress for Success.* New York: Peter H. Wyden.
McGaw, Judith
 1982   "Women and the History of American Technology: Review Essay." *Signs* 7:798–828.
 1989   "No Passive Victims, No Separate Spheres: A Feminist Perspective on Technology's History." In *In Context: History and the History of Technology,* edited by Stephen H. Cutcliffe and Robert C. Post, 172–91. Bethlehem, Pa.: Lehigh University Press.
 1994a   "Introduction: The Experience of Early American Technology." In *Early American Technology: Making and Doing Things from the Colonial Era to 1850,* edited by Judith A. McGaw, 1–15. Chapel Hill: University of North Carolina Press.
 1994b   "'So Much Depends upon a Red Wheelbarrow': Agricultural Tool Ownership in the Eighteenth-Century Mid-Atlantic." In *Early American Technology: Making and Doing Things from the Colonial Era to 1850,* edited by Judith A. McGaw, 328–57. Chapel Hill: University of North Carolina Press.
 1996   "'Say It!' No Ideas but in Things: Touching the Past through Early American Technological History." In *The World Turned Upside: The Reorientation of the Study of British North America in the Eighteenth Century,* edited by William G. Shade. Bethlehem, Pa.: Lehigh University Press.
McKendrick, Neil, John Brewer, and J. H. Plumb
 1982   *The Birth of a Consumer Society: The Commercialization of Eighteenth-Century England.* Bloomington: Indiana University Press.
McMurry, Sally
 1988   *Families and Farmhouses in Nineteenth Century America.* New York: Oxford University Press.
Quimby, Ian M. G., ed. *Material Culture and the Study of American Life.* New York:
 1978   W. W. Norton and Company.
Rosaldo, Michelle Zimbalist, and Louise Lamphere, eds.
 1974   *Women, Culture, and Society.* Stanford, Calif.: Stanford University Press.

St. George, Robert Blair
    1986   "'Set Thine House in Order': The Domestication of the Yeomanry in Seventeenth-Century New England." In *Common Places: Readings in American Vernacular Architecture*, edited by Dell Upton and John Michael Vlach. Athens: University of Georgia Press.
Shammas, Carole
    1980   "The Domestic Environment in Early Modern England and America." *Journal of Social History* 14:3–24.
Staudenmaier, John M.
    1985   *Technology's Storytellers: Reweaving the Human Fabric.* Cambridge, Mass.: MIT Press.
Strasser, Susan
    1982   *Never Done: A History of American Housework.* New York: Pantheon Books.
Tanner, Nancy, and Adrienne Zihlman
    1976   "Women in Evolution, Part I: Innovation and Selection in Human Origins." *Signs* 1:585–608.
Upton, Dell, and John Michael Vlach, eds.
    1986   *Common Places: Readings in American Vernacular Architecture.* Athens: University of Georgia Press.
Vanek, Joann
    1974   "Time Spent on Housework." *Scientific American* 231:116–20.
Zihlman, Adrienne
    1978   "Women in Evolution, Part II: Subsistence and Social Organization among Early Hominids." *Signs* 4:4–20.

Part II
Gender and Production

Chapter 3
Technology, Gender, and Class: Worlds of Difference in Ur III Mesopotamia

Rita P. Wright

The images of men and women conveyed in textual and representational sources from early Mesopotamia suggest that there were great disparities of wealth and status within the society that cut across gender, class, and ethnic lines. On a variety of art forms, priests and priestesses are shown performing ritual functions, and kings engage in victories over important enemies. Similarly, from texts we hear of large quantities of goods being brought as tribute to or produced in workshops at temple, palace, and private estates. In marked contrast, there are few depictions of nonelites, but a substantial number of documents that record activities to which both men and women contributed, especially as workers in agricultural projects and craft production. Although texts attest to the abilities of some workers to accumulate wealth, own land, and participate actively in temple and palace functions, many agricultural workers and craft producers appear to have led relatively impoverished lives. Some clearly were among the lowest in social status. Perhaps the most dramatic examples of the latter are the women and children known only from texts who worked as millers, oil pressers, and weavers at state, temple, and private estates or "households" (Waetzoldt 1987:117). The available data about these women are substantial but in this chapter, I confine my discussion to weavers during the Ur III period (ca. 2112–2004 B.C.). Further, I do not attempt to work through this data comprehensively but rather focus on several specific factors relevant to the issues addressed in the chapter.

My principal interest here is in investigating differences in status and role between men and women and among women of different classes and ethnic groups, using the texts on craft production and other labor

records as one basis and some images of women from art and archaeological sources as another. My entry point is through the examination
of the policies of public institutions (principally royal households and
temples, the two major public institutions in Mesopotamia), principally
among female weavers, that affected the social position of women. In
this I follow Henrietta Moore (1990), who states that, although it would
be misleading to generalize about states as if they were single, monolithic entities, there are ways in which certain types of state policies
affect the social position of women. She notes that as state regulations
govern wages and taxation, they

reproduce the segregated occupational structure of the labour force and the
sexual division of labor within the family. These policies are not necessarily designed with the intention of oppressing or discriminating against women, but
they are designed according to prevailing assumptions and ideologies about the
role of women, the nature of the family and the proper relations between men
and women. (1990:129)

Here, I compare the differences in temple and state policies for women
and men, and I follow Moore's suggestion that these are a reflection
of deeper ideologies and assumptions. A second area of investigation
is whether the low status of *some* women affected the status of women
in general, as Robert Adams (1982) suggested in a discussion of the
potential implications of the "large stream of dependent or enslaved
women" (Adams 1982:116), who appear to have been primary producers
of textiles. I therefore draw on evidence that highlights relationships
among women and the dynamics by which gender and class differences were created through cloth production and consumption. Finally,
a major catalyst for my discussion is Judith McGaw's contribution in
Chapter 2. In the Mesopotamian context, I attempt to unravel the intertwined nature of technology and gender through an analysis of those
people who produced cloth and others who used and consumed it.
Cloth and textiles are particularly well suited to these kinds of inquiries,
since throughout history they have served as major carriers of culture,
whether as valued goods in the marketplace, items of exchange among
groups wishing to establish alliances, or as emblems of status and role
in secular and nonsecular rituals (Weiner and Schneider 1989).

While there are many societies in which a discussion of cloth and textiles would make sense (for example, see Costin in Chapter 4 of this volume and Brumfiel 1991), the documentary sources from early Mesopotamia provide an important set of evidence, since cloth and textiles were
central to the Mesopotamian economy and social relations and served
as a medium of exchange and an important signifier of status. These

sources have great significance for anthropologists, especially to scholars with interests in gender, class, and issues of the political economy.

My argument follows McGaw's central thesis that technology is a social
phenomenon, that it cannot be separated from the social relations of
the producers and consumers that use its end products, and that, in
general, scholars have downplayed society's relation to technology. To
illustrate the differences between McGaw's approach and the perspective usually taken by archaeologists, I briefly discuss how archaeologists
have viewed technology in the past. This section is followed by a review
of some recent rethinking about technology, drawing from McGaw's
work on the history of technology and from others in anthropology.
These discussions are followed by a brief introduction to the representational images of women and others known from documentary sources.
I also discuss the value of cloth in Ur III Mesopotamian society and
the weavers' workshops in which cloth was produced. Finally, I outline
the wage structure for weavers and workers in other crafts, in order to
assess the relative value of men's and women's labor and the effect of
state policies on the social position of women.

Technology and Archaeology

From archaeology's inception, archaeologists have placed a strong emphasis on technologies, often attaching to them major significance as
causal factors in critical transformations in human society. Indeed, some
of the earliest attempts to systematize the course of human development in prehistory were in technical terms, where "ages" were defined
as Stone, Bronze, and Iron and "cultures" as Basket Maker, Post-Basket
Maker.

In American archaeology, in the 1950s through the 1980s archaeologists developed various theories to explain the mechanisms behind
the apparent influence of technologies on increased sociocultural complexity and other advances in "cultural evolution." Although there were
other voices,[1] these theories were dominated by an "adaptive" bias in
which the primary importance attached to technologies was their ability
to overcome a variety of environmental constraints (Brumfiel 1983). In
the 1960s through the 1980s, archaeologists maintained strong interests
in technology as central to "process." Lewis Binford (1965), for example,
emphasized the interrelatedness of technology, social organization, and
ideology, but concentrated almost exclusively on technology, as if it
were disembedded from social and ideological constraints. A heavy emphasis was placed on accommodations to the natural landscape made
by technologies, and entire cultures were characterized by these adapta-

tions. Bryan Pfaffenberger (1992) has characterized as mechanistic and circumscribed the view that technologies were self-propelled ("digging sticks develop into ploughs, drums into telephones" [1992:496]) rather than subject to social action. The strong adaptive bias of this approach has had the effect of extracting technologies from the historical circumstances by which they came into existence, as if they were "out of time" (Dobres 1995). Bruce Trigger has suggested that this bias may be a reflection of contemporary attitudes about technologies in that they frequently are viewed as incomprehensible and somehow beyond our control (1989:320), a view that echoes McGaw's discussion in Chapter 2 in which she articulates the various ways in which we have misunderstood how technologies work and excluded all but high-tech technologies from our contemporary definition of "technology" itself.

One of the ways in which archaeologists have successfully approached the social aspects of technologies and contextualized them historically is through the study of craft specialization. This position is most apparent in the influential works of V. Gordon Childe (Trigger 1989:297). Building on the earlier typologies discussed above, Childe attempted to explain the social processes behind technologies. For him, a principal factor in technologies was the acquisition of skills through training and practice; but what made technologies crucial to societal developments was their exploitable qualities. Childe viewed them as major factors in social evolution because they provided an opportunity for elites to appropriate a surplus and to control the production process itself. His approach, with modifications, continues to influence archaeological research among scholars with primary interests in the political economy who focus on craft production, specialization, and exchange (Brumfiel and Earle 1987). While this approach continues to contribute to theory building and our knowledge of the past, there have been few studies in which gender has been adopted as a central problematic (although see Brumfiel 1991, 1992; Wright 1991; Zagarell 1986). The relevance of an engendered approach to craft specialization is exemplified by Costin's important contribution in Chapter 4 of this volume.

Technology as Social Phenomena

A focus on the political economy and craft production is compatible with McGaw's discussion of technology since both examine the social actions behind technologies. However, there is a significant shift in emphasis. Whereas discussions of craft specialization focus primarily on artisans and the organization end of the production process, historians of technology place technologies as the pivotal point of analysis. Their rationale is that in the process of the production and use of technologies sets of social relationships and ideologies become attached to them that underlie important social, political, economic, and symbolic processes. The principal advantage of a focus on technology is that it serves as an entry point into examining sets of social relationships (craft producers, managers, administration, for example) at the same time that it is possible to observe the formulation of ideologies that produce and reproduce differences in how producers and users of the end products of technologies are perceived. These concepts and insights are relevant to technology and gender, as discussed by McGaw in Chapter 2, but they similarly impact on class, ethnicity, and age, for example.

An investigation of technology using concepts developed by McGaw in Chapter 2 and elsewhere (McGaw 1982, 1989, 1994) and the significant literature on technology and gender (cf. Bush 1983, Rothschild 1983, and McGaw's "References" this volume) effectively transforms how we view technologies. It does so in three ways. First and most decisively it demystifies technologies by removing them from the world of high-tech science to the mundane practices of everyday life, forcing us to question why certain things have come to stand for technology while others have been excluded. Second, having been alerted to, in this case, the gendered nature of technologies, we can analyze the specific ways in which they have become labeled as feminine or masculine. And third, it leads us to explore the "software" or knowledge component of technologies, to find the sometimes hidden sets of relationships and technical knowledge that become attached to specific technologies. This component, elaborated on by McGaw in the several examples she develops in Chapter 2, has been extensively discussed by others in anthropology, although from somewhat different perspectives (cf. Basalla 1988, Dobres and Hoffman 1994, Lechtman 1977, Lemmonier 1992, Pfaffenberger 1992, for example).[2]

In the preceding chapter, McGaw articulated the closely intertwined nature of technology and gender. She pointed out that, although the analysis of contemporary technologies may appear to have little relevance to the analysis of technologies in the past, they, in fact, have broad significance. She persuasively argued that embedded within our conceptions about technology are hidden assumptions and ideologies, and she provided several examples of how gendered approaches to technology reveal some of their hidden social dimensions.

For archaeologists, the advantages of a gendered approach to technology are numerous. It especially is effective in shifting attention from the mechanistic and dehumanized view of technology that has dominated archaeology over the past several decades to one that emphasizes its dynamic qualities and the social actors that promote, produce, control, and use its end products. Further, although archaeologists already are familiar with mundane, low-tech technologies given the nature of our evidence, a biased hierarchy of technologies dominates the archaeological literature. In the archaeological hierarchy of technologies, for example, metallurgy appears somehow more important or revolutionary than weaving or cooking (Wright 1995). Rethinking technologies is useful in correcting possible misunderstandings about the relevance of particular technologies to the people who produced and consumed their products in the ancient past. Finally and perhaps the most important advantage is that it provides a more inclusive analysis in which knowledge is not confined to decision-making strategies and management control but includes numerous other social acts in which social relations and ideologies are embedded. Whereas the hardware components of technologies refer to materials, techniques of construction, and certain pragmatic and physical reasons why a technology might be useful, software refers to a technology's knowledge systems and the various social, political, economic, and symbolic factors that affect its production and use. Hardware establishes basic limitations, while software factors the day-to-day knowledge base and social relations by which objects come into existence and are consumed. A pot, mortar and pestle, blade or weaver's tool were made and used by people and their production and use are felt by other people. If we now assume that there is an interaction between social phenomena and technology, then the logical next step is to ask, who were the human actors and how did their acts affect their social status and roles?

In this chapter I utilize the concepts discussed above to examine weaving technology and the producers and consumers of cloth in a specific historical period. I place weaving technology at the center of the analysis, and examine its end product, cloth, in its production and consumption contexts. In the chapter, I approach technology and cloth in Mesopotamia by raising a series of questions about those places in which gender and technology meet, drawing on the analyses of historians of technology. These questions include asking, for example, who benefits from technology and who does not, whose opportunities increase and whose decrease, who creates and who accommodates to technologies, and, especially, how do technological decisions reflect particular class, individual, or institutional interests (Bush 1983:153). Ignoring these questions is, as McGaw suggests in this volume, an implicit technological determinism in which technology is segregated as though it is a *cause* of social change rather than a phenomenon that ramifies throughout social life.

In the following essay, I first examine the importance of cloth in the Ur III context and the intertwined nature of gender and the political economy of the period. These sections are followed by discussions of the organization of cloth production, the value attached to cloth production, and the ideologies attached to cloth production and use.

Why Cloth and Technology?

The concepts introduced in the above discussion are the basis ón which I approach cloth and technology in the Ur III context. By the Ur III period, Mesopotamian society was organized into a number of different social strata visible through occupational categories (but not a caste system) in which rulers were at the top, followed by priests and priestesses of high rank, bureaucratic and military personnel, merchants, craft people, agricultural and menial laborers, some of whom belonged to a semifree class of "serfs" and others that were slaves. There also were private citizens of high rank who had acquired land and significant other holdings (Postgate 1992:183); some people who were not of high rank held land allotments (Maekawa 1987, Steinkeller 1987)—prebend lands that could not be sold or inherited but that the holder could cultivate or lease to a third party (Postgate 1992:187).

Textiles and cloth were an essential part of life as they touched virtually all aspects of social, political, economic, and religious functions and people at all levels of society. The most obvious institutions in which we actually see cloth represented is in the public displays of temple and palace personnel, where cloth and clothing played a prominent role in important ceremonies, government, and administration (Figure 3.1). Similarly, there is evidence that textiles were emblems of status in temples and palaces where the display of cloth wealth and prestige would be most apparent. For example, J. N. Postgate (1992:243) believes that tapestries and woven rugs may have hung on palace walls.

In addition to representation, textual accounts list items that served as decorative embellishment in ritual and as mediums of exchange in social, political, economic, and religious transactions. These accounts are replete with references to cloth being offered as gifts and donations at celebrations and festivals to temple and palace; as dowries in marriage contracts; as gifts in alliances between foreign governments, between city-states, and between city-states and rural areas; as gifts to gods in other cities (Gordon, Rendsburg, and Winter 1987:126); and as objects of trade and exchange outside of southern Mesopotamia itself (ibid.: 125). These exchanges were carried out by temple and palace personnel and possibly by private individuals.

There were many different types of cloth, produced from wool and flax, some of which were designated for the use of women and men of high rank while others were distributed to people in a wider range of occupations and ranks. In iconography rulers can be identified by

Figure 3.1. Impression of the cylinder seal of a governor in the Ur III period. A man is being led into the presence of a god. (Courtesy of the British Museum)

a type of cap and the special cloths draped over the stools on which they are seated.[3] Further, as W. J. Reade and D. T. Potts (1993) recently noted, during the Ur III period linen cloth was reserved for individuals of the highest rank, such as kings and governors, priests, and other temple personnel. Linen garments and hangings also were draped on the statues of deities (Reade and Potts 1993:104).[4]

Two roles that gave high visibility to women and to cloth were those of wives of rulers and priestesses, women who appear to have had control over some economic activities and to have possessed significant authority. These assessments are based upon their ownership of personal seals and the types of imagery on them. In at least one instance, a woman is represented on her own seal (Winter 1987:190) and in others owned by women goddesses are depicted in direct parallel to the male gods on the seals of their husbands, suggesting that personal seals were tailored in subject matter to the rank of their owners. In periods that preceded Ur III, women carried out important public roles, donating statues and textiles used in ceremonies involving the building of temples, in weddings, and in birth and ancestral cults (Asher-Greve 1985:183), and we have no reason to believe they did not continue to do so during Ur III. Queens, priestesses, and the wives of governors played active roles in ceremonies and feasts, to which they brought offerings of food, jewels, and cloth. This participation is apparent from images on seals, where they are shown carrying emblems and pictured alongside temples and on ships (Asher-Greve 1985:182). These representations follow mythological accounts of gods and goddesses visiting one another and may "reflect actual ceremonies in which the divine image was physically transported up or downstream" (Postgate 1992:124) for annual festivals, consecrations of temples, and settlement of legal disputes. In some cases priestesses of different ranks, accompanied by other female cult personnel, are represented, and women appear as equal to or of a higher status than men represented in the same scene. Thus although these women appear in auxiliary roles that are "socially integrative" (Winter 1987:189), the depictions of their actions place them in complementary roles. Further, among high-ranking individuals, it is the representation of office that supersedes gender.

The images of high status women in these positions was a highly developed form of communication (Winter 1987:201). In addition to placement of figures and performance of certain gestures, decorative variation and styles of cloth and garments conveyed important information about the rank and office of individuals.[5] As with cloth elsewhere, it appears to have been a major medium by which important rules were communicated and divine sanction legitimated (Weiner and Schneider 1989). Some cloth and finished clothing worn by priestesses and wives of rulers and others holding government and religious offices appear to have been reserved for them alone. For example, a special type of headgear served to identify priestesses (Winter 1987:192). The overwhelming impression of these representations is that different types of cloth were restricted to individuals of specific rank and gender, suggestive of images from other courts in history, in which rulers, priests, priestesses, and other high-ranking individuals "lived in a world of textiles, where cloth was created with elaborate rules that restricted the wearing of some emblems and types of cloth to certain ranks in society" (Cohn 1989:316). This impression is complemented by documentary sources.

Texts indicate that in addition to linen, many other types of cloth were allocated to individuals of specific rank. These records are from weavers' workshops at temple, palace, and private estates where cloth referred to as high quality or sumptuous was recorded and distributed to high ranking men and women. The lists include diverse types of cloth, such as hand-loomed, plaited, or fleeced cloth; linen woven into robes and garments; and wool woven into saddle cloth, shaggy garments, fleeced skirts, head bands, headdresses, loincloths, menstruating garments,[6] menstruating bandages, and underwear. Both old and new cloth was curated, as suggested by entries for worm-eaten cloth, even worm-eaten, ordinary underwear! Further, cloth was graded in categories such as sumptuous, best, third, or fourth grade; and by size, as small, middle, and large (Kang 1973:297ff., Postgate 1992:237). While higher grades were distributed to high-ranking persons or gods and goddesses, other products from the weavers' workshops were internally distributed as payment to the weavers and to other personnel on estates.

While these items were distributed to a broad spectrum of individuals, the best qualities were reserved for rulers (or representatives such as governors) and their wives and priests and priestesses for ritual purposes. At Umma special garments for priests and kings were prepared, and different types of cloth were required as garments for statues, gifts, and tribute (Kang 1973:14ff). The use of cloth in ritual display and its high volume of consumption are exemplified by an account from Umma that lists various types of cloth. This account records activities in a year when a high priestess was installed; it includes "120 best woven garments, 1061 woven garments, 42 woven garments, small (size)" as well as "141 man-(size) garments, 13 man-(size) black . . . [and] . . . 7 medium-(size)" garments (Kang 1973:303) in a single transaction.

Given the importance of cloth as a symbolic and communicative device and the variety and volume in which it was produced, it is reasonable to ask "Who produced the cloth worn by these women and men and other members of Mesopotamia society?" Here, I turn to the production of cloth and to documentary sources that reveal a dramatically different side to the political economy.[7]

Gender and the Mesopotamian Political Economy

During the Ur III period, Mesopotamian society was deeply stratified. This stratification had its basis in state policies and in the fact that large tracts of agricultural land were controlled by state, temple, and private institutions. Taken together, these institutions employed large numbers of individuals as agricultural laborers and/or as craft producers who were paid in "rations" principally consisting of barley, wool, and oil. Some workers also received land allotments. The conditions of compensation for these laborers varied, and here I provide only a brief outline of recent attempts to disentangle the wage structure and the status of individuals who participated in what are referred to as "men in gangs," discussed below.

Clearly, the textual sources are skewed in that they only document economic activities carried out by large temple, palace, and private organizations. These sources contain records of activities on craft production and various types of work related to agriculture. In many of them, detailed accounts are available on specific tasks performed, time devoted to completion, numbers of people employed, wages allocated to them, and information on individuals and institutions to whom products were distributed.

The numbers of people employed in workshops varied. In many cities large numbers of individuals received barley and other "rations" for labor services. According to Waetzoldt (1987:118), in the city of Ur individuals who received allotments of barley may have amounted to 40,000. These numbers can be broken down using texts for the period from various locations; for example, a small temple might employ 150 to 270 persons; larger ones, 500 or more (Waetzoldt 1987:118); a governor's household in the city of Girsu controlled 2,000 workers while a single temple employed 4,000 (Maekawa 1987:64). In the city of Girsu as a whole 6,000 weavers were employed (Maekawa 1987:63). Waetzoldt (1987:119) has estimated the total number of workers in state and temple service during the Ur III period at 300,000 to 500,000.

Compensation for labor services varied according to the work performed and the status of the worker. It should be stated that translating the meaning attached to specific terms for workers is subject to interpretation and, as new texts are translated, the nuances of terms are continually reevaluated. For our purposes, two major categories that have been identified among the "men in gangs" are "semifree serfs" and "slaves." The former comprised a broad class of state dependents with varying degrees of access to land or a means of production, the latter, a class of unfree slaves.

Semifree workers were employed in a variety of occupations. Males worked as managers, scribes, overseers, carpenters, canal construction and maintenance workers, agricultural field workers, basket makers, and fishermen, for example (Kang 1973:5). Among the tasks performed by women were harvesting, irrigating fields, carrying and winnowing barley, hauling barley into granaries, working in mill houses and weaving establishments; more rarely, they loaded goods into boats and sieved beer-bread (ibid.: 10).

In addition to the legal status of workers as free or dependent, other issues surrounding these terms concern their freedom to control their own means of production, to possess land, and to have a "family life," a phrase that appears to refer to whether individuals lived in households with their nuclear families. Speaking of a group of male foresters designated as erin$_2$ in the province of Umma, Piotr Steinkeller notes that these semifree serfs worked with their sons and brothers, "their blood relations and natural heirs" (1987:99), since land allotments were passed from father to son. In lists of their activities and allotments, workers were distinguished by patronym rather than profession and worked together in teams in neighborhoods near their home villages. Based upon this evidence Steinkeller argues that these male workers did possess a family life (1987:99). Although Kazuya Maekawa points out that it would be difficult to determine whether all men in gangs had families, he is "tempted to assume that they did" (Maekawa 1987:64).

Other evidence also indicates that many workers controlled their own means of production and some received allotments of land. There is, for example, evidence that allotments of land were disbursed to individuals who received higher rations. These included individuals working for the state, temple, and private institutions who were compensated with "fields as subsistence allotments" and "persons of higher rank (more empirically stated, persons in higher pay scales) usually received land allotments" (Waetzoldt 1987:128). Hartmut Waetzoldt reports allotments of as much as ninety-six acres to a priest as against two and a half acres to "obligatory service personnel" (1987:129). This evidence is consistent with allotments to the foresters at Umma, where Steinkeller indicates that workers were "prebenders and that they worked and received rations only during a part of the year" (1987:100). It also is consistent with categories of male workers engaged in collective labor in Girsu, where records of "men in gangs," of whom there were more than four thousand under "direct control of the governor," were engaged in service at the lowest end of the compensation scale for men (Maekawa 1987:64).[8] Since they received low compensation (see Table 3.1), they did not receive land allotments.

The belief once held by many that the Ur III state exercised monolithic control of production is not supported by the current evidence (Lamberg-Karlovsky 1994). Steinkeller (1994) has articulated the case of potters and demonstrated that in addition to their employment in the "great households," potters were able to produce and distribute their products without intervention of the state during those times when they were not working for the state. They then were free "to produce pots and other clay artifacts to satisfy the needs of the general population" (1994:xx). Marc van de Mieroop has noted the same practice among craft workers in Isin in a slightly later period (1987:87). These reconstructions are consistent with Postgate's suggestion that workers were free to work outside of temple, state, and private workshops and controlled their own means of production for at least part of the year (1992:239).

The texts on which the above cases are based deal exclusively with men, since few women are discussed, and to determine the work they performed, their status, their wage compensations, and whether they possessed a means of production, it is necessary to consult other sources. Describing the work status of women weavers designated by the terms geme$_2$ and sag,[9] Waetzoldt (1987) notes that "the term geme$_2$ seems to designate a person who is in a legal status of dependence, perhaps semi-free, since her master could force her to work as a weaver or miller. The term sag on the other hand seems to denote a person whose legal status was that of slave . . . 'bought with silver' " (1987:119n. 19).

Weavers, therefore, were either semifree workers without land or purchased slaves. They also included war captives and indentured workers. This interpretation is based upon a separation of workers into "weavers since former times" and "purchased ones" (Maekawa 1973–74:98ff., n. 23). The category indentured workers included daughters or wives brought to the workshops for debt payments, perhaps belonging to the semifree category during the term of "employment" (for example, a man's wife or daughter might be "seized and forced to work as weavers" (Waetzoldt 1987:139) or a female slave could be substituted if the farmer had one).[10]

The compensation for all of these women was based upon allotments of food; they did not receive any land allotments, consistent with their wage compensation at the lowest end of the scale. As far as I know, there are no records that indicate that women weavers controlled their own means of production for any part of the year. Where they appear on lists, names of women are carried throughout the entire year, although they may be shifted from one weaving team to another (Maekawa 1973–74:125). Furthermore, it seems unlikely that they had the type of family life (husband, wife, children) implied by texts in which the work of men is recorded. For example, women are listed by name only, without reference to their husbands, as in "wife of," a practice used in naming high-ranking women. In addition, the children of women in weaving workshops are referred to by their matronym; in one specific case, children born to a woman while in the weaving workshop are recorded as "orphans" after her death, suggesting that she may not have been married. Finally, the status of children of women weavers as semifree or slave appears to follow that of their mothers.

Cloth and Production

The production of cloth and the organization of labor in workshops attached to temple, palace, or private organizations was tightly regulated and specialization within the industry was fostered. Even in the earliest archives, textile production is divided according to workplace with one place for working wool, another for working flax (Postgate 1992:235).

Production was organized in a number of ways, but in general, there appear to have been fairly large numbers of individuals employed in each workshop. All of the workshops for which we have evidence were owned by leaders of palaces, temples, and private households; although the majority of owners were men, there are records of women, for example a priestess who "owned fields, herds, and buildings, among which was a weaving establishment" (Waetzoldt 1987:117). Just to give an idea of scale, one ruler's household employed 750 individuals in a weaver's

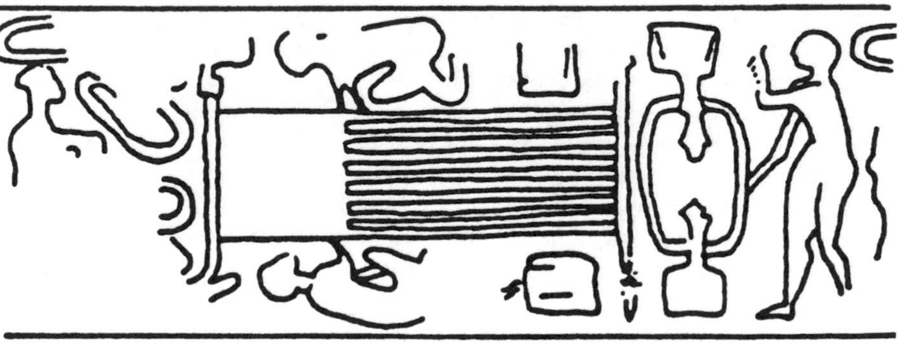

Figure 3.2. Early cylinder seal from Susa, fourth millennium B.C., showing a ground-loom, weavers, and preparation of a warp. (Drawing courtesy of Dominique Collon)

workshop (Maekawa 1980:82ff.).[11] In Lagash, a "gang" of female workers consisted of twenty women, supervised either by a male or female leader (Maekawa 1980:87). There might have been as many as thirty-seven teams altogether. Whether the group was led by a male or female fluctuated; for example, in one year five were led by females and one by a male. Fluctuations of this kind may have been due to military crises when fewer men were available or may be a reflection of the availability of suitable female supervisors.[12]

The production of cloth was a labor-intensive industry and virtually all production work was carried out by women. Women were employed in the shearing (actually plucking) of sheep, spinning of wool (possibly including carding), weaving on a horizontal hand loom as depicted in Figure 3.2, plaiting (wrapping and binding threads or interlacing two or more threads), cleaning cloth, trimming the cloth to size, and possibly sewing garments. In visual representations of clothing, many garments were embellished with embroidery and fringes, although there is no evidence from accounts of the weaving workshops that women participated in this kind of finishing.[13]

Three categories of male workers were involved in cloth production. First, male children of the female weavers, who received a "wage" according to their age, began working inside the workshop, perhaps as early as age six (Waetzoldt 1987:134), although they received a small amount of food "rations" before that. They were separated from their mothers "at a certain age" and sent from the weavers' workshops to other types of labor. Second, male workers were employed in a supervisory capacity. And the third category of males worked as fullers and felters, weaving related professions. Cloth produced in the weaving workshops was brought to fullers for final finishing and sizing of the cloth, but it is unclear whether their activities were conducted in the weavers' workshop or in separate locations. Felters produced felted cloth in separate workshops, using a production process that is technically different from loom weaving. The cloth produced was "a special textile, possibly a coarsely woven fabric, which was tassled or matted" (Steinkeller 1980:93). As far as I know, there are no known workshops in which women were employed as felters. Moreover, the description of felting suggests that these fabrics were totally unlike those produced in the women weavers' workshops.

Important distinctions were made between the daughters and sons of the women in the workshops. Although male and female children are recorded in workshop accounts, it is not always possible to identify the women with whom they are listed as their mothers or surrogates. At any rate, when the daughters of women weavers achieved adulthood (apparently between thirteen and fifteen) they continued to work in the workshops. Boys, on the other hand, left the weavers' workshop and were assigned to tasks such as towing boats or other menial labor (Maekawa 1980:112). Further, a considerable number of them were castrated just before they attained puberty, when they left the weavers' workshop (ibid.).[14] A related phenomenon is a male supervisor, who is recorded under the name Gàl-si (gala), a term associated with non-masculine characteristics, gala having been translated as "cantor" but also as men who "had certain feminine characteristics which connect them with women" (Gelb, cited in Maekawa 1980:117). Further, according to Maekawa, the number of female children always exceeded males, and he suggests that male children were purposefully excluded from the workshops (Maekawa 1980:107).

As a contrast to the treatment of the sons of weavers, it is useful to look at the conditions of the sons of fullers. Fullers were responsible for a finishing process carried out after cloth was removed from the loom.[15] According to Maekawa, "fullers are listed by name with their fathers," which means that "fullers were ordinarily succeeded by their sons, not by the sons of female weavers" (1980:112), so that while we might have expected the sons of women weavers to follow that craft, they appear to have been excluded. These differences in the experiences of adult females and males are evidence for a pervasive ideology that associated weaving with feminine characteristics and that imposed sanctions that excluded men from the weaving workshops, an issue I return to below.

Conditions in the weavers' workshops, as well as in other female and male workshops, were not good, as records of people's running away and dying attest. For example, one account records the deaths of one-third of a group of women and children in a single year (Maekawa 1987:110);

another shows that 5 of 224 fled, then were returned and forced to work at a lower wage (Waetzoldt 1987:140). Further, to be discussed in more detail below, the average wages or "rations" that they received were low, barely at a subsistence level.

In spite of their poor working conditions, women in cloth production possessed significant technical skills, as is attested by the variation in the lists of cloth and clothing items. This variation indicates that many different types of weaving techniques were employed to produce them. Although there is no direct evidence, since there are few archaeological textiles, the techniques employed no doubt were drawn from the producers' different regional and ethnic groups. There would have been, for example, a constant flow of technical knowledge between women from different ethnic groups captured in battles or purchased as slaves and local women serving indentured or other service from urban and rural settlements who worked together in workshops. While it is possible that different techniques and styles were suppressed, the knowledge, tools, and skills they brought with them constitute the technical options at the society's disposal. Therefore, whatever innovations or technical expertise developed within the workshops most likely came through the experimentation of the women themselves. I don't think we should imagine that textile engineers who were not weavers devised new techniques. There is no suggestion that the individuals who recorded workshop output were very knowledgable about weaving. The categories used in recording cloth are decidedly nontechnical; words like sumptuous or ordinary or even third grade are social categories. We do not read about records of thread counts per unit of measure, for example, a technical means of assessing the value of cloth, indicating that recorders (scribes?) either were not knowledgable about the technical aspects of the craft or preferred the social categories.

The previous discussion indicates that textile production differed from that of all other crafts in important ways. First, it required a large trained workforce that was permanently employed (Postgate 1992:235), since textile production requires skilled laborers and is a labor-intensive craft. In addition, large quantities of cloth were needed by the temple and the palace for allotments to workers, for social and ritual display and for local consumption, trade, and exchange. Second, individuals, whether semifree or slaves, worked full-time and were permanently attached to temple or palace production, as is attested by lists of individual names recorded on a month-to-month and year-to-year basis. Unlike other craft producers who were employed part-time and were free to distribute the products of their labor, women weavers appear not to have been free to produce, distribute, or consume their products. Although women wove cloth in noninstitutional contexts, they may not

TABLE 3.1. Allotments received by males and females for compensation in
Ur III.

	Male	Female	Children
Monthly barley allotments			
Range in liters—all professions	40–5,000	20–100	10–20
Average in liters for males performing menial tasks and women and children weavers	60	40	10 (0–5 years) 15 (5–10 years) 20 (10–15 years)
Yearly wool allotments			
Average in minas*	4	3	1
Clothing allotments	When available	When available	When available
Oil allotments (when barley was unavailable or for special occasions)			
Average in liters	2.5–5	2–5	1–2

Source: Data compiled from Maekawa (1980, 1987); Waetzoldt (1987).
*One mina equals half a kilogram; four minas was sufficient wool for one garment.

have had access to the technical knowledge and quality standards developed in the workshops.

Compensation for Weavers and Others

An important consideration in assessing the status of women weavers and the value attached to their labor is the compensation they received. Compensation is, of course, relative; therefore, I include comparative data for males and females in other occupations and for differences within workshops.

Table 3.1 compares the allotments recorded in documents for females and males who were engaged in a wide range of occupations. A comparison of the compensation for males who worked at menial tasks to that for women weavers shows clear disparities, with women workers receiving the lowest compensation (except for children). Disparities are most apparent in their average compensations, since only small numbers of individuals received the highest and lowest levels (for example, at the one-hundred-liter level for females). Women millers never reached such a high level.

Table 3.2 compares the compensation of women weavers and millers with several male professions. Although the disparities between weavers

TABLE 3.2. Compensation for male and female professions in Ur III.

Male Profession	Allotments (in liters of barley)*
Scribes	60–5,000 (in increments of 120–300)
Boat captains	60–510
Herdsmen	60–900
Farm supervisors	150–1,200
Craftsmen	60–300
Foresters	60–75

Female Profession	Allotments (in liters of barley)
Weavers	30–100
Millers	30–35
Oil pressers	Not available

	Allotments (in minas of wool)
Priestesses	10–15

Source: Data compiled from Maekawa (1980, 1987); Steinkeller (1987); and Waetzolt (1987).
*See Table 3.1 for yearly allotments of wool. Some of the foresters received grants of land. Foremen or head workers "held land allotments in exchange for services. In return for these allotments prebenders worked, together with their junior kinsmen, several months each year in specific forests" (Steinkeller 1987:88). The rights to cultivate the land were inherited by the eldest son upon the death of the individual to whom it had been alloted, as was his official status as supervisor.

and millers were significant, the greatest differences in the compensations were between men and women, regardless of occupation.[16] Even at the lowest end, males with low levels of technical skill are compensated higher than women in any occupation. The weavers fare better than the millers, but not as well as the men, despite the fact that the technical skills and level of specialization required of them were more comparable to those of the male occupations listed. Further, in compensation for many of the male occupations, land allotments also were given, and the harvest from land would have yielded additional food supplies. One other relevant comparison from Table 3.1 and 3.2 is the gap between the allocation of cloth to women of a different status; for example, note the large allotment of wool to a priestess and the minimal amount to female occupations listed, an indication of the significant differences among women (and men) of different classes.

Tables 3.3 and 3.4 compare different types of "extra" compensation allocated to female weavers and millers and disparities among female weavers based upon types of cloth produced, age, ethnicity, job performed, or amount of service. As discussed above, weaving groups within workshops were organized, ideally, into groups of twenty, and in some instances, the quality of cloth produced varied among groups

TABLE 3.3. Compensation for various female weaving work.

Job	"Extra" or occasional compensation
Shearing (plucking) sheep	5 liters of dates $\frac{1}{6}$ liter of sesame oil Barley, fish, meat

	Monthly compensation based on on quality of final product or rank
Representing or supervising a "gang"	60–100* liters of barley
Leading a group producing first-class cloth	60 liters of barley
Leading a group producing second-class cloth	50 liters of barley
Leading a group producing third-class cloth	40 liters of barley
Working as a rank-and-file member of a group producing first-class cloth	40 liters of barley
Working as a rank-and-file member of a group producing second-class cloth	40 liters of barley
Working as a rank-and-file member of a group producing third-class cloth	30 liters of barley

Source: Data compiled from Maekawa (1980) and Waetzoldt (1987).
*One hundred liters is rare; the average appears to be sixty liters.

TABLE 3.4. Compensation disparities among female weavers based on age, ethnicity, experience.*

Weaver group	Monthly allotment (in liters of barley)
Adult women	40–60
"Young" women	25–30
"Old" women	20
Newly purchased	18
Non-Sumerian names or prisoners of war	18

Source: Data compiled from Maekawa (1980).
*See compensation for children in Table 3.1.

within a single workshop. In those instances, the supervisors of better quality cloth were given greater compensation, although rank-and-file workers apparently did not benefit from their greater expertise. Disparities based upon age (young and old women were compensated at the lowest end of the scale) were significant but not as dramatic as those among newly "purchased" workers and those with non-Sumerian names or prisoners of war. Finally, jobs performed within the profession also were graded; spinners, for example, were given lower compensation (Maekawa 1980:93), whereas supervisors and others in a category of workers "working since former times" (Maekawa 1980:93) received higher compensation. As discussed above, some of the supervisors were women, but the majority appear to have been men, although this varied over time. Workers who performed specialized tasks, such as shearing (plucking) of sheep, perhaps because it was an unusually strenuous activity, occasionally received extra compensation. In some years, depending upon availability, women received a ration of sesame oil and wool or cloth, in amounts equivalent to or enough for one garment.

These wage scales, although they acknowledged certain types of expertise, were significantly lower than any other crafts, where males were predominant. In other crafts the average compensation was sixty (Table 3.1), but sometimes as much as three hundred liters of barley. These wage differences indicate that men's labor was more highly valued than women's labor, even though cloth was an important commodity.

Regarding the participation of children in the workshops and their circumstances, newly purchased women did not bring children with them. This does not mean that children were excluded from the workshops, however, since other workers already in the workshop had their children with them. In fact, many women in workshops from "former times" had from two to four children for whom they were responsible. Judging by the ages of some of the children, many were born after the women joined the workshop. As Table 3.1 shows, children were compensated according to their ages.

What may at first glance appear to be small discrepancies in allotments between men and women represents major differences in food and sustenance. Waetzoldt (1987:134) has calculated just how well provisioned workers would be based upon the average compensations outlined on Table 3.1. He calculated the subsistence basis of a "family" consisting of a father, mother, and four children. Their combined amounts would be sufficient to keep them alive, but if a "father or mother were unable to work for a month or more, then immediate difficulties would have arisen" (Waetzoldt 1987:135). Although in recent discussions there now appears to be a consensus that most male workers lived in nuclear families, there is no way to assess whether this was the case for women. Records for the workshops show the range of ages for children from birth to fifteen. As I have indicated above, these births do not necessarily indicate that the women were married or that they and their children had a family life, if the term *family life* is restricted to the nuclear family. Using Waetzoldt's calculation, we can see the potential for devastation of these women and their children as "families" if they were unable to work for a month or more. Without land allotments and without the freedom to produce and distribute cloth independent of the large workshops—a freedom that now appears to have been the norm for other craft workers—women weavers were among the lowest economic status.

Weaving as a Feminine Technology

The textual accounts discussed above indicate that weaving was a craft strongly linked to women and that men were purposefully excluded. Three types of evidence lead to this conclusion. First, the occupation of fullers in the final finishing process of cloth is the only association of adult males with cloth production, but these men did not weave. Second, male children of weavers were excluded from the workshop after they attained adulthood. This situation is dramatically different from other professions where children in work groups followed their parent in that profession. Finally, some young males were castrated before they left the weaving workshops, suggesting that important distinctions were made between desirable masculine and feminine traits and that weaving was associated with the latter. The association of "feminine characteristics" in a supervisor, as discussed above, supports this conclusion.

Textual sources both before and after the Ur III period support the view that a strong gender ideology linked weaving with women.[17] In Mesopotamian religious ideology, the weaving deity, Uttu, is female; she does not have a male counterpart (Lambert 1987:126). The circumstances of her birth are narrated in the myth "Enki and Ninhursaga," where she is described as "shapely and decorous" (Jacobsen 1987:184), an apparent allusion to Mesopotamian concepts of femininity. Further, another name for Uttu is Sig, "Wool," and in the royal love song "My 'Wool' Being Lettuce" is a provocative association of wool with female pubic hair and sexual reproduction (ibid.: 93). In another royal love song, "The First Child," the king refers to his queen's fertility as the warp on the loom and the mother of a large family as "the clothbeam with its finished cloth" (ibid.: 85). This sentiment both links weaving with women and conveys Mesopotamian ideals of womanhood, following Samuel Noah Kramer's suggestion that the wife "as child-bearer" was of crucial importance (Kramer 1987:109). Other textual references are to dowries which include items used in textile production such as wool, wool combs, loom woods, spindles, and cloth (Postgage 1992:192).

These ideological links of weaving and women indicate that even outside of the large workshops, women were responsible for the production of cloth. Entries for the disbursal of wool to workers are a clear indication that weaving was carried out independent of the large workshops. This association apparently cut across class lines, as there are depictions of the spinning of yarn by women of high rank. In addition, there are entries that record cloth brought by individuals to temples and palaces as donations or tribute from households within the city and in rural areas. Although many of these were brought by men, it is reasonable to assume, given the association of women with weaving, that the cloth was produced by women.

There is very little archaeological evidence for textile production in either domestic or workshop contexts, cities or villages. It consists of a small number of spindle whorls and loom weights known from surface surveys at several small settlements, documented by Adams (1981), that indicate that cloth production did occur in rural areas. However, it is possible that production at small settlements was attached to the workshops of larger state, temple, or private institutions (Jacobsen 1970:222). Archaeological remains of textile or other craft workshops are limited to a few locations, where scatters of evidence leave doubt as to the specific craft being practiced (van de Mieroop 1987:x–xii; Postgate 1992:115).[18]

Conclusion

But what of the interaction of technology and gender and the ways in which weaving technology was played out in the wider political economy? Considering the large numbers of women employed in the weavers' workshops, the lists of cloth produced by them, and the degree to which the state and other powerful institutions regulated their production and appropriated products for their distribution, there was a clear desire to control and regulate weaving. This comes as no surprise given its importance in ritual display, as badges of office, and in trade. Above, I have discussed the qualities of cloth, styles of garments, and decorative variation that conveyed rank and attachment to powerful organizations, such as the temple and palace. As discussions of cloth in other contexts attest, cloth accrues great significance in ceremony and important meanings become attached to it, providing a source of legitimacy to powerholders (Weiner and Schneider 1989:3). And the high quality grades for women of high rank clearly served to demarcate social status.

In the Ur III context, textiles also constituted a major export essential to the procurement of raw materials and other products. The "high value-to-weight ratio" of cloth made it particularly sustainable in long-distance overland and maritime commerce (Adams 1982:116), and cloth served important functions in the formation of alliances that bound elite groups together within Mesopotamia and across cultural boundaries. Workshop organization was an efficient means to produce larger quantities of cloth than could have been procured through taxation or tribute from individual households. It also served to mark certain kinds of cloth as state or temple cloth through the control of its style and quality.

Yet, weaving technology had a strong association with women; given the wage scale by which they were compensated, their low status as slaves and even perhaps "semifree," female textile workers were rendered entirely subservient.[19] Ironically, the differences in status between them and other women and men were reinforced by the very cloth they wove, for it socially reproduced the society that they served. Cloth stated the sameness and difference within and between classes, as would have been apparent by the plain garment/cloth of the weaver and the high quality, perhaps sumptuous grades for women of high rank. Further, although cloth in Mesopotamian society was highly visible and highly valued, the women who produced it were not.

The specific situation of women weavers in contrast to other craft producers requires explanation. As conceived, the system placed these women in a position inferior to all other craft producers through lower compensation and in assigning them slave or a semifree status that differed from other craft workers, since the weavers lacked their own means of production. As stated, there now appears to be a consensus that, unlike women weavers, many craft workers possessed land and/or worked for the state for only *limited* periods, enabling them to produce and exchange or distribute their products outside of institutional distribution systems. Further, the familial links among fathers, sons, and brothers in professions suggest that men did possess a "family life." If this was generally the case, then, the status of weavers was unique among craft workers. Records indicate that weavers worked *full time*, since names on lists are carried for the full year and not parts of years or months as described for male workers. Therefore, it seems unlikely that the women weavers worked outside of the workshops for a portion of the year and therefore unlikely that they were able to distribute cloth independently. Both the low rates of compensation of barley rations to weavers and the absence of land allotments placed them among the lowest ranks of workers during the Ur III period. Finally, since women weavers are listed only by name and not designated "the wife of" or "daughter of," as is the case for high-ranking women, it is unclear whether they were married and had a "family life" in the sense that other craft workers did. However, it seems unlikely.

The particular circumstances of female weavers was conditioned by the vested interests of the state and other powerful institutions to control both the production *and* distribution of cloth for economic and social reasons. Textiles were central to the economy as a major export product and for distribution to workers. In addition, the social use of cloth as adornment and as a signifier of status and affiliation in important ceremonies and rituals was a compelling reason to control its production and distribution. From an economic perspective cloth production appears to have been more tightly regulated than other crafts, since among other craft workers, there was a certain freedom to produce products and distribute them to the local population. As I have said, there were independent producers of cloth who worked in household contexts, but they appear to have been loosely integrated into the production system, the only link being women who were indentured to workshops in debt payment who presumably returned to their homes. The majority of women outside of the workshops were effectively excluded from innovations and conventions behind desirable types of cloth (criteria for assessing what constituted high quality or sumptuous cloth, for example) and conceivably from the technical knowledge developed in the workshops. Control of both production and distribution by large institutions promoted efficiency but, more importantly, it insured that particular grades and styles were produced *and* distributed for the "right" people.

The policies described effectively regulated the economic and social control of cloth production and its end products, but they did more. The exclusion of males from the weaving process (I assume supervisors did not weave and the "logical" males to move into this craft, following other occupations, were the male children of weavers) reinforced a strong gender ideology known from myths and poetry that connected weaving to women. Further, if male children who worked in the workshops were indeed castrated, their association with weaving clearly disqualified them from the types of "family lives" other men in the society possessed. That this control of reproductive functions may have been due to the foreign status of some of the workers seems unlikely, since other foreign individuals were assimilated into Mesopotamian society. At stake here was the feminine association with weaving, which appears to have been an ideology deeply embedded in the society. The exclusion from the male category of the sons of female weavers by neutering them suggests that attached to weaving were ideals about appropriate female and male roles.

In addition to their control of the reproductive functions of the sons of weavers, the state may have intervened in the reproductive functions of women. As noted above, the ratio of female to male children was greater in all instances reported, indicating that there were policies that specifically limited the number of males in the workshops. There are no records to clarify whether male children simply were brought to other types of work groups or other more drastic measures were taken when they were born. However, the male-female child ratio suggests that there were regulations that governed the disposition of children in the workshops and women's reproduction. The fact that workers with longer service and greater expertise had greater numbers of children than those receiving the lowest compensations (Maekawa 1980:106) is added evidence for this practice. Finally, the accounts are clear that the majority of children were born while their mothers worked in the workshop, although it is not known whether these women were married.[20] One recorded instance that suggests that at least some were not married is the purchased worker, referred to earlier, whose children were born while she was employed in the workshop and who were orphaned at her death.

Attempts to control female reproduction are well known from other states, although the particular circumstances in Mesopotamia differ. Given the social and economic importance of cloth and a gender ideology that associated women with weaving, it was in the best interests of major institutions to continue employment of females but not males. The policies I have described made it possible to control a resource in a way that reinforced the prevailing gender ideology at the same time that it preserved ideals of family life for the majority of the population. Although many of the women weavers and their offspring were excluded from these ideals of family life, the marginal status of large numbers of them as purchased, indentured, or captured foreigners meant their exclusion was minimally disruptive to societal values.

At the same time that these policies served to reinforce gender roles and ethnicity, they also created class differences among women. Therefore, gender did not carry a unitary status. The active participation of high-ranking women in the temple and palace in complementary roles in the elaboration of ceremonial and administrative apparatus enhanced the status of some women. Further, although large numbers of women were employed in the weaving and milling workshops and in a variety of menial tasks, women in general may have been minimally involved in conscripted service. As I have noted, most other professions are associated with men. Therefore, at the same time that gender differences were reinforced, important class differences also were established among women and between men and women. Thus gender and class differences transformed Mesopotamian society with dramatically different effects on the lives of men and women.

In addition, the production and distribution system relates to broader processes of Mesopotamian state development. Allen Zagarell (1986) has argued that the appropriation of female labor in the Mesopotamian textile workshops was instrumental in replacing the kin-corporate system of property ownership with a centralized, state-ordered mode of production. In that sense, control of the allocation of women's labor and their production was a "metaphor for the appropriation of kin group community" and the control of the dual potential of reproduction and production (Gailey 1985:83). The evidence discussed in this chapter suggests that, while the appropriation of female labor clearly was instrumental in the centralization of textile production, the relationship of kin groups to the temple and palace organization was more complex than previously believed. During Ur III the administrative records list only a few occupations for women, principally the weavers and millers; in the case of women weavers, large numbers of them appear to have been from outside the local community. In contrast, men were employed in a wide variety of occupations (see Table 3.2) and were engaged in conscripted service for only part of the year, after which they were free to engage in productive activities outside of the major institutions. While the period of corvée service clearly would have weakened the productive relations of kin groups, the men appear to have remained active contributors to the political economy independent of their service to the temple and state.

Finally, the Mesopotamian data fit patterns known from other states; for example, they closely follow Moore's suggestion that state policies reflect deeply embedded ideologies. In the Mesopotamian case, there appears to have been a conscious effort to accommodate gender ideologies, while at the same time the productive economy of major institutions was enhanced. Thus the appropriation of female labor in the weaving workshops was purposeful, and it played to historical circumstances. Here, it appears that the state and other powerful institutions attempted to preserve a sexual division of labor in which gender roles were maintained, although in the particulars they inevitably were altered by the circumstances they created. The historical specificity of the Mesopotamian case does not make it less interesting but rather more so: given its close historical connection to the development of Western society, here we may have the roots of ideas and sets of mind embedded in our own Western traditions.

Acknowledgments

An earlier version of this essay was presented in October 1993 at Queens College, the City University of New York, and Northwestern University. I would like to thank the students and faculty at both universities for their encouragement and criticisms of the essay; Liz Brumfiel, Michelle Marcus, Susan Pollock, and Alison Wylie for comments on a previous draft; Megan McCormick for sharing her Mesopotamia weaving bibliography with me; and Judy McGaw for stimulating discussions on technology and gender and inspiration through her published works.

Notes

1. The settlement pattern studies of Robert Adams (1965, 1981 and Adams & Nissen 1972) in southern Mesopotamia very significantly challenged this view.

His research reversed the widely held belief that irrigation systems were, by virtue of some inner logic or driving force, causal factors in the development of civilizations by demonstrating how human forces altered the natural and social landscape.

2. In a number of recent discussions, these scholars address the essentially social nature of technology, articulating its position within societies' wider systems of knowledge and meaning. Lemmonier, for example, views the unconscious and conscious mental operations or models of technological elements brought to technical activities as embedded in the wider system of *meaning* within a culture (Lemmonier 1992:82ff.) and not simply to available resources or known *techniques*. In other words, technologies are "integral components of the larger symbolic system" (ibid.:3).

3. Postgate (1992) identifies three symbols—"a hat, a stick and a stool"—associated with kings in iconography and a recurrent theme in hymns. He also states that during the earlier Uruk period, a particular type of "flat cap and a 'net skirt'" are associated with an individual who "wields authority" (1992:261).

4. Their original source for this assertion is Waetzoldt (1983:592ff.)

5. Ornaments similarly served as markers of gender and status. In the preceding Early Dynastic III period, Susan Pollock (1991) has noted gender divisions based upon archaeological evidence from the Royal Cemetery at Ur and the Kish A cemetery. Differences of status were found among high-ranking females whose graves were marked by "the types and quantities of jewelry that they wore" (Pollock 1991:376). Michelle Marcus (1994) also has documented the use of personal adornment to clarify "social roles and relations" and as symbolic and rhetorical devices. Although her evidence for the use of shroud pins on women's garments to mark life-cycle stages, provide personal protection, and convey "the illusion of an armed society" (1994:3) is from Iranian Azerbaijan in the late second and early first millennia B.C., and therefore, geographically outside of the southern Mesopotamian region, she convincingly argues that its roots may be in the representation of the Mesopotamian goddess Ishtar, goddess of war and sex, who frequently is represented with weapons protruding from her shoulders (see Marcus 1994:9ff., figure 12).

6. Listed as "bloody bandage or bandage for menstruation," "bandage used by women>menstruation bandage," "bandage of a menstruating woman" (bloody bandage), "garments for menstruating women" (Kang 1973:379).

7. In this essay I have relied on sources that represent activities in three locations during the Ur III period—Lagash, Girsu, and Umma, as discussed by Maekawa (1980, 1987), Waetzoldt (1972, 1987), Kang (1973), Steinkeller (1987), and to a lesser extent van de Mieroop (1987).

8. Maekawa (1987) describes two types of male work groups: (1) Men working "for hire" while "waiting for service," referring to regular service (corvée labor), and (2) men "engaged in regular service" (corvée labor). The work of men in the first group occurred in interim periods between the corvée labor. The two systems alternated, suggesting that men in gangs served obligatory corvée for, perhaps five or six months a year when they worked every day for thirty days, but when "hired," they usually worked twenty days (Maekawa 1987:65). Seasonal corvée may be related to the agricultural cycle; many of the jobs assigned to these "men in gangs" involved repairing or constructing irrigation canals and seeding and plowing fields. This distinction apparently represents a shift from preceding periods, when there does not appear to have been the "for hire" category and the free time away from work.

9. The term geme$_2$ is a female category, whereas sag refers to both male and female slaves (Gelb 1982:82).

10. Men also were "seized and forced" to work. Waetzoldt lists the following in grain grinding establishments: "gardeners, singers, 'lamentation priests,' fullers, porters, potters, reed mat weavers, and even merchants" (1987:139). It is unclear whether their service was for payment of debt or "some kind of deficiency in carrying out their professional obligations" (ibid.).

11. In addition to workshops in cities, there were others in villages and towns. These workshops appear to have operated in the same way as those in cities. They were directly responsible to either the temple or royal interests (Jacobsen 1970:216).

12. Maekawa, for instance, refers to an earlier period when there was a prolonged military crisis during which female supervisors were the norm. Still there is dispute about whether there was a shift from the period preceding Ur III. It is possible that during that period, regardless of military crises, there were fewer male supervisors. I am not sure what evidence contributes to the following comment by Maekawa: "At any rate, it seems possible to assume that male supervisors were not with female weavers during the actual work of shearing, spinning or weaving. In other words, one or two experienced women under a male supervisor might have led the other women under a male supervisor" (1980:88).

13. Textile production involved a large labor investment. Postgate reports of an account from Larsa in which "384 textile workers (days)" were required to produce one fine robe (1992:236).

14. Maekawa states the term "amar-KUD . . . was not only applied to animals but also to men in the meaning of 'young castrated animal/man' in the Ur III period. I have noticed that several Lagash texts of Ur III refer to young castrated sons of female weavers" (1980:81).

15. The process refers to a procedure in which cloth is pommeled, heaved, and trampled. Its purpose is to shrink and thicken the cloth and to "mat the fibers together into an impermeable sheet" (Barber 1991:178). Textual accounts speak of "walking on the cloth" (Jacobsen 1970:226).

16. These low compensations are attested in earlier periods and in the state of Ebla and other Mesopotamian cities (Waetzoldt 1987:122).

17. In addition to the references cited here, the pictorial imagery on cylinder seals from Susa (Figure 3.2) may represent women weaving (Asher-Greve 1985).

18. One textual account from Umma records 120 female workers employed for one day laying "reed mats on the roof/beam at the house of the weavers" that may refer to a separate establishment in which cloth production occurred (Kang 1973:152).

19. Such sentiments have been noted for women more generally as attested by Sumerian proverbs cited by Adams (1982, from Gordon 1959:12): "A rebellious male may be permitted to reconciliation (?); a rebellious female will be dragged in the mud."

20. A disturbing instance is a female child who, since she received a twenty-liter compensation, was between 13 and 15 but already had a child. According to Waetzoldt, "it is clear that she must have been reckoned among the nongrownups even after puberty. If one assumes puberty at twelve years of age, birth could have occurred around 13 or 14 years of age" (1987:133).

References

Adams, Robert McC.
  1965   *Land Behind Baghdad: A History of Settlement on the Diyala Plains.* Chicago: University of Chicago Press.
  1981   *Heartland of Cities.* Chicago: University of Chicago Press.
  1982   "Mesopotamian Social Evolution: Old Outlooks, New Goals." In *On the Evolution of Complex Societies: Essays in Honor of Harry Hoijer,* edited by Timothy Earle, 79–129. Malibu, Calif.: Undena Publications.
Adams, Robert McC., and Hans J. Nissen
  1972   *The Uruk Countryside: The Natural Setting of Urban Societies.* Chicago: University of Chicago Press.
Asher-Greve, Julia
  1985   *Frauen in altsumerischer Zeit.* Malibu, Calif.: Undena Publications.
Barber, E. J. W.
  1991   *Prehistoric Textiles: The Development of Cloth in the Neolithic and Bronze Ages with Special Reference to the Aegean.* Princeton, N.J.: Princeton University Press.
Basalla, George
  1988   *The Evolution of Technology.* Cambridge: Cambridge University Press.
Binford, Lewis R.
  1965   "Archaeological Systematics and the Study of Culture Process." *American Antiquity* 31:203–10.
Brumfiel, Elizabeth M.
  1983   "Aztec State Making: Ecology, Structure and the Origin of the State." *American Anthropologist* 85:261–84.
  1991   "Weaving and Cooking: Women's Production in Aztec Mexico." In *Engendering Archaeology: Women and Prehistory,* edited by Joan Gero and Margaret Conkey, 224–51. Oxford: Basil Blackwell.
  1992   "Distinguished Lecture in Archaeology: Breaking and Entering the Ecosystem: Gender, Class and Faction Steal the Show." *American Anthropologist* 94(3):551–67.
Brumfiel, Elizabeth M., and T. K. Earle, eds.
  1987   *Specialization, Exchange and Complex Societies.* Cambridge: Cambridge University Press.
Bush, Corlann Gee
  1983   "Women and the Assessment of Technology." In *Feminist Perspectives on Technology,* edited by J. Rothschild. New York: Pergamon Press.
Cohn, Bernard S.
  1989   "Cloth, Clothes, and Colonialism: India in the Nineteenth Century." In *Cloth and Human Experience,* edited by Annette Weiner and Jane Schneider, 303–53. Washington, D.C.: Smithsonian Institution Press.
Costin, Cathy L.
  1994   "Gender, Technology and Power: Cloth Production in the Inka Empire." Paper presented at the 93d annual meeting of the American Anthropological Association, Atlanta, Ga.
Dalley, Stephanie
  1980   *Old Babylonian Dowries. Iraq* 42:53–74.
Dobres, Marcia-Anne
  1995   "Of Paradigms Lost and Found: Archaeology and Prehistoric Technology, Sleepwalking through the Past." Paper presented in the

session *Cultural Logic, Social Agency, and the Political Dynamics of Technology: Beyond the Tangible.* Society for American Archaeology, Minneapolis, Minn., May 1995.

Dobres, Marcia-Anne, and Christopher R. Hoffman
1994   "Social Agency and the Dynamics of Prehistoric Technology." *Journal of Archaeological Method and Theory,* vol. 1, no. 3:211–58.

Englund, J.
1991   "Hard Work—Where Will It Get You: Labor Management in Ur III Mesopotamia." *Journal of Near Eastern Studies* 50(4):255–80.

Gailey, Christine Ward
1985   "The State of the State in Anthropology." *Dialectical Anthropology* 9:65–89.

Gelb, I. J.
1972   "The Arua Institution." *Revue d'Assyriologie* 66:1–32.
1973   "Prisoners of War in Early Mesopotamia." *Journal of Near Eastern Studies* 32:70–98.
1979   "Household and Family in Early Mesopotamia." *Orientalia Lovaniensia Analecta* (5):1–97.
1982   "Terms for Slaves in Ancient Mesopotamia." In *Societies and Languages of the Ancient Near East: Studies in Honour of I. M. Diakonoff.* Warminster, England: Aris and Phillips.

Gordon, Cyrus H., G. A. Rendsburg, and N. H. Winter, ed.
1987   *Eblaitica: Essays on the Ebla Archives and Eblaite Language.* Winona Lake, Ind.: Eisenbrauns.

Jacobsen, Thorkild
1970   *Toward the Image of Tammuz and Other Essays on Mesopotamia History and Culture,* edited by W. Moran. Cambridge, Mass.: Harvard University Press.
1987   *The Harps That Once . . . Sumerian Poetry in Translation.* New Haven, Conn.: Yale University Press.

Kang, Shin T.
1973   *Sumerian Economic Texts from the Umma Archive: Sumerian and Akkadian Cuneiform Texts in the Collection of the World Heritage Museum of the University of Illinois, Volume II.* Urbana: University of Illinois Press.

Kramer, Samuel Noah
1987   "The Women in Ancient Sumer: Gleanings from Sumerian Literature." In *La Femme dans le Proche-Orient antique,* edited by J.-M. Durand, 107–15. Paris: Éditions Recherches sur les Civilisations.

Lamberg-Karlovsky, C. C.
1994   "The Archaeological Evidence for International Commerce: Public and/or Private." Paper presented at New York University, September.

Lambert, W. G.
1987   "Goddesses in the Pantheon: A Reflection of Women in Society?" In *La Femme dans le Proche-Orient antique,* edited by J.-M. Durand, 125–30. Paris: Éditions Recherches sur les Civilisations.

Lechtman, Heather
1977   "Style in Technology: Some Early Thoughts." In *Material Culture: Styles, Organization and Dynamics of Technology,* edited by Heather Lechtman and Robert Merrill, 3–20. St. Paul, Minn.: American Ethnological Society.

Lemmonier, P.
    1992   *Elements for an Anthropology of Technology.* Museum of Anthropology, University of Michigan Anthropological Papers, No. 88, Ann Arbor.

McGaw, Judith
    1982   "Women and the History of American Technology: Review Essay." *Signs* 7:798–828.
    1989   "No Passive Victims, No Separate Spheres: A Feminist Perspective on Technology's History." In *In Context: History and the History of Technology*, edited by Steven H. Cutcliffe and Robert C. Post, 172–91. Bethlehem, Pa.: Lehigh University Press.
    1994   "Introduction: The Experience of Early American Technology." In *Early American Technology: Making and Doing Things from the Colonial Era to 1850*, edited by Judith A. McGaw, 1–15. Chapel Hill: University of North Carolina Press.

Marcus, Michelle I.
    1994   "Dressed to Kill: Women and Pins in Early Iran." *The Oxford Art Journal* 17:3–15.

Maekawa, Kazuya
    1973–74 "The Development of the é-mi in Lagash during Early Dynastic III." *Mesopotamia* 8–9 (pub. in 1976): 77–144.
    1980   "Female Weavers and Their Children." *Acta Sumerologica* 2:81–125.
    1987   "Collective Labor Service in Gursu-Lagash: The Pre-Sargonic and Ur III Periods." In *Labor in the Ancient Near East*, edited by M. A. Powell, 49–72. New Haven, Conn.: American Oriental Society.

Moore, Henrietta L.
    1990   *Feminism and Anthropology.* Minneapolis: University of Minnesota Press.

Pfaffenberger, B.
    1992   "Social Anthropology of Technology." *Annual Review of Anthropology* 21:491–516.

Pollock, Susan
    1991   "Women in a Men's World: Images of Sumerian Women." In *Engendering Archaeology: Women and Prehistory*, edited by Joan Gero and Margaret Conkey, 366–87. Oxford: Basil Blackwell.

Postgate, J. N.
    1992   *Early Mesopotamia: Society and Economy at the Dawn of History.* London and New York: Routledge.

Reade, W. J., and D. T. Potts
    1993   "New Evidence for Late Third Millennium Linen from Tell Abraq, Umm al-Qaiwain, UAE." *Paleorient*, vol. 19/2:99–106.

Rothschild, Joan
    1983   "*Machina ex Dea* and Future Research." In *Feminist Perspectives on Technology*, edited by J. Rothschild, 213–22. New York: Pergamon Press.

Steinkeller, Piotr
    1980   "Mattresses and Felt in Early Mesopotamia." *Oriens Antiquus* 19:79–100.
    1987   "The Foresters of Umma: Toward a Definition of Ur III Labor." In *Labor in the Ancient Near East*, edited by M. A. Powell, 73–116. New Haven, Conn.: American Oriental Society.

1994   "The Organization of Crafts in Third Millennia Babylonia: The Case of Potters." Paper delivered at the Eleventh International Congress of Economic History, Milan, Italy, September.

Stone, Elizabeth C.
1986   "Comment to Zagarell." *Current Anthropology* 27(5):424–25.

Trigger, Bruce
1989   *A History of Archaeological Thought.* Cambridge: Cambridge University Press.

Uchtel, Alexander
1984   "Daily Work at Sagdana Millhouse." *Acta Sumerologica* (Hiroshima) 6:75–98.

van de Mieroop, Marc
1987   *Crafts in the Early Isin Period: Study of the Isin Craft Archive from the Reigns of Isbi-erra and Su-ilisu.* Leuven: Departement Orientalistiek.

Waetzoldt, Hartmut
1972   *Untersuchungen zur neosumerischen Textilindustrie.* Studi economici e tecnologici 1. Rome: Centro per le antichita e la Storia dell'a vicino Oriente.
1983   "Leinen (Flachs)." *Reallexikon der Assyriologie* 6:583–94.
1987   "Compensation of Craft Workers and Officials in the Ur III Period." In *Labor in the Ancient Near East,* edited by M. A. Powell, 117–42. New Haven, Conn.: American Oriental Society.

Weiner, Annette B., and Jane Schneider, eds.
1989   *Cloth and Human Experience.* Washington, D.C.: Smithsonian Institution.

Winter, Irene
1985   "After the Battle Is Over: The Stele of the Vultures and the Beginning of Historical Narrative in the Art of the Ancient Near East." In *Pictorial Narrative in Antiquity and the Middle Ages,* edited by H. Kessler and M. Simpson, 11–32. Washington, D.C.: National Gallery of Art.
1987   "Women in Public: The Disk of Enheduanna, the Beginning of the Office of En-Priestess, and the Weight of Visual Evidence." In *La Femme dans le Proche-Orient antique,* edited by J.-M. Durand, 189–201. Paris: Éditions Recherches sur les civilisations.

Wright, Rita P.
1991   "Women's Labor and Pottery Production in Prehistory." In *Engendering Archaeology: Women and Prehistory,* edited by Joan M. Gero and Margaret W. Conkey, 194–223. Oxford: Basil Blackwell.
1993   "Technological Styles: Transforming a Natural Material into a Cultural Object." In *History from Things: Essays on Material Culture,* edited by S. Lubar and W. D. Kingery, 242–69. Washington, D.C.: Smithsonian Institution Press.
1995   "Knowledge and Cultural Choice, Cultural and Practical Reasons." Paper presented in the session *Cultural Logic, Social Agency, and the Political Dynamics of Technology: Beyond the Tangible.* Society for American Archaeology, Minneapolis, Minn., May 1995.

Zagarell, Allen
1986   "Trade, Women, Class, and Society in Ancient Western Asia." *Current Anthropology* 27(5):415–30.

Chapter 4
Exploring the Relationship Between Gender and Craft in Complex Societies: Methodological and Theoretical Issues of Gender Attribution

Cathy Lynne Costin

> Men [*sic*] are known by their work. It is no accident that when strangers meet, a standard opening gambit is the question, "what sort of work do you do?" for this information provides the best single clue to the sort of person one is. It marks a person as "someone to be reckoned with" or as one who can be safely ignored, one to whom deference is due or from whom deference can be expected. Moreover, it permits at least crude inferences regarding attitudes, experiences, and style of life. In short, occupational roles locate individuals in social space, thereby setting the stage for their interaction with one another.
> —Donald Treiman, *Occupational Prestige in Comparative Perspective*

> Gender attribution is not even a necessary stage in the process whereby we engender the past, although it *is* certainly and inextricably part of the inquiry. While it would be extremely helpful to attribute specific features to a specific gender, and while gender associations are integral to research that takes gender as a subject, we refuse to feel limited by the notion that we must provide gender attributions and *must* do so with a certain "fixity."
> —Margaret Conkey and Joan Gero, in *Engendering Archaeology*

The value of conducting research into specific gender attributions and roles in prehistory has recently come under some scrutiny (for example, see comments by Costin [1994a], Gero [1994], and Klein [1994] on

McCafferty and McCafferty [1994]; Dobres 1993), largely when it becomes an end in and of itself, as we recognize that the "add women and stir" approach is not sufficient for engendering the past. Yet we should not read cautions about the limitations of gender attribution as justification to shun gender attribution altogether. Gender is a major structuring principle in social life, and our engendered past must make use of this concept to understand social process and social change in ways analogous to ways we use class and faction. Thus, while we might successfully explore gender theory and gender relations without associating specific genders with particular features in some contexts, I suggest it is more critical to make specific gender attributions in others. In fact, there are important anthropological questions that likely can only be addressed if one is able to ascribe gender with a relatively high degree of explicitness and confidence. Studies of the division of labor and social relations of production constitute one such domain of inquiry.

This essay addresses the central importance of gender attribution as an endeavor that is broader than just a "search for prehistoric women" in studies of the division of labor generally and craft production in complex societies more specifically. Such studies are particularly desirable because there are no known cases of complex society—modern or historic—in which a gendered division of labor is not a critical factor in the domestic and political economies and because gendered relations of production are tied into other complex social and political relations. Yet it may be that the gendered division of labor is too idiosyncratic cross-culturally to neglect direct research in gender attribution before using the gendered division of labor to address other complex social issues in historically specific or comparative cases.

I have two purposes in this essay. First, I explore the reasons why gender attribution is so critical to studies of the division of labor and gendered relations of production. Second, I argue that gender attribution is an approachable problem that can be addressed with specificity and rigor, since there are several different types of data that can be used effectively to interpret the archaeological record. I enumerate several methods appropriate for reconstructing plausible gender attributions in prehistory, and then present a case study to demonstrate how, when used as multiple lines of evidence to address a single issue, they are particularly effective for exploring the gendered division of labor in craft production and the sociopolitical implications of the gendered social relations of production in ancient societies.

Gender and the Division of Labor

Gender is a fundamental component of one's social identity. I view gender as comprised of *learned* behaviors and culturally communicated symbols that "materialize" (to use the term introduced by DeMarrais, Castillo, and Earle 1996) a set of beliefs about masculinity and femininity—most fundamentally that men and women are different and have different roles and responsibilities in social reproduction and maintenance.[1] The gender system includes beliefs; activities (including things entailed in the gendered division of labor); characteristics of personal appearance (such as hair length, placement of jewelry, and so on); modes of interaction (such as servility, acquiescence, domination) and reaction (violence, crying, and so on); all of which mediate and reflect the identities of and relationships between members of gender categories.

The productive tasks for which one is consistently responsible are another key element of social identity. Especially in complex societies, prestige and status—not to mention wealth—are often derived from the work one performs *for* the social group (cf. Joyce 1992, this volume, Chapter 6). The androcentric language in the quote from Treiman above is unfortunate, but his point is well made: the type(s) of labor one performs and the type(s) of services or goods one offers to the social group help to define one's place in society. Especially in complex societies, occupation is often a real determinant of power as well as a metaphor for social position.

These two key aspects of social identity—gender and productive responsibilities to the group—intersect in the gendered division of labor. The gendered division of labor is generally accepted to be universal in anatomically and behaviorally "modern" human groups, although it is uncertain when in the evolution of our species it developed. It is a common presumption that the primary function of gender is to organize labor. While I don't subscribe to the implicit causal link in this construct—that gender arose specifically as a means of organizing economic and other activities—I do believe there is an inextricable link between gender and division of labor.[2] In kin-based societies, gender, along with age, is often the primary factor in determining who does what. The division of labor within the household is held by some to be the most rudimentary form of specialization (e.g., Rueschemeyer 1986; Gero 1995), although most definitions of specialization specifically exclude the division of labor within the household when products are used only by household members (recent examples include Clark and Parry 1990:297; Costin 1991:4; Rice 1991a:263).

The need to engender our discussions of the organization of production in complex societies is especially acute. Heretofore, class has been the primary aspect of social identity investigated for its role as a structuring principle in the organization of production (e.g., Rice 1981; Feinman 1980, 1985; Brumfiel and Earle 1987; Sinopoli 1988; Clark and Parry 1990). Gender largely has been excluded from such discussions (Zagarell [1986], Billigmeier and Turner [1985], Brumfiel [1991], and Wright [1991] are a few notable exceptions within the large literature on the organization of production). Clearly, gender relations do not disappear as active means of forming and organizing economic relations in ranked and stratified societies (see discussions by Gailey 1987; Costin 1993a; Silverblatt 1987). Rather they are transformed as different institutions of social integration define reproductive categories (genders) and their "appropriate" roles in social maintenance and reproduction. The gendered relations of production in complex societies become more multifaceted as rank and class intersect with gender (and age) to define productive and reproductive roles and create highly complex sets of economic relationships in chiefdoms and states.

Understanding the gendered relations of production in economies characterized by specialized production—which requires the transfer of goods between individuals likely unrelated by blood or marriage—is particularly important for two reasons. First, direct participation in an economy characterized by specialization of production and exchange creates social ties and connects one to social networks. Second, specialization is social labor that enriches and empowers. This later point has been elaborated for class relationships, focusing on the material and ideological powers that accrue to those who ostensibly control certain types of production, particularly elite sponsorship of attached production (e.g., Friedman and Rowlands 1977; Earle 1982; Brumfiel and Earle 1987; DeMarrais, Castillo, and Earle 1996; Costin in press). I suggest that analogous, potentially unequal social relations of production obtain when divisions of labor are based on gender.

The Importance of Gender Attribution in Studies of Craft Production

As I will discuss below, craft production is highly gendered in complex societies. In noncapitalist societies, I would argue artisanship is a particularly important determinant of social roles and social positions. As creators of material goods, artisans create items of indispensable domestic utility and of wealth. Artisanship can be a metaphor for sociopolitical power (Helms 1993). Craft is often integral to gender identity (e.g., McCafferty and McCafferty 1991). Because one's gender often establishes the range of economic activities permissible and because participation in certain kinds of productive activities situates one in specific socioeconomic networks, we can see the importance of investigating the associations between gender and craft and how they change over time as a key element of social process and social change. Gender-based differences in craft production can lead to gendered differences in social participation, wealth, and legitimation because specialization is social labor that serves to create networks beyond the resident group, and because crafting in complex societies is materially and ideologically connected to power hierarchies of all sorts.

Yet despite the significance of the gendered division of labor in craft production for structuring social and power relations in complex societies, there are surprisingly few systematic, sustained works ascribing gender in studies of craft production (and distribution). Such studies are clearly necessary for several reasons. The first reason to engage in explicitly documented gender attribution is to demonstrate that gender exists as a relevant social category structuring or mediating roles and relationships within the cultural domain under study, here craft production. To assert with confidence that gender is a relevant dimension of social identity factoring into the relations of production, we must identify some of those symbols or behaviors that marked differences between gender groups in terms of access to resources, technology, occupational roles, and so on. When class is considered a "factor" in the social relations of production, it is incumbent upon us to demonstrate that there were *classes*, by identifying evidence that can distinguish between rich and poor, powerful and powerless, and that the different classes somehow controlled, participated in, and/or enjoyed the output of productive activities in different ways. Since we are hard pressed to demonstrate convincingly that class or other social differences such as faction or ethnicity existed *and mattered* in the absence of concrete data, by analogy I question how we can argue that gender was a relevant category in the social relations of production without some elemental recognition that gendered differences existed within the particular economic processes under investigation.

Second, while the ethnographic record suggests strongly that gender is indeed a relevant and primary social category in allocating resources, technologies, and other factors of production, we must continue with studies of craft production that include a rigorous program of explicit gender attribution to avoid the risk of perpetuating stereotypes and to develop plausible alternative models for gender roles and gendered relations of production in the past. I am concerned about implicit gender attributions made in the absence of concrete data that argue convincingly for the association of particular activities with a specific gender. Unsubstantiated gender attributions are likely to follow the same stereotypes and limits that we argue should be questioned with the archaeological data. Ultimately, we must make explicit the assumptions behind our analogies, and in doing so demonstrate that they are justified in historic as well as cross-cultural terms. As McGaw (1989:173) has pointed out, we must substantiate the differences between men and women, rather than merely assume them. Perhaps our most relevant lesson from the ethnographic data is that craft production is gendered in largely idiosyncratic, historically contingent ways, making sweeping generalizations and general analogies problematic in many cases. If we are not to be bound to analogy with societies from the ethnographic present, then we *must* have concrete examples from the past with which to broaden our understanding of the range of human experiences and to more fully explore the contexts in which labor is gendered in specific ways.

Third, specific gender attribution ultimately provides the detail necessary to evaluate and substantiate theories of gender process. Without specific gender attributions, we create a "genderless" gender theory. While such an endeavor may be useful for posing research questions about the nature of gender relations and structure within the larger social whole and for developing alternative scenarios for how and why certain events and processes may have occurred, it affords little opportunity for resolution of competing explanatory frameworks (assuming, of course, that such resolution is desirable or necessary) and little specificity about particular historical cases. As Elizabeth Graham (1991:470) has stated, "Even the most comprehensive of theories . . . must, to be viable, account for specifics."

Methods of Gender Attribution in Studies of Craft Specialization

I suggest that no "methodological breakthrough" is needed to concretely ascribe gender in studies of the division of labor and relations of production; what is at issue is the creation of new research questions. In this, I agree with Alison Wylie (1991) that the key change we require is to view women and gender as conceptually appropriate subjects of inquiry. Women, men, and gender have always been "directly accessible as subjects," but we have ignored them. Given the definition of gender as a cultural construction that elaborates and extends fundamental sexual/reproductive differences to mark one's place in social maintenance and reproduction, whenever there are *cultural* distinctions made between men and women we in fact have evidence for a *gender* system. Such differential treatment can be recognized in such things as diet (Hastorf 1991); degenerative diseases indicative of activities (Hollimon 1992; Molleson 1994); burial practices (Arnold 1991; Damm 1991), and figurative portrayals that go beyond depictions of anatomical and biological characteristics (Proskouriakoff 1961; Ehrenberg 1989: chapter 4; Joyce 1992 and this volume).

Several types of data routinely used by archaeologists can be used to ascribe gender in studies that model and explain the gendered division of labor and social relations of production in complex societies. *Ethnographic analogy* can be used to inform studies of craft production when data on contemporary artisans are considered an appropriate analogy for attributing gender to specific activities at a specific locale or among a specific people in the past. Many studies that use such analogies have not focused on the division of labor or relations of production, per se, but rather sought to use to division of labor to reconstruct other aspects of social organization. Such studies include the classic attempts to identify matrilineal descent by tracing patterns of similarities in pottery designs, under the assumption that if mothers taught their daughters to make pottery in matrilineal societies, design elements would be clustered in the residential units associated with matrilineal social units (Deetz 1968; Hill 1968; Longacre 1968). In these cases, the twentieth-century division of labor was *presumed* to hold for the prehistoric past, but few data were presented to support the supposition. In a more rigorous analysis, Yvonne Marshall (1985) has attempted to systematically engender Lapita pottery production, by looking for what she called "signature traits": the cultural and environmental contexts where potters of a particular gender would be more likely to be found. Direct and more general analogies may be of great utility in those parts of the world where such data are available, but there are likely a limited number of useful cases, and in all instances we must pay careful attention to the effects of hundreds of intervening years of internally driven culture change, colonialism, and Western capitalist influence. Moreover, some form of independent, corroborating evidence would increase greatly the rigor of the analysis.

Text is an important source of information regarding the gender of artisans in complex societies. There are many types of textual sources available for use in studies of the organization of production: indigenous writings and transcribed native oral traditions, including myths, legends, poetry, literature, genealogical histories, and legal codes; accounts and descriptions by outsiders such as traders, explorers, missionaries, and conquerors; and colonial administrative documents, including censuses, official questionnaires, tribute lists, court transcripts, and legal codes.

None of the ethnohistoric sources is without problems and/or biases. Few of these works are consciously "ethnographic" investigations of native culture and are likely limited in the scope of subjects they cover and subjective in their presentation of many "facts." The topics and domains covered are often narrow, usually focusing primarily on things of interest to the ruling class (such as political organization, taxation, the management of economy, warfare, and official religious practice). The information was often collected from and recorded by men—usually, upper-class men—and therefore, represents the viewpoint of only a small segment of society. Women rarely participated in the creation of these texts, as subjects, sources, or scribes. The comments of Inga Clendinnen (1991:154) on documentary sources for Mexica women are likely near universal:

Sources, as is usual for the female half of the human race, are deficient. We hear no Mexica women's voices at all. . . . In pre-contact times public and therefore recorded matters were the business of men. . . . After the conquest those who recalled or commented on the Mexica past were males, and often celibate foreign males at that. . . . Mexica women (like Mexica children, like Mexica commoners) were neither the makers nor keepers of the records, but something of their circumstances of life, and even, with luck, some sense of their experience of those circumstances, can reasonably be sought for.

In addition to gender and class bias found in most textual sources, we must also consider that colonial chronicles, censuses, court proceedings, and other administrative records often fail to represent the native point of view.

Despite their shortcomings, the documentary sources are particularly valuable as sources of certain kinds of information, especially for those intangibles of culture that often leave no material record. These include rules, ideas, abstract beliefs, marriage patterns and practices, systems of access to resources, and historical information. Among the important information contained in many of these records is the identification of gender in the division of labor and the sociopolitical contexts in which that production was pursued. Elizabeth Barber (1991, 1994) relied extensively on textual and linguistic evidence to reconstruct textile production in the Aegean and Near East, primarily enumerating textile technology, the contexts of cloth manufacture, and the organization of production over thousands of years of prehistory. The great value of ethnohistorical materials may be as a complementary/contrastive data set used in conjunction with other archaeological materials, as exemplified by Elizabeth Brumfiel's (1991) analysis of the impact of Aztec conquest on women in the Basin of Mexico, where she demonstrated changes in women's activity load and discussed how men and women may have experienced the Aztec conquest differently because of these different demands on their labor.

Sex and gender are generally readily accessible in *mortuary contexts*. However, few studies have used mortuary remains to establish the nature and effects of the gendered division of labor in craft production.

Mortuary analysis has been used most often to assess the general relative "status" of gendered groups, usually through analysis of nutrition and disease, burial types and locations, and the quality and quantity of grave goods. Brief mention is sometimes made of general associations between sex and a particular class of tools. Some interesting recent studies have analyzed how particular patterns of labor in food procurement and processing have affected women (e.g., Hollimon 1992; Molleson 1994). I suggest it would be constructive to adopt these methodologies to studies of non–food related activities: for example, to use skeletal data along with other mortuary evidence to associate crafting with other patterns of work, health, and stress.

Some have argued that mortuary analysis can be problematic because burial practices sometimes mask organizational structures and aspects of practice actually operating in a society. Yet the grave goods displayed and then deposited with an individual clearly must reflect *someone*'s version of reality: there must be an underlying ideological, ritual, sociological, or political, if not operative, reason why the dead and/or those who have buried them would choose to mark a person in death in a particular way. When such marking is patterned, it must have some meaning; our responsibility is to identify the plausible meanings. While in isolation patterns in burial practices may be "misleading," when they are contextualized in time, space, and/or relative to other cultural domains, we may in fact gain important insight into important historical factors or processes such as structural discontinuities or changing gender roles.

Figurative representations have been one of the most common sources of information about gender (e.g., Miller 1988; Nelson 1990; Gero 1992; Brumfiel this volume; Arsenault 1991; Joyce 1992, this volume; Barber 1991, 1994). Such images reflecting the gendered division of labor are extremely useful because they provide not only a catalog/inventory of activities but also, when properly contextualized, yield evidence for social attitudes and the subtleties of social interactions associated with economic activities.

In a thought-provoking essay, Dyfri Williams (1985) discusses many of the difficulties inherent in using figurative representations in gender studies. One problem is recognizing which categories of women are represented in the scenes. For example, among the vases she looks at, many scenes lack sufficient clues to differentiate among slaves, professionals (that is, hetairai) and family women; mortals, legendary figures, and immortals. Second, Williams demonstrates that we must be careful to identify the function (in her case, for example, funerary or male drinking-party) and "consumer" (for example, male or female; housewife or hetaira) of the representations, as different messages/stories are appropriate and different meanings can be read in different contexts.

Third, Williams notes the importance of identifying the "viewpoint" of the artist, or what she calls the "natural bias" of the vase-painters (Williams 1985:97), a perspective influenced by their gender, status, the neighborhood in which they lived, and the market for which they produced.

Like historical texts, figurative representations are best interpreted within the context of where they were made, for whom they were made, why they were made, and the background of their creators. One problem, of course, is that we rarely know the social identities of those who created the art we are interpreting. The existence of marked individual artisans is extremely rare in prehistoric contexts (cf. Gunter 1991; Reents-Budet 1994) and little work has been done by archaeologists and prehistorians to investigate the social identities of anonymous artisans. Although unfortunate, the assumption is often made that figurative artisans were male (cf. Handsman 1991; Russell 1991). Williams's observations make clear that we ought to try harder to discover the social identities of ancient artisans. What this means, of course, is that we must learn the gender of the artisans whose images we are using to engender craft production!

It is well to consider that, while each type of data has its own strengths and weaknesses, they do share a common characteristic: to a great extent, all reflect normative or idealized views of gender roles, albeit for different reasons. Gender, like most organizational and structural phenomena, is a conceptual category: members of a group share a core identity and set of attributes, but the boundaries of the category are "fuzzy," not only across time and space but within any one society at a single point in time. Given that the archaeological record is a palimpsest of the cultural categories that we considered "gender," I suggest we begin our inquiry by identifying that core of meaning that was relatively fixed and widely shared within the society under study. From this, we can then expand our investigation to move toward the fuzzy, negotiable boundaries of the conceptual category, to see how the division of labor figures into the process of gender categorization/classification. We can also phrase our research questions in ways that explicitly recognize the nature and function of norms and ideals within society. For example, it is important to understand how/why certain activities become labeled as "masculine" or "feminine," in what contexts those appellations change, and the implications of such gender correlations for social relations of production and the allocation of power and wealth within a society. Similarly, we might want to understand what happens when individuals perform activities considered the domain of another gender. If those activities convey prestige and/or wealth, are other producers empowered in the same way as the stereotypical group? How is their contribution recognized or acknowledged? What are the implications for their more broadly defined "status" within the community?

More often than not, the different types of data are most useful as complementary and/or contrastive sets of information. In fact, addressing complex issues like gender may depend upon using multiple lines of evidence that reflect different aspects and different parts of the system. Analyses of multiple data sets are particularly worthwhile because it is likely that the different types of evidence suffer from different sorts of biases or lacunae and were likely created independently of one another (Costin 1995).

Gender and Craft in the Ethnographic Literature

A currently underutilized source of information relevant to our studies of the gendered division of labor is the cross-cultural ethnographic literature. I find it useful in two ways. First, it provides a baseline against which we can better understand our archaeological data. Second, it is a rich source for questions about the gendered division of labor and gendered relations of production that are well-suited to study using an archaeological perspective. One of the most fundamental of these is the very nature and structure of the gendered division of labor. In a classic cross-cultural study of the division of labor, George Murdock and Caterina Provost (1973) scored fifty activities by gender participation and calculated means to indicate whether activities were best characterized as "masculine" or "feminine" (Table 4.1). Their study is most often cited to justify general analogies ascribing gender to particular activities. Yet I am not sure the most useful lesson from this study is that women are slightly more likely to pot or weave or that men are more likely to make stone tools, thus universalizing a particular division of labor (cf. Gero 1991; Rice 1991b; Wright 1991). Rather, two key implications of this and other cross-cultural studies of craft production are that (1) the gendered division of labor in craft production is remarkably strong, perhaps more so than in food production,[3] and (2) despite this, the actual allocation of tasks is remarkably idiosyncratic when considered on a worldwide basis. While many activities have median scores of sex participation when such scores are calculated on a worldwide or even regional basis—because they may be pursued by men or women in different societies—within a single society there is usually a strong division of labor, with either men *or* women pursuing a particular occupation or task within a sequence of production steps. As indicated in Table 4.1, the percent of societies where men and women are reported to work in the same industry in the same society is relatively low; the percent of societies where crafts are exclusively male or female is conversely quite high. We can conclude

TABLE 4.1. Crafts rated by "sex participation" worldwide.

Craft	Number of societies with craft (percent)	Index of sex partici- pation[a]	Percent equal partici- pation	Percent predominantly one gender	Percent exclusively one gender
Metalworking	86	99.8	0	1	99
Woodworking	164	98.8	1	2	97
Stoneworking	73	95.9	8	0	92
Bone, horn, shellworking	82	94.6	9	2	89
Netmaking	65	71.2	8	4	88
Rope and cord making	111	69.9	16	11	73
Leatherwork	74	53.2	3	11	86
Mat-making	103	37.6	9	8	83
Loom weaving	88	32.5	7	9	84
Potting	105	21.1	6	10	84
Spinning	91	13.6	4	9	87

Source: Data after Murdock and Provost (1973: Table 1).
[a]Calculated on a scale of one hundred (100), with one hundred (100) equaling exclusive male participation, and zero (0) equaling exclusive female participation.

that although many industries are considered "swing" activities in that they have mid-range scores of gender participation on a worldwide average, the division of labor in any one society is usually highly gendered. For example, leatherworking has a worldwide sex participation score of 53.2, which indicates near equal distribution between male and female practitioners (Table 4.1). This does not mean, however, that leatherworking is not gender-specific in individual societies. In 86 percent of the cases, it is the domain of one gender or the other. A similar pattern holds for almost all crafts reported by Murdock and Provost.

I have used data from the Human Relations Area Files to expand upon the Murdock and Provost study (Costin 1993a) to suggest that in those cases where women and men ostensibly work in same activity, there is actually a gendered division of labor by subtasks or a distinction between female and male artisans by material, technology, products, or markets. In my own coding of craft production in complex societies, there were only three observations (3 percent) where women and men apparently participated together in the production of the same goods for the same set of consumers. Of these three, two were in the same society (Cuna pottery and cloth production) and were production for domestic use, not specialized production.

In most cases where men and women pursued the same general craft—for example, weaving—they either used different technologies, made different kinds of products, worked for different kinds of consumers/patrons, and/or were organized in a different mode of production. For example, among the Ashante, women produced utilitarian domestic pottery, while men produced special, ritual ceramic vessels. Among the Hausa, women wove cotton blankets on a wide loom for long-distance exchange, while men wove cotton cloth on narrow looms for local use in clothing manufacture. In the Inka empire, both female and male weavers produced cloth for the state. However, as I discuss below, male and female weavers were physically and conceptually distinguished in many ways.[4]

The systematic cross-cultural analysis of ethnographic data suggest there may be a remarkably consistent ideal of keeping men's and women's labor distinct. I cannot argue that this practice is universal. But because the division of labor and gender identity are so deeply entwined, it is an interesting and important observation that can help us understand the nature of origins of gender as a structuring social principle, namely the incredible strength of the tendency to mark men and women as separate, as well as the dynamic that gender played in the organization of production in complex societies.

Cross-cultural research suggests other patterns in the gendered division of labor that warrant further study both comparatively and within particular historical sequences. For example, men are generally more likely to be craft producers than are women. Overall, in nearly three-quarters of the observations, men were the artisan, while women produced crafts in only one quarter of the industries identified. A number of measures—aggregated across all crafts and measured within each craft—indicated that men are much more likely to be craft *specialists*, not only craft producers, in complex societies. If a craft is produced domestically for household use, it is likely to be produced by women; if it is produced for extra-household exchange, it is much more likely to be produced by a *male* specialist (Costin 1993a).

Cloth Production and Gender in the Inka Empire

In addition to cross-cultural investigation, I have tapped multiple lines of evidence to engender cloth production and discuss the social, political, and economic implications of the gendered relations of production in one historically specific case, namely the Inka empire of the Late Horizon period (ca. A.D. 1400–1533) in the Andean highlands. Of particular interest has been the changes that occurred when the expansionist Inka conquered other highland societies and incorporated them into their empire.

The importance and value of cloth and cloth production in pre-

Hispanic Andean societies are well attested in the documentary sources. Relying on key colonial texts, John V. Murra (1962, 1989) has discussed the centrality of cloth in basic survival; its role in many important ceremonies and rituals, including puberty rites, marriage, and burial; and the functions of cloth as the primary form of wealth in most Andean societies. In particular, the activities of the elites and state institutions were financed by tribute levies consisting largely of agricultural products and cloth, which were imposed on subordinate populations. Studies of cloth production can serve as an important entrée into social relations of production, political economy, and sociopolitical dynamics more generally.

Ethnohistoric materials were the point of embarkation for my analyses (Costin 1993b, 1994b, 1995). The precolonial Andean peoples were nonliterate; however, there are a number of colonial sources from which to draw basic information about the gender of artisans and the sociopolitical contexts in which they worked. These include the rich Andean oral traditions which were recorded soon after the Spanish conquest of Peru in A.D. 1533; a large body of legal documents, including censuses, official questionnaires (*visitas*), and court documents from the early colonial era; and a relatively large corpus of diaries, letters, and other written works of the conquerors, European administrators, and literate natives from the first century after Spanish conquest.

The gender of cloth producers in the Inka empire is of much interest. Most agree that both females and males contributed to cloth production. When we consider *all* the tasks involved in textile production—herding and shearing camelids; growing and harvesting cotton; preparing raw fiber; spinning and plying; dying; weaving; sewing; embroidering; finishing—there is no question but that almost all members of pre-Inka and Inka Andean societies were involved in the various stages of cloth production in the Andes (Gayton 1973; Rowe 1979; Bruhns 1991; Benavides 1993). However, there is disagreement on the nature, context, and relative importance of the contribution of men and women, especially in state-sponsored production. This issue is important as we try to discern various contributions to the political economy, changing relations of production, and the impact of imperial incorporation on various social groups.

Cloth production in the Inka empire took place in several distinct contexts, and it is important to understand how gender roles may have differed in these contexts as well as how they changed over time. Most cloth was produced in a household context, and this is the context in which weaving is most closely associated with women (Gero 1992; Costin 1993b). Nonreproductive males may have spun to assist their female kin (see below), but we have no indication they wove. In pre-Inka times, even most of the finest cloth for elite use was made in an elite domestic context, employing women of the (polygynous) household in a form of production I call elite intensified household production (Costin 1993b).

Domestic cloth production was transformed after the Inka conquest as all households—commoner as well as elite—were drawn into the Inka political economy through a cloth tax enacted on subjugated populations. State tax collectors requisitioned certain amounts of cloth from each community on a regular basis; local leaders divided the work among the villagers under their control. Not surprisingly, the cloth tax burden imposed by the Inka fell on the "traditional" spinners and weavers, that is, largely on girls and women. Thus, in addition to spinning and weaving to make clothing and blankets for their own families—as they had done before the Inka conquest—under the Inka, women additionally spun thread and wove cloth that was turned over to state tax collectors.

Archaeological data from the Upper Mantaro Valley were analyzed in conjunction with the ethnohistoric materials to broaden our understanding of the impact of Inka policy on the local Wanka population beyond the information available in the ethnohistoric documents. Using ethnographic analogy and the ethnohistorical documents, I associated spindle whorls recovered in a domestic context primarily with female labor. The distributions and densities of whorls recovered from pre-Inka and Inka contexts indicate the amount of spinning in local communities doubled after the Inka conquest (Figure 4.1). From this I conclude women worked harder after the conquest, as there is no indication in either the ethnohistorical literature nor in the archaeological record to indicate that other aspects of their work load were proportionally decreased. Now, men also worked harder after the Inka conquest. However, the contexts of female and male tribute labor were different, resulting in different experiences of and consequences for the tribute burden. Women met their tribute levies by working (more or less) alone within their homes, apparently receiving little in return from the state. In contrast, men met their tribute requirements by working collectively on large-scale land modification and construction projects, and were regularly feted by the state in the course of completing their labor assignments (cf. Hastorf 1991). Thus, differential participation in craft and other labor may have resulted in men and women perceiving their conquerors very differently, and therefore developing gender-specific attitudes toward the state and its incursions into household and community life.

Additionally, in the Late Horizon period two sets of specialists—*aqlla-kuna* and *qompi-kamayoq*—wove for the state, presumably in state facilities. It is in state contexts that we find evidence for male as well as female

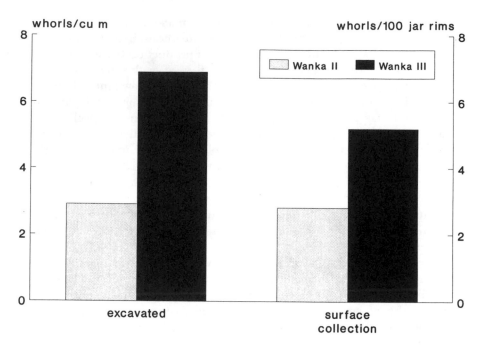

Figure 4.1. Concentrations of spindle whorls from the Upper Mantaro Valley, Peru. Recovered in household contexts, Pre-Inka and Inka. (Courtesy of Cathy Costin)

weavers. The *aqllakuna* were women removed from their natal communities at a young age and sent to special state facilities (*aqllahuasi*) where they were instructed in the arts of weaving and brewing. Some of them were sacrificed or given as second wives to Inka nobles and provincial elites, but the vast majority lived out their lives as sequestered virgins in the *aqllahuasi*, brewing beer for consumption at state-sponsored feasts and weaving fine cloth for the nobility and religious institutions. The second group of state weavers, the *qompi-kamayoq*, are everywhere assumed to be male. *Kamayoq* in general were skilled specialists. Some worked full-time for their elite and state patrons; others only part-time. While not all *kamayoq* retained ties to their natal communities, as far as we know all were permitted to marry, have children, and were not cloistered by the state. Importantly, female and male specialists worked wholly apart from one another.

I wish to turn now to the issue of ideology and practice, because it is disjunctions between cultural norms and actual behavior that can lead to the disruption I suggest may have been feared as the state began to recruit male weavers. Although, as discussed above, men and women variously contributed to cloth production, I suggest that spinning and weaving were generally *conceptualized* as women's work.[5] Indeed, as in many other societies, making cloth was the archetypal feminine activity. As Michael Moseley (1992:68) has written: "Pride in clothing one's family is a hallmark of Andean femininity. . . . All women wove, from the humblest of peasants to the wives of kings. Queens and empresses wove as an Andean symbol of their femininity." The normative association between cloth production and women is represented in myth and in burial practices. According to Inka creation myths, weaving was a craft brought to humans by the first empresses. While spinning and weaving implements are found in the graves of both men and women in Formative times (ca. 3500–200 B.C.), by the Early Intermediate Period (roughly 200 B.C. to A.D. 600)—which is perhaps not coincidentally the period in which true state-level societies arose in the Andes—it appears that tools associated with cloth production (spindle whorls, weaving baskets, loom parts) are found almost exclusively in female burials (Stone-Miller 1992:68; C. Donnan personal communication, 1994). While this may not mean that only women spun and wove in life, it does argue for a strong ideological association between cloth production and femininity.

There are other indications of an ideological association between weaving and femininity—or perhaps we should say between cloth production and nonmasculinity!—by Late Horizon times in the Andes. In his thousand-page treatise on Inka history, native Andean lifeways, and the Spanish conquest, the native Guaman Poma (1980[1615]) includes numerous illustrations of tasks related to cloth production, primarily spinning and weaving. His images are largely of females performing these tasks. Females of all ages are shown spinning and weaving in precolonial contexts (Figure 4.2). In contrast, his only male weaver appears in a clearly marked *colonial* image (Figure 4.3, left). He describes other males spinning, but gives us only one image of a man involved in thread production (Figure 4.3, right). This man is actually plying along side a woman (his wife?) who is spinning. Importantly, Guaman Poma describes this scene as occurring in a mythological past. According to colonial sources, those Inka-period males who *assisted* in cloth production at the household level—primarily by spinning thread—were males who were unable to fulfill other "masculine" roles such as serving in the army or participating in "masculine" corvée labor assignments (such as large-scale construction and working in the mines) because they were too young, too old, or "crippled" in some way. This allocation of labor continues into the present: in many parts of the Andes spinning is performed by very young and very old males as well as females of all ages. It is notable that women of reproductive age, but not men of reproductive age, spin. Indeed, Karen Bruhns (1991:426), who is ostensibly argu-

Figure 4.2. Illustrations from Guaman Poma of females of all ages spinning (top) and weaving (bottom). (Courtesy of Cathy Costin)

Figure 4.3. Illustrations from Guaman Poma of a colonial man weaving (right) and a man in a mythical past plying thread as a woman (his wife?) spins (left). (Courtesy of Cathy Costin)

ing that cloth production is not necessarily gender-based in the Andes, writes, "it is the [adult] women who are most commonly seen spinning in public." This correlation between *all* females and nonreproductive males is, I think, quite important in understanding gender ideology: male spinners were and continue to be men who were in some physical way "emasculated"; might we turn the equation around and wonder whether, traditionally, participating in cloth production was in some way itself an emasculating act?

We have many clues that the state was "sensitive" to the gender of its weavers—that is, it was cognizant of the social symbolism of productive roles in defining gender identity and reproductive roles. Documentary evidence suggests that male weavers were treated and conceptualized quite differently from female specialist weavers. The state clearly marked—by gender—categories of specialist weavers working in institutional contexts. First, male and female weavers were marked lexically. The female specialists (*aqllakuna*) were identified by a social role/status, while the male weavers (*gompi-kamayoq*) were called by an occupational title that stressed the parallel between them and other specialists—

both craft and service—working for the state. *Aqllakuna* were "chosen women"; *qompi-kamayoq* were "specialists skilled in the weaving of fine cloth." *Aqllakuna* were women chosen by the state to fulfill their traditional feminine roles solely in service to the state. Women in general and *aqllakuna* in particular were *expected* to weave. Although the *aqllakuna* produced some of the finest cloth in the empire, this crucial aspect of their social contribution did not need to be specifically marked because it was, as ascribed activity, almost an innate part of their femininity. No attention needed to be called to the occupation of female weavers, because in some ways these terms—woman and weaver—were redundant. In contrast, I would suggest that male weavers were designated by the specific occupational title of *qompi-kamayoq* because participation in this activity was an achieved role, extraordinary to these particular male specialists and not an activity expected of all males. Hence, their contribution needed a specific marker and a special acknowledgment. The title *kamayoq*—skilled specialist—was applied to many categories of workers with different social identities and life circumstances, all of whom produced for the state. The first group consisted of skilled artisans obliged to manufacture their specialized crafts to meet their tribute (*mit'a*) obligations. The second group, called *mitmaqkuna*, were kin-based groups of specialists removed from their natal lands and resettled into new communities to establish or expand production in areas that the state desired to develop economically. The third group, the *yanakuna*, were individual specialists who had been permanently separated from all traditional kin ties, and served as retainers to specific state institutions or to particular individual patrons (Costin in press; see Rowe 1982 for a somewhat different interpretation of the differences among these classes of workers). Importantly, the title *kamayoq* was not applied to the *aqllakuna*.

Second, male and female weavers may have been differentiated by the use of different types of looms. Both verbal descriptions and visual images from the colonial era associate female weavers with the traditional backstrap loom (see Figure 4.2, bottom) and male weavers with a vertical frame loom (Figure 4.3, right). John Rowe (1979) believes this is because they wove different kinds of cloth, while I have suggested this technological difference was more a means of visually marking the difference between masculine and feminine weavers (Costin 1994a).

Third, male and female weavers were treated far differently by the state in terms of the context of their activities and state control over aspects of their lives other than their productive activities. *Aqllakuna* were sequestered in special state facilities where they were carefully supervised at all times. Once recruited into state service, the *aqllakuna* lost all contact with their kin. The state in essence stood *in loco parentis* to these females, having direct control over both their production and reproduction. They were wholly dependent on the state—including for their very lives—and lacked any form of personal or social freedom. In contrast, while male weavers may have worked in special state facilities, most apparently preserved long term their traditional family structure, lived among their kin, and often maintained their traditional lands or were granted lands by the state, which allowed them to meet their own subsistence needs. Male weavers, in contrast with female weavers, apparently had their social lives and social identities far less disrupted as they served the state.

Why did the state distinguish between male and female weavers in so many ways? At the time of the Spanish conquest, Inka state institutions were intensifying cloth production. But there were no technological innovations among the Inka that allowed for greater efficiencies in production that could increase output per unit time (Costin 1992, 1994c). In this nonindustrial milieu, output could only be increased by increasing the amount of time spent spinning and weaving. Under the "traditional" system of production in a household context—using women as the primary cloth producers—the amount of time that could be reallocated to cloth production was limited by the other demands on women's time, especially child rearing and other household maintenance activities. Although the state increased cloth production somewhat by increasing the work burden on existing domestic producers, the primary options to increase output were to relieve some women of their other responsibilities or to recruit men into cloth production. In fact, both solutions were state strategies. Specially recruited female weavers were basically excused from other "feminine" responsibilities—notably cooking and child rearing—to concentrate full-time on production of cloth and beer for the political economy. This strategy of creating a class of women whose reproduction was fully controlled (actually, denied) by the state was not highly disruptive *ideologically*: rather, it reinforced a developing hierarchical gender ideology that stressed women in service to men (Silverblatt 1987; Costin 1993b). Although the *aqllakuna* were largely denied the reproductive aspects of their sex/gender identity, they continued to produce in appropriately feminine sorts of ways.[6] Indeed, their hyperfemininity was stressed in state ideology.

The second state strategy to increase textile production—recruiting male weavers—was potentially problematic, however, because weaving was associated traditionally with femininity. The state sought to avoid resistance to new social roles and to minimize ideological disruption by distinguishing between male and female weavers through linguistic, technological, and structural means. In sum, the gendered division of labor as well as the gendered social relations of production were changing at the time of Spanish conquest, necessitating important structural changes to balance traditional gender ideologies (including gender identity and gender relations), state ideologies, and state logistical demands for increased output in textile production. This differential conceptualization and treatment of male and female weavers ostensibly supported a traditional gender ideology that emphasized complementarity between men and women, but also likely contributed to gender hierarchy and an ideology in which women/conquered peoples depended upon and served men/the state.

Given the extreme importance of cloth in Inka subsistence and political economies, it should not be surprising that the many aspects of the production of that cloth—the actors, the tools, the techniques—should all be imbued with important social and political meanings, as well as economic "worth." It is precisely because of these *social* meanings, however, that changes in any aspect of production could potentially be so highly disruptive.

Gender consists of, among other things, sets of behaviors and symbols that function to express one's appropriateness as a reproductive partner *because* one adheres to appropriate gender roles. Those individuals who don't conform to appropriate roles run the risk of being considered substandard or undesirable mates. I have tried to show that certain—if not all—aspects of cloth production were ideologically associated with femininity. Males "too deeply" involved in cloth production, then, may have run the risk of being labeled inappropriate reproductive partners.

Neither individuals nor the state can afford high levels of disruption in the reproductive domain, which can occur with a disruption of the gender system more generally. If the Inka were making changes in the division of labor to facilitate production within the political economy, disrupting gender ideology (woman the weaver) by employing male weavers for political means (the need to intensify cloth production and bring it under greater state control), the potential existed for resistance to these new, state-sponsored productive strategies. I suggest that the state manipulated the way the division of labor was conceptualized in part to disassociate state-sponsored male specialists from household (female) weaving.

Summary and Conclusions

The purposes of this essay have been severalfold: to stress the importance of gender attribution in studies of specialized production in prehistoric complex societies, to suggest how we might credibly engender our data and our interpretations of those data, and to give a brief example of how a gendered discussion of craft production more fully elucidates the social relations of production and the sociopolitical contexts in which they are situated. Because gender is such a fundamental structuring principle in human societies, I argue that we must understand how it operates in practice, not simply in theory. I have stressed that without reasonable gender attribution, we have a theory of occupation in the abstract but not an explication of the gendered division of labor or the gendered social relations of production, whether our research is cross-cultural or historically specific in nature. The organization of production—so fundamental to social relations in all tiers of social interaction—is clearly an area where we have only just begun to develop a mature, sophisticated method and theory within the engendered archaeology. I have high hopes for our research in the coming years.

Acknowledgments

I would like to thank Rita Wright and an anonymous reviewer for their detailed comments on earlier versions of this essay. Liz Brumfiel and Joan Gero have commented on the substantive portions of the examples from my own work, originally presented at the 1993 and 1994 Annual Meetings of the American Anthropological Association (Costin 1993a, 1994b). Their input has greatly strengthened the critique and the argument. All errors and omissions remain my responsibility.

Notes

1. In contrast with gender—a cultural construct—"sex" is a biological construct that describes the genetically determined, physiological differences between males and females that relate directly to their respective roles in biological reproduction. Sex is universal in the sense that no matter where you go, all females have the same genitalia and the same potential roles in biological reproduction (they gestate and lactate), while males have a distinctive set of genitalia and their own role in biological reproduction (they impregnate). Gender defines groups that aspire to the same cultural reproductive strategy; that is, to the same ideal mating or marriage practice and the same ideal degree and type of parental investment in child rearing. All individuals with the same biological sex may or may not pursue the same reproductive strategy. When these broadly defined reproductive strategies are institutionalized, they are genders. Hence, while there are only two biological sexes, they may be more culturally defined genders.

2. Rather, I suggest the primary function of gender is to regulate reproduction, by signaling one's appropriateness as a mate (Costin 1994b). I believe the *practice* of gender developed as a means of signaling one's reproductive strategy (especially relative willingness to practice long-term pair bonding and sexual exclusivity) during the evolution of "human" mating and marriage patterns. This was necessary as males and females began to practice increasingly distinctive sets of food procurement strategies and juvenile males required long-term adult male parental investment to learn "male" skills. Gender later became "codified" as a series of culturally specific sets of symbols and behaviors that structure social as well as biological reproduction. These ideas are developed more fully in Costin (n.d.).

3. This contrasts with food production, where instances of multigender task groups are much more common. My hunch is that the separation of genders in craft production is stricter than it is in food production because (1) food procurement requires the participation of *all* able-bodied individuals (to exclude capable individuals on the basis of gender might compromise success); and (2) those societies where we have more craft specialization are likely to be those where gender separation is played out more strongly across many different domains.

4. Yvonne Marshall's (1985) survey of Papua New Guinean potters suggests that where females and males work together in one workshop ("shared pottery"), specific tasks tend to be allocated to either women (primarily vessel formation) or men (decoration), thus preserving a structural gendered division of labor within the workshop. Similar differences in products made by female and male artisans have been reported for potters in the Yucatan (Thompson 1958) and the Philippines (Scheans 1977).

5. There is strong ethnographic data for male weavers in some parts of the Andes, but the extent to which these examples represent a direct historical continuation of pre-Hispanic practice is something that requires careful evaluation. For example, there are many male weavers in modern Ecuador, but this is an area that had a distinctive pre-Inka economic order (e.g., Salomon 1986) and that more recently has been the locus of economic redevelopment, including the reintroduction/"revitalization" of a hand-weaving industry (Salomon 1973; Meisch 1987). In other cases—such as southern Peru—we must be careful to distinguish between continuities with pre-Inka practice and continuities in practices introduced by the Inka.

6. Brewing beer was a second traditionally "feminine" role that was translated on a larger scale into the Inka political economy through the labor of the *aqllakuna*.

References

Arnold, Bettina
    1991   "The Deposed Princess of Vix: The Need for an Engendered European Prehistory." In *The Archaeology of Gender*, edited by D. Walde and N. Willows, 366–74. Calgary: Archaeological Association of the University of Calgary.

Arsenault, Daniel
    1991   "Representations of Women in Moche Iconography." In *The Archaeology of Gender*, edited by D. Walde and N. Willows, 313–27. Calgary: Archaeological Association of the University of Calgary.

Barber, Elizabeth
    1991   *Prehistoric Textiles: The Development of Cloth in the Neolithic and Bronze Ages with Special Reference to the Aegean.* Princeton, N.J.: Princeton University Press.
    1994   *Women's Work: The First 20,000 Years.* New York: Norton.

Benavides, Oswaldo
    1993   "Where Are the Men? Gender and Textile Production in Pre-Capitalist States: The View from the Central Andes." Paper pre-

sented at the 92d annual meeting of the American Anthropological Association, Washington, D.C.

Billigmeier, Jon-Christian, and Judy Turner

1985   "The Socio-Economic Roles of Women in Mycenaean Greece: A Brief Survey from Evidence of the Linear B Tablets." In *Reflections of Women in Antiquity*, edited by H. Foley, 1–18. New York: Gordon and Breach.

Bruhns, Karen O.

1991   "Sexual Activities: Some Thoughts on the Sexual Division of Labor and Archaeological Interpretation." In *The Archaeology of Gender*, edited by D. Walde and N. Willows, 420–29. Calgary: Archaeological Association of the University of Calgary.

Brumfiel, Elizabeth

1991   "Weaving and Cooking: Women's Production in Aztec Mexico." In *Engendering Archaeology: Women and Prehistory*, edited by Joan M. Gero and Margaret W. Conkey, 224–51. Oxford: Basil Blackwell.

Brumfiel, Elizabeth, and Timothy Earle

1987   "Specialization, Exchange, and Complex Societies: An Introduction." In *Specialization, Exchange, and Complex Societies*, edited by E. Brumfiel and T. Earle, 1–9. Cambridge: Cambridge University Press.

Clark, John, and William Parry

1990   "Craft Specialization and Cultural Complexity." *Research in Economic Anthropology* 12:289–346.

Clendinnen, Inga

1991   *Aztecs: An Interpretation*. Cambridge: Cambridge University Press.

Conkey, Margaret W., and Joan M. Gero

1991   "Tensions, Pluralities, and Engendering Archaeology: An Introduction to Women and Prehistory." In *Engendering Archaeology: Women and Prehistory*, edited by Joan M. Gero and Margaret W. Conkey, 3–30. Oxford: Basil Blackwell.

Costin, Cathy L.

1991   "Craft Specialization: Issues in Defining, Documenting, and Explaining the Organization of Production." In *Archaeological Method and Theory*, volume 3, edited by M. B. Schiffer, pp. 1–56. Tucson: University of Arizona Press.

1992   "Conquest and Technological Stability in Highland Peru." Paper presented at the 25th Annual Chacmool Conference: "The Archaeology of Contact: Processes and Consequences." Calgary, Alberta, Canada.

1993a   "Gender and the Organization of Craft Production in Complex Societies." Paper presented in the symposium "Gender and the State" at the 92d annual meeting of the American Anthropological Association, Washington, D.C.

1993b   "Textiles, Women, and Political Economy in Late Prehispanic Peru." *Research in Economic Anthropology* 14:3–28.

1994a   Comment on McCafferty and McCafferty, "Engendering Tomb 7 at Monte Albán: Respinning an Old Yarn." *Current Anthropology* 35(2):143–66.

1994b   "Gender, Technology, and Power: Cloth Production in the Inka
             Empire." Paper presented in the symposium "The Social Dy-
             namics of Technologies Past and Present: Exploring New Per-
             spectives" at the 93d annual meeting of the American Anthro-
             pological Association, Atlanta, Ga.
1994c   "Weaving Technology in the Domestic and Political Economies."
             Paper presented in the symposium "The Social and Political
             Contexts of Craft Technology," at the 59th annual meeting of
             the Society for American Archaeology, Anaheim, Calif.
1995   "Cloth Production and Gender Relations in the Inka Empire."
             In *Research Frontiers in Anthropology—Advances in Archaeology and
             Physical Anthropology*, edited by P. Peregrine, C. Ember, and
             M. Ember, pagination varies. Upper Saddle River, N.J.: Pren-
             tice Hall.
In press   "Craft Production and Mobilization Strategies in the Inka Em-
             pire." In *Craft Specialization and Social Evolution: In Memory of
             V. Gordon Childe*, edited by B. Wailes. Philadelphia: University of
             Pennsylvania Museum Publications.
N.d.   "Gender and the Division of Labor." Ms. in preparation.
Damm, Charlotte
1991   "From Burials to Gender Roles: Problems and Potentials in Post-
             Processual Archaeology." In *The Archaeology of Gender*, edited by
             D. Walde and N. Willows, 130–36. Calgary: Archaeological As-
             sociation of the University of Calgary.
Deetz, James
1968   "The Inference of Residence and Descent Rules from Archaeo-
             logical Data." In *New Perspectives in Archaeology*, edited by S. Bin-
             ford and L. Binford, 33–40. Chicago: Aldine.
DeMarrais, Elizabeth, Luis Jaime Castillo, and Timothy Earle
1996   "Ideology, Materialization, and Power Strategies." *Current An-
             thropology* (February): 15–32.
Dobres, Marcia-Anne
1993   "Beyond Gender Attribution: Some Methodological Issues for
             Engendering the Past." In *Proceedings of the Women in Archaeology
             Conference*, edited by J. Balme et al. Armidale, Australia: Depart-
             ment of Archaeology and Paleoanthropology, University of New
             England.
Earle, Timothy
1982   "The Ecology and Politics of Primitive Valuables." In *Culture and
             Ecology: Eclectic Perspectives*, edited by J. Kennedy and R. Edger-
             ton, 65–83. Washington, D.C.: American Anthropological Asso-
             ciation Special Publication 15.
Ehrenberg, Margaret
1989   *Women in Prehistory*. Norman: University of Oklahoma.
Feinman, Gary
1980   *The Relationship between Administrative Organization and Ceramic
             Production in the Valley of Oaxaca*. Ph.D. dissertation, Department
             of Anthropology, CUNY Graduate Center.
1985   "Changes in the Organization of Ceramic Production in Pre-
             Hispanic Oaxaca, Mexico." In *Decoding Prehistoric Ceramics*, edited

by B. Nelson, 195–224. Carbondale: Southern Illinois University Press.

Friedman, Jonathan, and Michael Rowlands
1977   "Notes towards an Epigenetic Model of the Evolution of 'Civilization.' " In *The Evolution of Social Systems*, edited by J. Friedman and M. Rowlands, 201–78. London: Duckworth.

Gailey, Christine Ward
1987   *Kinship to Kingship: Gender Hierarchy and State Formation in the Tongan Islands.* Austin: University of Texas Press.

Gayton, Anna
1973   "The Cultural Significance of Peruvian Textiles: Production, Function, Aesthetics." In *Peruvian Archaeology*, edited by J. Rowe and D. Menzel, 275–92. Palo Alto, Calif.: Peek Publications.

Gero, Joan
1991   "Genderlithics: Women's Roles in Stone Tool Production." In *Engendering Archaeology: Women and Prehistory*, edited by Joan M. Gero and Margaret W. Conkey, pp. 163–93. Oxford: Basil Blackwell.
1992   "Feasts and Females: Gender Ideology and Political Meals in the Andes." *Norwegian Archaeological Review* 25(1):15–30.
1994   Comment on McCafferty and McCafferty, "Engendering Tomb 7 at Monte Albán: Respinning an Old Yarn." *Current Anthropology* 35(2):143–66.
1995   "Household Production as Glue: Insights from the Early Formative of Northwestern Argentina." Paper presented at the 60th annual meeting of the Society for American Archaeology, Minneapolis, Minn.

Graham, Elizabeth
1991   "Women and Gender in Maya Prehistory." In *The Archaeology of Gender*, edited by D. Walde and N. Willows, 470–78. Calgary: Archaeological Association of the University of Calgary.

Guaman Poma de Ayala, Felipe
1980[1615]   *El Primer Nueva Corónica y Buen Gobierno.* Edición Crítica de John Murra y Rolena Adorno; Traducciones y Análisis textual del Quechua por Jorge Urioste. Madrid and Mexico: Siglo Veintiuno Editores, SA.

Gunter, Ann
1991   "Artists and Ancient Near Eastern Art." In *Investigating Artistic Environments in the Ancient Near East*, edited by A. Gunter, 9–20. Madison: University of Wisconsin Press.

Handsman, Russell
1991   "Whose Art Was Found at Lenenski Vir? Gender Relations and Power in Archaeology." In *Engendering Archaeology: Women and Prehistory*, edited by Joan M. Gero and Margaret W. Conkey, 329–365. Oxford: Basil Blackwell.

Hastorf, Christine A.
1991   "Gender, Space, and Food in Prehistory." In *Engendering Archaeology: Women and Prehistory*, edited by Joan M. Gero and Margaret W. Conkey, 132–59. Oxford: Basil Blackwell.

Helms, Mary
1993   *Craft and the Kingly Ideal.* Austin: University of Texas Press.

Hill, James
1968   "Broken K Pueblo: Patterns of Form and Function." In *New Perspectives in Archaeology*, edited by S. Binford and L. Binford, 103–42. Chicago: Aldine.
Hollimon, Sandra
1992   "Health Consequences of Sexual Division of Labor among Prehistoric Native Americans: The Chumash of California and the Arikara of the North Plains." In *Exploring Gender through Archaeology: Selected Papers from the 1991 Boone Conference*, edited by C. Claassen, 81–88. Monographs in World Archaeology No. 11. Madison, Wis.: Prehistory Press.
Joyce, Rosemary
1992   "Images of Gender and Labor Organization in Classic Maya Society." In *Exploring Gender through Archaeology: Selected Papers from the 1991 Boone Conference*, edited by C. Claassen, 63–70. Madison, Wis.: Prehistory Press.
Klein, Cecilia
1994   Comment on McCafferty and McCafferty, "Engendering Tomb 7 at Monte Albán: Respinning an Old Yarn." *Current Anthropology* 35(2):143–66.
Longacre, William A.
1968   "Some Aspects of Prehistoric Society in East-Central Arizona." In *New Perspectives in Archaeology*, edited by S. Binford and L. Binford, 89–102. Chicago: Aldine.
Marshall, Yvonne
1985   "Who Made the Lapita Pots? A Case Study in Gender Archaeology." *Journal of the Polynesian Society* 94:205–33.
McCafferty, Sharisse, and Geoffrey McCafferty
1991   "Spinning and Weaving as Female Gender Identity in Post-Classic Central Mexico." In *Textile Traditions of Mesoamerica and the Andes: An Anthology*, edited by M. Schevill, J. C. Berlo, and E. Dwyer. New York: Garland.
1994   "Engendering Tomb 7 at Monte Albán: Respinning an Old Yarn." *Current Anthropology* 35(2):143–66.
McGaw, Judith
1989   "No Passive Victims, No Separate Spheres: A Feminist Perspective on Technology's History." In *In Context: History and the History of Technology*, edited by S. H. Cutcliffe and R. C. Post, 172–91. Bethlehem, Pa.: Lehigh University Press.
Meisch, Lynne
1987   *Otavalo: Weaving, Costume, and the Market*. Quito: Ediciones Libri Mundi.
Miller, Virginia, ed.
1988   *The Role of Gender in Pre-Columbian Art and Architecture*. Lanham, Md.: University Press of America.
Molleson, Theya
1994   "The Eloquent Bones of Abu Hureyra." *Scientific American* 271(2): 70–75.
Moseley, Michael
1992   *The Incas and Their Ancestors*. London: Thames and Hudson.

Murdock, George, and Caterina Provost
    1973   "Factors in the Division of Labor by Sex: A Cross-Cultural Analysis." *Ethnology* 12:203–25.

Murra, John V.
    1962   "Cloth and Its Functions in the Inca State." *American Anthropologist* 64:710–28.
    1989   "Cloth's Function in the Inca State." In *Cloth and Human Experience*, edited by A. Weiner and J. Schneider, 275–302. Washington, D.C.: Smithsonian Institution Press.

Nelson, Sarah M.
    1990   "Diversity of the Upper Paleolithic 'Venus' Figurines and Archaeological Mythology." In *Powers of Observation: Alternative Views in Archeology*, edited by Sarah M. Nelson and Alice B. Kehoe, 11–22. Washington, D.C.: Archaeology Papers of the American Anthropological Association, no. 2.

Proskouriakoff, Tatiana
    1961   "Portraits of Women in Maya Art." In *Essays in Pre-Columbian Art and Archaeology*, edited by S. K. Lothrop et al., 81–99. Cambridge, Mass.: Harvard University Press.

Reents-Budet, Dorie
    1994   *Painting the Maya Universe: Royal Ceramics of the Classic Period.* Durham, N.C.: Duke University Press.

Rice, Prudence
    1981   "Evolution of Specialized Pottery Production: A Trial Model." *Current Anthropology* 22:219–40.
    1991a   "Specialization, Standardization, and Diversity: A Retrospective." In *The Ceramic Legacy of Anna O. Shepard*, edited by R. Bishop and F. Lange, 257–79. Niwot: University Press of Colorado.
    1991b   "Women and Prehistoric Pottery Production." In *The Archaeology of Gender*, edited by D. Walde and N. Willows, 436–43. Calgary: Archaeological Association of the University of Calgary.

Rowe, John V.
    1979   "Standardization in Inca Tapestry Tunics." In *The Junius Bird Pre-Columbian Textile Conference*, edited by A. Rowe, 239–64. Washington, D.C.: Dumbarton Oaks.
    1982   "Inca Policies and Institutions Relating to the Cultural Unification of the Empire." In *The Inca and Aztec States 1400–1800: Anthropology and History*, edited by G. A. Collier, R. I. Rosaldo, J. D. Wirth, 93–118. New York: Academic Press.

Rueschemeyer, Dietrich
    1986   *Power and the Division of Labor.* Oxford: Polity Press.

Russell, Pamela
    1991   "Men Only? The Myths about European Paleolithic Artists." In *The Archaeology of Gender*, edited by D. Walde and N. Willows, 346–51. Calgary: Archaeological Association of the University of Calgary.

Salomon, Frank
    1973   "Weavers of Otavalo." In *Peoples and Cultures of Native South America: An Anthropological Reader*, edited by David Grove, 463–92. New York: Doubleday/Natural History Press.

1986   *Native Lords of Quito in the Age of the Incas: The Political Economy of North Andean Chiefdoms.* Cambridge: Cambridge University Press.

Scheans, D. J.
1977   *Filipino Market Potteries.* Monograph 3. Manila: National Museum.

Silverblatt, Irene
1987   *Moon, Sun, and Witches: Gender Ideologies and Class in Inca and Colonial Peru.* Princeton, N.J.: Princeton University Press.

Sinopoli, Carla
1988   "The Organization of Craft Production at Vijayanagara, South India." *American Anthropologist* 90(3):580–97.

Stone-Miller, Rebecca
1992   *To Weave for the Sun: Andean Textiles in the Museum of Fine Arts, Boston,* edited by Rebecca Stone-Miller. Boston: Museum of Fine Arts.

Thompson, R.
1958   *Modern Yucatecan Maya Pottery Making.* Memoirs of the Society for American Archaeology, no. 15.

Treiman, Donald
1977   *Occupational Prestige in Comparative Perspective.* New York: Academic Press.

Williams, Dyfri
1985   "Women on Athenian Vases: Problems of Interpretation." In *Images of Women in Antiquity,* edited by A. Cameron and A. Khurt, 92–105. London: Croom Helm.

Wright, Rita
1991   "Women's Labor and Pottery Production in Prehistory." In *Engendering Archaeology: Women and Prehistory,* edited by Joan M. Gero and Margaret W. Conkey, 194–223. Oxford: Basil Blackwell.

Wylie, Alison
1991   "Gender Theory and the Archaeological Record: Why Is There No Archaeology of Gender?" In *Engendering Archaeology: Women and Prehistory,* edited by Joan M. Gero and Margaret W. Conkey, 31–54. Oxford: Basil Blackwell.

Zagarell, Allen
1986   "Trade, Women, Class, and Society in Ancient Western Asia." *Current Anthropology* 27:415–30.

Part III
Gender and
Representation

Chapter 5
Figurines and the Aztec State: Testing the Effectiveness of Ideological Domination

Elizabeth M. Brumfiel

According to Margaret Conkey and Joan Gero (1991), studying gender in prehistoric societies involves much more than determining which activities were carried out by women and which by men. A gendered prehistory presents gender roles, gender relations, and gender ideology, and it explores the ways in which gender intersects with and is influenced by other aspects of social life. Such a vision of a gendered past is both inspiring and daunting. It is inspiring because striving to realize it will teach us so much about women's and men's lives and the dynamics of social change. It is daunting because it seems to require a knowledge of mental categories and patterns of social interaction that are not easily gleaned from the archaeological record.

This problem can be attacked from two sides. On the one hand, we can refine techniques of symbolic interpretation and contextual study so that we can reconstruct the subjective meanings of gender categories. On the other hand, we can sidestep the issue of content momentarily and explore the structure of gender ideologies and their intersection with other aspects of social life without specifying the meanings attached to gender in a particular culture. I follow the latter strategy.

This chapter explores the changes in gender that occurred in Late Postclassic central Mexico under the influence of the Aztec state. A rich historical record exists for Aztec culture, but the current analysis relies primarily upon the analysis of archaeological materials. It is hoped that the strategies of inquiry employed in this chapter will be applicable to other cultures, particularly cultures in "deep" prehistory, which may lack a historical record but which, like the Aztecs, produced visual images of gendered subjects that are available for analysis.

Do definitions of gender change in communities that are incorporated into highly stratified regional states? If so, what is the direction of change? Do community definitions of gender come to resemble those disseminated by the state or do local communities retain a distinctive view? Answers to these questions are obtained by studying variation in the representation of women in Aztec material culture. Two types of variation are analyzed.

First, I examine temporal change in the abundance and style of representation in a single genre, ceramic figurines. As Sharisse McCafferty and Geoffrey McCafferty (1991) suggest, studying symbols diachronically enables us to monitor the construction of gender ideologies and transformations in negotiation of gender. Second, I compare the representation of women in several media at a single point in time. As Susan Pollock (1991) observes, women in different representational media may be portrayed in inconsistent and contradictory ways, and these very inconsistencies can inform us of the synchronic variation in gender ideology within a single society, and how this variation was negotiated.

This study of change in Aztec gender systems suggests some general conclusions about the effectiveness of ideological domination in states. The flow of discussion from "gender" to "nongender" issues demonstrates how gender is entwined with other aspects of social life. It suggests the broad relevance of gender as a focus of archaeological investigation.

The Problem

In recent years, some sharp disagreement has developed concerning the status of women in Aztec society. The debate centers upon whether Aztec gender relations were hierarchical or complementary and whether Aztec women accepted an ideology of male dominance or vigorously contested it. In her classic article "The Aztecs and the Ideology of Male Dominance," June Nash (1978) argues that Aztec imperial expansion resulted in the subordination of Aztec women. Warfare and conquest were men's work, and while men gained wealth, power, and prestige from imperial conquests, the status of women declined. Older deities expressing the balanced opposition of masculine and feminine were replaced by male warrior deities. Blood sacrifice and ritualized battles became common forms of religious devotion that excluded women from participation. As the empire expanded, the cult of warfare and male dominance was elaborated.

However, Nash believes that the influence of the male dominant ideology was circumscribed. It was resisted by Aztec women.[1] And it was not accepted by commoners or by hinterland peoples among whom older patterns of balanced opposition between male and female continued. Militarism and ideologies of male dominance were strongest among the ruling elite in the Aztec capital.

Nash's depiction of heightened gender inequality among the Aztecs is confirmed and extended by María Rodríguez (1988) in her book *La Mujer Azteca*. Rodríguez differs from Nash in arguing that the oppression of women was by no means a fortuitous outcome of militarism; rather, the oppression of women was pursued by men of the Aztec ruling class because it was very much in their interests. Control of women's labor increased their wealth, and control of women's sexuality increased their ability to make advantageous alliances and to reward male participation in the economy of conquest and tribute extraction.

Aztec religion constituted a primary avenue of male domination. In Aztec hands, female deities became secondary figures: the spouses, concubines, and subordinates of powerful male gods. They also assumed warlike elements of costume and character, indicating that no separate sphere of supernatural power was reserved to women, outside the male sphere of warfare and conquest.

Rodríguez paints a bleak picture of extreme male dominance. She suggests that Aztec women were systematically exploited, demeaned, and controlled by both brutal coercion and psychological terror. Unlike Nash, Rodríguez argues that Aztec women accepted their subordination and even participated in its perpetuation: mothers encouraged their daughters to suppress all their autonomous impulses. In another departure from Nash, Rodríguez maintains that the statuses of noble and commoner women were not very different; both were subject to powerful mechanisms of ideological control and both were thoroughly dominated. Furthermore, this domination characterized not only the Aztec capital but most of central Mexico; Rodríguez's (1989) analysis of the status of women in Tlaxcala suggests conditions that were not significantly different from those in Tenochtitlan.

Rodríguez's views are clearly different from those of McCafferty and McCafferty (1988, 1989, 1991), who argue that, even at the height of the empire, Aztec gender roles were characterized by "structural complementarity" and "parallelism" rather than dominance and submission. They also argue that women controlled important spheres of activity in Aztec culture including household production and sexual reproduction. Control of these spheres was associated with an ideology of female power that women exercised vigorously to resist male dominance. Spinning and weaving, archetypical female activities, linked Aztec women to Tlazolteotl, Xochiquetzal, Mayahuel, and Toci, four aspects of the Aztec mother goddess who controlled human reproduction.

These differing views raise two interesting general questions. The first

concerns the general relationship between state formation and the oppression of women. Rayna Rapp (1978), Christine Gailey (1985), and
Irene Silverblatt (1987) have argued that the rulers of states will always
make an effort to subordinate women because the control of women is
both a metaphor and a mechanism for the state's control over kinship-
based households. The figurine data provide one gauge of the subordination of women in the process of state expansion.

The second question concerns the effectiveness of ideology as a
mechanism of state dominance. Rodríguez (1988:102) argues that ideological state apparatuses (see Althusser 1971) played an important role
in the subordination of Aztec women and that ideological domination
serves as an effective means of implementing state goals. McCafferty
and McCafferty (1988:46), citing Silverblatt, argue that there is always
reciprocal interplay between ideologies of domination and resistance,
implying that ideological domination is a less important mechanism of
control.

An examination of the frequencies of different types of ceramic figurines at three Aztec-period sites in the Basin of Mexico enables us to
address these arguments.

Aztec Figurines

Figurines occur in low frequencies at almost every Aztec-period site
in the Basin of Mexico. They are small, molded ceramic figures, between ten and twenty centimeters in height, and apparently made of the
same orange paste that was used in Aztec orange ware pottery (Cook
1950:94). Mary Parsons (1972) defined three varieties of Postclassic figurines in collections from the Teotihuacan Valley. Solid, standing, flat-
backed figurines were the most common (accounting for 84 percent of
the Teotihuacan collection). Hollow figurines were next most common
(constituting 14 percent of the collection). Jointed figurines, which have
holes at the four corners of the trunk of the body for the attachment of
limbs (which also have holes drilled through their ends), are quite rare
(accounting for only 2 percent of the collection).

These figurines were apparently made by craft specialists. Possible
figurine workshops have been reported from Tlatelolco (Cook 1950) and
Otumba (Otis Charlton 1994). The figurines were used in household
contexts, for they are usually found in association with household debris
and, occasionally, in association with burials (Pasztory 1983:282, Evans
1990). They very rarely occur as offerings; Esther Pasztory (1983:282) reports that there were no ceramic figurines among the more than seven
thousand objects excavated from the Aztec Templo Mayor in Mexico

City.[2] Clearly, then, figurines were utilized in activities carried out at the household level.

Most figurines are anthropomorphic (77 percent of the figurines in Parsons's Teotihuacan collection), and many of these clearly bear the insignia of Aztec deities (Seler 1902–23 1:305–13; Preuss 1901:87–91; Barlow and Lehmann 1956:157–76; Kaplan 1958; Parsons 1972; Millian 1981). This implies a ritual function for the figurines, but it has been difficult to define their use in any detail.

Various sixteenth-century chroniclers comment upon the Aztecs' use of effigies or idols. Toribio Motolinía (1969:26), for example, states that the Aztecs had idols of stone, wood, fired clay, and dough. Diego Durán (1971:235, 452) and Bernardino de Sahagún (1950–69: Bk. 2, chap. 9, p. 16; chap. 12, p. 21; chap. 19, p. 36) mention that idols were kept on household altars; such images became the focus of ritual offerings during certain calendrical ceremonies and when household members were away at war. Durán (1971:419) states that "small effigies, cloth images" were hung from ropes strung from tree to tree in the cornfields, perhaps to promote agricultural fertility.[3] Motolinía (1969:201) and Durán (1971:419) record that children were given idols as protection against evil and illness; they were given idols at birth and at the ages of one and four years. However, the chroniclers never specify whether the idols used in these various contexts were ceramic figurines.

The archaeological evidence pertaining to figurine function is also sparse. Susan Evans (1990) observes that most Aztec figurines have been found in archaeological contexts such as the plow zone and midden that reflect patterns of discard rather than patterns of use. However, at Cihuatecpan, Evans found that most (90 percent) of the figurines with good behavioral contexts occurred in habitation rooms or in courtyards containing steam baths; the latter suggests an association between figurines and female reproduction and curing rituals, which frequently employed steam baths as a ritual procedure.

Suggestions that the figurines were concerned with health and curing have also been based upon the appearance of the figurines themselves. One common figurine type (Figure 5.1) depicts a bare-breasted woman with a looped headdress ending in two projections. Often, she holds one or two children in her arms. It has been suggested that this figurine represents either the Aztec goddess Xochiquetzal or Coatlicue, and that it expresses a concern with healthy sex, fertility, and birth (Cook 1950; Parsons 1972; Millian 1981; Evans 1990; cf. Pasztory 1983:284). Alva Millian (1981) suggests that the male deities represented among the figurines were the patrons of various diseases.[4] Another link between figurines and health and curing is suggested by several figurines

Figure 5.1. Aztec-period ceramic figurine of a woman holding two children. Height 19 centimeters. Musée de l'Homme, Paris. (Courtesy of Elizabeth Brumfiel)

that depict individuals with physical abnormalities: hunchbacks, dwarfs, people with protruding chests such as might be associated with rickets, and possibly individuals afflicted with dementia (Cook 1950; Morss 1952; Parsons 1972; Millian 1981; Evans 1990).

However, not all figurines are anthropomorphic, and not all can be related to health and curing. There are zoomorphic figurines of various types (monkeys, rabbits, birds, coyotes, toads, and mountain lions, Parsons 1972:112–13). And there are replicas of temple pyramids that may reflect the integration of peasant households into the state religion (Parsons 1972:105–8; Kaplan 1958, cited in Pasztory 1983:291). In addition, figurine heads from the Formative and Classic eras sometimes occur in what are otherwise undisturbed Postclassic strata. This implies that Postclassic peoples collected and curated figurines from earlier periods, perhaps incorporating them into their own household rituals. While these figurines are anthropomorphic, they most commonly occur as figurine heads lacking bodies, and although some wear fairly elaborate headgear, most lack attributes that would specifically define them as male or female. Therefore, for Postclassic peoples, these Formative and Classic figurines may have been ungendered, representing the general domain of ancestral authority.

In summary, then, Aztec figurines appear to represent ritual activity at the household level. Whether this ritual was carried out by folk practitioners, heads of households, or any household member, the figurines should reflect popular estimations of the importance of various supernatural powers and popular concern over the spheres of life where well-being was threatened. Thus, the frequencies of different types of figurines in hinterland communities before and during the period of Aztec dominance should provide a valid gauge of the extent to which popular consciousness was affected by state ideology (also see Kann 1989).

If there are no differences in the composition of the figurine assemblage or in the presentation of the female figure, then popular gender ideologies would appear unaffected by Aztec dominance. Such evidence would indicate that while male-dominant ideologies may be elaborated by political elites, they are not necessarily accepted by the rural, nonelite segments of state systems. On the other hand, the existence of differences in the composition of the figurine assemblage or in the presentation of the male or female figure would indicate that existing gender ideologies among commoners were challenged by the male dominant ideology of the Aztec elites. Whether the response to the elite ideology was one of acceptance or resistance is indicated by the degree of similarity between popular images of men and women as seen in the figurines from hinterland communities and elite images of men and women as presented in the official arts of the Aztec state, such as manuscript painting and monumental sculpture.

Figurine Frequencies at Huexotla, Xico, and Xaltocan

Representative samples of figurines are available from three Postclassic sites in the Basin of Mexico (see Figure 5.2). Huexotla and Xico have

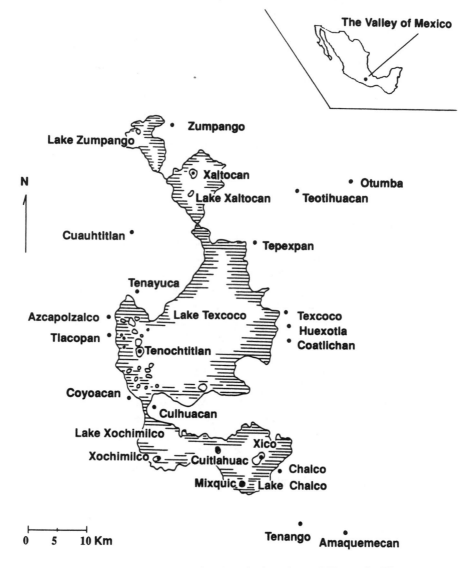

Figure 5.2. The Basin of Mexico, showing the locations of Huexotla, Xico, Xaltocan, and the Aztec capital, Tenochtitlan. (Courtesy of Elizabeth Brumfiel)

been sampled using intensive systematic surface collection (Brumfiel 1976, 1980, 1985, 1991a, 1991b). Sample sizes range from 1 percent in the urban core at Huexotla to 11 percent in Huexotla's piedmont sector and at Xico. At Xaltocan, figurine samples are available from seventeen excavation units, each a two-by-two-meter square. All three sites were occupied during the Middle Postclassic (A.D. 1150–1350) period, prior to Aztec rule; they were also occupied during the Late Postclassic (A.D. 1350–1521), the period of Aztec dominance. Figurines in collections with predominantly Middle Postclassic ceramics can be compared with figurines in collections with predominantly Late Postclassic ceramics. Observed differences in figurine frequencies or images provide a good indication of stability or change in gender ideologies. (Frequency is the number of figurines per 1000 rim sherds in the collections. This ratio controls for differences in the extent and density of occupation debris dating to the Middle and Late Postclassic periods.)

Figurine data from the three sites are quite different, so it is best to discuss each site individually.

Huexotla was an important city-state in the eastern Basin of Mexico. Prior to Aztec dominance, Huexotla was an autonomous petty kingdom whose rulers were allied by marriage to the rulers of other major centers in the Basin of Mexico (Alva Ixtlilxóchitl 1975–77, 2:22–25; Guzmán 1938:92). With expansion of the Aztec empire, however, Huexotla became firmly affixed as one of the fourteen client states of nearby Texcoco. Huexotla's rulers served as counselors and judges in the Texcocan ruler's court, and Huexotla's commoners paid a tribute in goods and labor to their Texcocan overlord (Gibson 1956; Offner 1983:97–114). The proximity of Huexotla to the imperial capital of Texcoco, less than five kilometers away, suggests an early and very intense level of interaction with an emerging imperial capital and its elite ideology.

Archaeologically, Huexotla consists of a three hundred hectare area of dense occupational debris in what was once Huexotla's urban core. This core contained both elite and commoner residences as well as several large, still preserved temple mounds. The urban core was occupied during both the Middle and Late Postclassic. Small scatters of prehistoric artifacts extend up the piedmont slopes east of Huexotla for a distance of ten kilometers; these small clusters probably mark the residences of rural agriculturalists, subjects of the urban-based nobility. The piedmont zone was occupied only during the Late Postclassic, the period of Aztec dominance.

Table 5.1 shows the distribution of figurines at Huexotla. It compares figurine frequencies for Middle Postclassic (pre-Aztec) collections from the urban core with figurine frequencies of Late Postclassic (Aztec) collections from both the urban core and the rural piedmont. These

TABLE 5.1. Ceramic figurines at Huexotla, Mexico.

	Middle Postclassic urban sector	Late Postclassic urban sector	Late Postclassic piedmont
Female figurines	11 (46%)	44 (58%)	37 (63%)
Male figurines	8 (33%)	15 (20%)	8 (14%)
Human figurines (sex indeterminate)	—	2 (3%)	5 (7%)
Zoomorphic figurines	4 (17%)	9 (12%)	5 (7%)
Archaic figurines	1 (4%)	5 (7%)	1 (2%)
Temple replicas	—	1 (1%)	3 (5%)
Total	24	76	59
Rim sherds collected	3,225	11,874	7,659
Total per 1,000 rim sherds	7.4	6.4	7.7

distributions have several interesting features. First of all, the overall frequency of figurines is about the same for Middle and Late Postclassic occupations. Figurines are somewhat more common in the rural piedmont than in the urban core, and this is consistent with the idea that figurines are a part of nonelite ritual activity.

Anthropomorphic figurines are very common at Huexotla. Counting only those figurines that could be identified using Parsons's (1972) typology, anthropomorphic figurines account for 82 percent of all figurines from the site. Zoomorphic figurines are the next most common figurine category, accounting for 11 percent of the figurines. Archaic (that is, anthropomorphic, but clearly of a Formative, Classic, or Early Postclassic date) figurines account for 4 percent of the figurines, and temple replicas account for 3 percent.

Some interesting temporal differences are apparent. The proportion of female figurines increases from Middle to Late Postclassic times. Female figurines are particularly abundant in the piedmont collections where they outnumber male figurines by better than three to one.[5] At the same time, temple replicas are found only in Late Postclassic collections, and although the numbers are quite low, temple replicas are most common in the piedmont collections. Both these trends indicate a degree of penetration by the urban-based elite religion during the period of Aztec dominance. The temple replicas suggest growing popular concern with official religion, and the increasing ratio of female to male figurines suggests a changing gender role ideology under conditions of Aztec rule.

Xico is a nucleated Middle and Late Postclassic site of twenty-five hectares, located in the Chalco lakebed in the southern Basin of Mexico.

TABLE 5.2. Ceramic figurines at Xico, Mexico.

	Middle Postclassic	Late Postclassic
Female figurines	5 (20%)	—
Male figurines	5 (20%)	3 (25%)
Human figurines (sex indeterminate)	1 (4%)	—
Zoomorphic figurines	—	4 (33%)
Archaic figurines	14 (56%)	3 (25%)
Temple replicas	—	1 (8%)
Other	—	1 (8%)
Total	25	12
Rim sherds collected	5,062	3,248
Total per 1,000 rim sherds	4.9	3.7

It was a regional capital during the first half of the Early Postclassic, but its importance diminished by Middle Postclassic times. It was subject to Cuitlahuac during the Middle and Late Postclassic (*Anales de Cuauhtitlan* 1945:17, 31), and Cuitlahuac became a client state of Tenochtitlan during the Late Postclassic. Thus, Xico was at least two steps removed from imperial rule during the Late Postclassic, suggesting a low level of interaction with imperial capitals. Nevertheless, Xico did serve as a tribute collection center for the Aztec Triple Alliance (*Codex Mendoza* 1992: folio 20v), and the three substantial temple mounds on the site indicate elite-sponsored religion in the community.

Xico's figurine collection is quite different from Huexotla's (see Table 5.2). Figurines are less abundant than at Huexotla, and only 38 percent of the figurines are anthropomorphic, while 46 percent of the figurines are in archaic styles (anthropomorphic figurines from the Formative, Classic, and Early Postclassic periods). Animal figurines account for 11 percent of the figurines, and the single temple replica constitutes 3 percent of the sample. There is no temporal trend for a change in the frequencies of female or male figurines. There is perhaps a lower frequency of archaic figurines during the Late Postclassic, and a higher frequency of zoomorphic figurines, but the counts are low, and these differences may be fortuitous. While Huexotla's figurines suggest changes in commoner ideology under Aztec rule, Xico's figurines provide little evidence of change. The low proportion of anthropomorphic figurines indicate that, at Xico, gender was not contested.

Xaltocan, in the northern Basin of Mexico, was first occupied during the Early Postclassic, around A.D. 950. By the Middle Postclassic, it had attained a position of great regional importance as the capital of all Otomí-speaking peoples in the southern Hidalgo–northern Basin of

154   Elizabeth M. Brumfiel

TABLE 5.3. Surface collections of ceramic figurines at Xaltocan, Mexico.

	Early and Middle Postclassic	Late Postclassic
Female figurines	4 (40%)	1 (17%)
Male figurines	1 (10%)	—
Human figurines (sex indeterminate)	—	—
Zoomorphic figurines	—	1 (17%)
Archaic figurines	4 (40%)	4 (67%)
Temple replicas	—	—
Other	1 (10%)	—
Total	10	6
Rim sherds collected	6,562	6,587
Total per 1,000 rim sherds	1.5	0.9

Mexico region (Alva Ixtlilxóchitl 1975–77, 1:321; Nazareo de Xaltocan 1940:125–26; Carrasco 1950:260–61). Xaltocan's rulers were allied by marriage to the rulers of other major centers in the Valley of Mexico (Alva Ixtlilxóchitl 1975–77, 2:17, 18, 51; *Anales de Tlatelolco* 1947:28; Nazareo 1940:124). In 1395, Xaltocan was incorporated into the Tepanec empire, and after 1430 it was subject to the Aztec Triple Alliance.

After its defeat by the Tepanec, Xaltocan lay abandoned for thirty-five or forty years (*Anales de Cuauhtitlan* 1945:50). On the basis of archival research, Hicks (1994) suggests that the repopulation of Xaltocan occurred under the direct control of Aztec nobles based in Tenochtitlan and Tlatelolco. The Aztecs installed a military ruler to govern Xaltocan (Nazareo 1940:125), and Xaltocan paid tribute to both the ruler of Texcoco and the ruler of Tenochtitlan (Alva Ixtlilxóchitl 1975–77, 1:380; Nazareo 1940:120). Xaltocan represents a community whose level of interaction with imperial capitals was high, once it was brought under imperial control.

Archaeologically, Postclassic Xaltocan consists of sixty-eight hectares of archaeological debris within and surrounding the modern town of Xaltocan. Only sixteen figurines were recovered from the surface collections at Xaltocan, a much lower frequency than at Huexotla or Xico (Table 5.3). The types of figurines in the collections are rather similar to Xico: 38 percent are anthropomorphic, 50 percent are archaic, and 6 percent are zoomorphic. Again, there is no trend toward a higher frequency of female figurines in Late Postclassic collections. Few temporal differences of any kind can be discerned.

The very low frequency of figurines in surface collections from Xaltocan is probably a consequence of amateur collecting by modern

TABLE 5.4. Excavated ceramic figurines at Xaltocan, Mexico.

	Early Postclassic	Middle Postclassic	Late Postclassic
Female figurines	5 (21%)	11 (39%)	12 (63%)
Male figurines	4 (17%)	14 (50%)	5 (26%)
Human figurines (sex indeterminate)	—	—	—
Zoomorphic figurines	4 (17%)	3 (11%)	1 (5%)
Archaic figurines	11 (46%)	—	1 (5%)
Temple replicas	—	—	—
Total	24	28	19
Rim sherds collected	2,816	3,348	2,091
Total per 1,000 rim sherds	8.5	8.4	9.1

residents of town. This is suggested by recent excavations at the site, which produced figurine frequencies ten times greater than those obtained in the surface collections (Table 5.4). With higher counts and less mixing, two important temporal shifts become apparent. First, the frequency of archaic figurines falls off steeply in the transition from Early to Middle Postclassic (around A.D. 1150). This decrease might indicate a decline in the importance of ancestral history in determining household rights and obligations as the strength of the rulers of autonomous city-states reached its height during Middle Postclassic times. Second, as at Huexotla, the proportion of female figurines increased from Middle to Late Postclassic times. Again, this increasing ratio of female to male figurines suggests a changing gender role ideology under conditions of Aztec rule.

The Female Subject: Official and Popular Images

The figurine collections from Huexotla and Xaltocan suggest that gender was a topic of increasing concern to some Basin of Mexico communities during the period of Aztec dominance. The question remains, was the attitude of nonelite segments of the hinterland population one of accepting or resisting the male-dominant ideology of the Aztec state? The striking differences between official and popular images of the female subject suggest that hinterland populations did not accept the elite ideology. In fact, the popular images provide evidence of an ideology of resistance that sharply contested the official gender ideology of the state.

The male-dominant ideology of the state is most obviously expressed in Aztec monumental sculpture. Two of the best known and most power-

Figure 5.3. The headless Coatlicue. Height 3.2
meters. Museo Nacional de Antropología,
Mexico City.

ful pieces of Aztec sculpture present highly dramatic images of mutilated women. The colossal statue of Coatlicue (Figure 5.3) presents a decapitated woman whose head is replaced by two snakes representing two
streams of blood surging from her neck (Pasztory 1983:158). The relief
of Coyolxauhqui from the Templo Mayor presents a woman whose limbs
and head have been severed from her naked body (Figure 5.4). In both
of these sculptures, images of mutilated women represent the Aztec
state's subjugation of its enemies (Klein 1988); these images express the
fundamental misogyny that Rodríguez (1988:126) finds characteristic of

Figure 5.4. The dismembered Coyolxauhqui. Diameter 3.3 meters. Templo Mayor, Mexico City. (Courtesy of Elizabeth Brumfiel)

Aztec culture. The sculptures also seem to condone the use of physical violence against women to achieve male goals (Rodríguez 1988:140).

The ideology of male dominance is also expressed in Aztec manuscript painting. Goddesses are sometimes presented holding shields and phallic staffs (*Codex Magliabecchiano* 1983, 1:33; Pasztory 1983: colorplate 10; Sahagún 1950–69: Bk. 1, illustrations 6–12). McCafferty and McCafferty (1988) argue that such images are an example of gender parallelism: female deities were powerful in the same terms as were male deities. But Yólotl González (1979:17) and María Rodríguez (1988:182) point out that such images are androgynous negations of a power grounded in femaleness. Rather than affirming an equivalence of male and female power, these images suggest that power can be obtained only through maleness. Androgynous goddesses are an artistic solution to the conceptual problem of representing powerful females under the prevailing ideology of male dominance (Figure 5.5).[6]

Figure 5.5. The goddess Coatlicue holding a shield and swordlike
weaving batten, from the *Codex Magliabecchiano*. (Courtesy of
Elizabeth Brumfiel)

Less dramatic, more common expressions of male dominance are
provided by smaller stone sculptures from Tenochtitlan in which women
are posed in a kneeling position (Figure 5.6). This pose is so common
in both sculpture and manuscript painting that it has been designated
the "Aztec women's pose" (Caso 1960:14; Robertson 1964:430; Baird
1993:127). According to Pasztory (1983:210), the kneeling position "expressed the Aztec ideal of women, who were supposed to be modest and
industrious. Quintessentially feminine activities, such as weaving and
grinding corn, were performed in a kneeling position." Such images are
the visual counterparts of verbal statements that emphasize the role of

Figure 5.6. Kneeling goddess with tasseled headdress. Height 30 centimeters. Museum für Völker-
kunde, Basel. (Courtesy of Elizabeth Brumfiel)

women as producers of food and cloth in Aztec texts (Sahagún 1950–
69; bk. 10, chap. 3, chap. 6, chap. 18). Men are more often depicted in a
crouched position that appears to be unrelated to their role in warfare.
A standing position is sometimes used for both women and men, but it
is more common for men.

Two images from official Aztec art, mutilated women and androgynous women, are not met with in popular representations of women
in figurines.[7] Kneeling poses sometimes occur, but they are rare.[8]
Most female figurines are posed standing, which, according to Pasztory

(1983:210), signifies higher status. In addition, female figurines often hold one or two children in their arms; such images are unknown in official Aztec art. In fact, official Aztec art contains only two cases of a woman being associated with children or reproduction. One is the *Codex Borbonicus* illustration of the goddess Tlazolteotl giving birth (Pasztory 1983: colorplate 32); the other is a realistic depiction in stone of a woman giving birth (Kubler 1984: figure 57). This lack of reproductive imagery is consistent with the underemphasis of women's reproductive roles in Aztec verbal texts.[9]

Thus, official images and popular images of women have few areas of overlap. The official images depicted women as mutilated or androgynous or emphasized their roles in production; popular images more frequently associated women with reproduction. The official images of women lend credence to claims by Nash and Rodríguez that the Aztec state subscribed to a male-dominant ideology that diminished the status of women in Aztec society. However, the differences between official images and popular images of women sustain claims by Nash and McCafferty and McCafferty that gender inequality had not suffused Aztec culture at all levels. In Huexotla and Xaltocan, Aztec dominance caused increased concern with gender ideology, but the result was not the acceptance of the state's point of view. Instead, the penetration of state ideology prompted a degree of ideological reformulation. Rejecting elements of official imagery, the reformulation stood in ideological opposition to official views; in other words, it constituted a kind of popular ideology of resistance.

Conclusions

Figurine data from Huexotla, Xico, and Xaltocan suggest two conclusions about the importance of dominant ideologies in premodern states. One is that dominant ideologies are dependent upon high levels of interaction with political capitals. If Black-on-Orange pottery is taken as a gauge of the level of interaction of hinterland communities with political (and market) centers in the Basin of Mexico, then Late Postclassic Huexotla and Xaltocan, with 13.3 and 14.2 percent Black-on-Orange pottery, respectively, show much higher levels of interaction than Xico, with only 7.2 percent Black-on-Orange pottery. Thus, the interaction that accompanied the highly integrated Basin of Mexico market economy (Smith 1979, Hassig 1985) was an important condition for the diffusion of the state ideology. In less commercialized economies with lower rates of capital-hinterland interaction, for example, premodern Europe, the apparatus of education and cultural transmission is much less effective (Abercrombie, Hill, and Turner 1980:69–70).

Second, where the influence of the dominant ideology is felt, it does not always result in ideological dominance. Official images may be opposed by popular images that offer an effective critique. While states have the ability to place certain issues on the popular agenda, they do not have an unfailing capacity to dictate popular consciousness. Definition of the sources of popular ideologies of resistance constitutes a major problem for future research, but daily experience with the sharp contradiction between elite ideology and the material interests of subordinate classes must play an important role in enabling subordinate classes to formulate their own world views (Scott 1985).

Acknowledgments

An earlier version of this essay was presented at the session "The Engendered Subject: Practice and Representation in Mesoamerica," organized by Veronica M. Kann and Geoffrey G. McCafferty for the eighty-ninth annual meeting of the American Anthropological Association, New Orleans, 1990. This version has benefited greatly from comments offered by John Clark, Susan Evans, Veronica Kann, Helen Pollard, Michael Smith, Lynn Stephens, James Taggart, and Alison Wylie. However, they have not seen the current version of this chapter and cannot be held responsible for its contents.

I am grateful to Susan Evans for making available to me the results of her archaeological and ethnohistoric research on Aztec figurines. Fieldwork at Huexotla, Xico, and Xaltocan was supported by grants from the National Science Foundation (GS-38470 and BNS-89-19095), the Mellon Foundation, and the H. John Heinz III Charitable Trust. This essay was completed while I was a Fellow at the Center for Advanced Study in the Behavioral Sciences. I am grateful for financial support provided by the Andrew W. Mellon Foundation and the National Endowment for the Humanities. Maggie LaNoue produced the drawings that illustrate the chapter.

Notes

1. As an instance of women's resistance to the male dominant ideology, Nash (1978) cites mourning that women assumed when warriors departed from Tenochtitlan; this she interprets as an expression of women's abhorrence of the destructiveness of war. Nash also suggests that when the women of Tlatelolco "flaunted their backsides" to insult visiting Tenochca warriors, they were protesting a military alliance negotiated between the two communities.

2. Recently, however, figurines were found in association with an offering at a public building in the ceremonial center of Tlatelolco (see Otis Charlton 1995).

3. Cook (1950:94) notes that some of the figurines she inspected were perforated in ways that would permit their suspension.

4. For a summary of the illnesses associated with the various Aztec deities, see Aguilar (1946).

5. In contrast, Kaplan (1958:217–18) reports that male figurines outnumbered female figurines at Nonoalco, a Late Postclassic site on the outskirts of Tenochtitlan-Tlatelolco.

6. However, Klein (1993) argues that the shield was a fundamentally feminine symbol, a visual metaphor for the female body itself.

7. Figurine heads attached to figurine bodies are very rarely encountered. Evans (1990) suggests that the heads may have been deliberately snapped from the body in an act of ritual sacrifice (in Aztec culture, women were conventionally sacrificed by decapitation; men were sacrificed by opening their chests to remove their still beating hearts). However, as Evans notes, heads are rarely attached to figurine bodies even in workshop contexts so the breakage pattern may be due to technical factors. Heavy, solid figurine heads attached to solid or hollow bodies by slender necks may be responsible for the breakage patterns (Cook 1950).

8. Interestingly, there are four kneeling figurines among the five female figurines in a photograph of artifacts recovered in archaeological salvage during the construction of Mexico City's Metro (Arana and Cepeda 1967:5). This suggests that the penetration of the state's male-dominant ideology was much greater in the imperial capital than in hinterland settlements such as Huexotla, Xico, and Xaltocan.

9. The popularity of reproductive imagery in female figurines may stem from a desire to define reproduction as a specifically female concern. This principle is also reflected in the symbolic association of women's implements such as spindles and cooking pots with human sexuality and childbirth (Sullivan 1982; McCafferty and McCafferty 1989, 1991; Brumfiel 1991c). This is consistent with McCafferty and McCafferty's (1991) observation that the goal of resistance was to delimit an arena within which female power could be negotiated. The popularity of reproductive imagery in female figurines may also reflect a growing concern with effective reproduction, perhaps because the state's demand for tribute, levied on a household basis, increased the need for household labor, and/or because the intensification of physical labor associated with imperial domination made pregnancy and childbirth more difficult, and/or because the increasing levels of violence associated with imperial expansion and control made less certain the survival of children to support parents in their old age. James Taggart (1990, personal communication) points out that the domain of reproductive success might include the reproductive capacity of the earth as manifested in agricultural production. If so, then the popularity of reproductive imagery in female figurines might also be explained by the need to increase agricultural production to meet increased demands for tribute or market exchange while continuing to meet household subsistence needs.

References

Abercrombie, Nicholas, Stephen Hill, and Bryan S. Turner
    1980   *The Dominant Ideology Thesis.* London: George Allen and Unwin.
Aguilar, Gilberto F.
    1946   "La medecina." In *México prehispánico,* edited by Jorge A. Vivó, 725–36. Mexico City: Emma Hurtado.
Althusser, Louis
    1971   "Ideology and Ideological State Apparatuses." In *Lenin and Philosophy and Other Essays.* New York: Monthly Review Press.
Alva Ixtlilxóchitl, Fernando de
    1975–77 *Obras históricas,* edited by Edmundo O'Gorman. 2 vols. Mexico

City: Universidad Nacional Autónoma de México, Instituto de Investigaciones Históricas.

Anales de Cuauhtitlan

1945   *Anales de Cuauhtitlan*. In *Códice Chimalpopoca*, translated by P. F. Velázquez, 1–118. Mexico City: Universidad Nacional Autónoma de México, Instituto de Investigaciones Históricas.

Anales de Tlatelolco

1947   *Anales de Tlatelolco*, translated by H. Berlin and R. Barlow. Mexico City: Antigua Librería Robredo.

Arana, Raúl, and Gerardo Cepeda

1967   "Rescate arqueológico en la Ciudad de México." *INAH Boletín* 30:3–9.

Baird, Ellen T.

1993   *The Drawings of Sahagún's Primeros Memoriales*. Norman: University of Oklahoma Press.

Barlow, Robert H., and H. Lehmann

1956   "Statuettes—Grelot Azteques de la Vallée de Mexico." *Tribus* 4–5:157–76.

Brumfiel, Elizabeth M.

1976   *Specialization and Exchange at the Late Postclassic (Aztec) Community of Huexotla, Mexico*. Ann Arbor, Mich.: University Microfilms.

1980   "Specialization, Market Exchange, and the Aztec State: A View from Huexotla." *Current Anthropology* 21:459–78.

1985   "The Division of Labor at Xico: The Chipped Stone Industry." In *Economic Aspects of Prehispanic Highland Mexico*, edited by B. L. Isaac, 245–79. Greenwich, Conn.: JAI Press.

1987   "Informe al Instituto Nacional de Antropología e Historia Sobre el Proyecto Xaltocan Azteca." Paper on file, Department of Anthropology and Sociology, Albion College, and the Instituto Nacional de Antropología e Historia, Mexico City.

1991a   "Agricultural Development and Class Stratification in the Southern Valley of Mexico." In *Land and Politics in the Valley of Mexico*, edited by H. R. Harvey, 43–62. Albuquerque: University of New Mexico Press.

1991b   "Tribute and Commerce in Imperial Cities: The Case of Xaltocan, Mexico." In *Early State Economics*, edited by H. J. M. Claessen and P. van de Velde, 177–98. New Brunswick: Transaction.

1991c   "Weaving and Cooking: Women's Production in Aztec Mexico." In *Engendering Archaeology: Women and Prehistory*, edited by Joan M. Gero and Margaret W. Conkey, 224–51. Oxford: Basil Blackwell.

Carrasco, Davíd

1990   "Give Me Some Skin: The Metamorphosis, Charisma, and Redistribution of the Aztec Warrior." Paper presented at the 55th annual meeting of the Society for American Archaeology, Las Vegas.

Carrasco, Pedro

1950   *Los Otomíes: Cultura e historia prehispánica de los pueblos Mesoamericanos de habla Otomiana*. Mexico City: Biblioteca Enciclopédica del Estado de México.

Caso, Alfonso

1960   *Interpretation of the Codex Bodley 2858*. Mexico City: Sociedad Mexicana de Antropología.

Codex Magliabecchiano
1983   *The Codex Magliabecchiano.* Notes and commentary by E. J. Boone. 2 vols. Berkeley: University of California Press.

Codex Mendoza
1992   *Codex Mendoza.* Edited by F. F. Berdan and P. R. Anawalt. Berkeley: University of California Press.

Conkey, Margaret W., and Joan M. Gero
1991   "Tensions, Pluralities, and Engendering Archaeology: An Introduction to Women and Prehistory." In *Engendering Archaeology: Women and Prehistory,* edited by Joan M. Gero and Margaret W. Conkey, 3–30. Oxford: Basil Blackwell.

Cook, Carmen
1950   "Figurillas de barro de Santiago Tlatelolco." *Memorias de la Academia Mexicana de la Historia* (Tlatelolco a Través de los Tiempos) 9(1):93–100.

Durán, Diego
1964   *Historia de las Indias de Nueva España.* 2 vols. Mexico City: Porrua.
1971   *Book of the Gods and Rites and the Ancient Calendar.* Translated by F. Horcasitas and D. Heyden. Norman: University of Oklahoma Press.

Evans, Susan
1990   "Household Ritual in Aztec Life." Paper presented at the 55th annual meeting of the Society for American Archaeology, Las Vegas.

Gailey, Christine Ward
1985   "The State of the State in Anthropology." *Dialectical Anthropology* 9:65–89.
1987   "Culture Wars: Resistance to State Formation." In *Power Relations and State Formation,* edited by T. C. Patterson and C. W. Gailey, 35–56. Washington, D.C.: American Anthropological Association.

Gibson, Charles
1956   "Llamamiento General, Repartimiento, and the Empire of Acolhuacan." *Hispanic American Historical Review* 36:1–27.

González Torres, Yólotl
1979   "El panteón mexica." *Antropología e Historia* 25:9–19.

Guzmán, Eulalia
1938   "Un manuscrito de la colección Boturini que trata de los antiguos señores de Teotihuacán. *Ethnos* 3:89–103.

Hassig, Ross
1985   *Trade, Tribute and Transportation: The Sixteenth-Century Political Economy of the Valley of Mexico.* Norman: University of Oklahoma Press.

Hicks, Frederic
1994   "Xaltocan under Mexica Domination, 1435–1520." In *Caciques and Their People,* edited by Joyce Marcus and J. F. Zeitlin, 67–85. Ann Arbor: Anthropological Papers 89. The University of Michigan Museum of Anthropology.

Kann, Veronica M.
1989   "Late Classic Politics, Cloth Production, and Women's Labor: An Interpretation of Female Figurines from Matacapan, Veracruz." Paper presented at the 54th annual meeting of the Society for American Archaeology, Atlanta, Ga.

Kaplan, Flora
    1958   "The Post-Classic Figurines of Central Mexico." Master's essay, Department of Anthropology, Columbia University, New York.
Klein, Cecelia F.
    1988   "Rethinking Cihuacoatl: Aztec Political Imagery of the Conquered Woman." In *Smoke and Mist: Mesoamerican Studies in Memory of Thelma D. Sullivan*, edited by J. K. Josserand and K. Dakin, 237–77. Oxford: British Archaeological Reports, International Series (402).
    1993   "The Shield Women: Resolution of an Aztec Gender Paradox." In *Current Topics in Aztec Studies: Essays in Honor of Dr. H. B. Nicholson*, edited by A. Cordy-Collins and D. Sharon, 39–64. San Diego: San Diego Museum Papers (30).
Kubler, George
    1984   *The Art and Architecture of Ancient America*. 3d ed. New York: Penguin Books.
McCafferty, Geoffrey G., and Sharisse D. McCafferty
    1989   "Weapons of Resistance: Material Metaphors of Gender Identity in Postclassic Mexico." Paper presented at the 90th annual meeting of the American Anthropological Association, Washington, D.C.
McCafferty, Sharisse D., and Geoffrey G. McCafferty
    1988   "Powerful Women and the Myth of Male Dominance in Aztec Society." *Archaeological Review from Cambridge* 7:45–59.
    1991   "Spinning and Weaving as Female Gender Identity in Post-Classic Central Mexico." In *Textile Traditions of Mesoamerica and the Andes: An Anthology*, edited by M. Schevill, J. C. Berlo, and E. Dwyer, 19–46. New York: Garland.
Millian, Alva C.
    1981   *The Iconography of Aztec Ceramic Figurines*. Master's essay, Department of Art History and Archaeology, Columbia University, New York.
Morss, Noel
    1952   "Cradled Infant Figurines from Tennessee and Mexico." *American Antiquity* 18:164–66.
Motolinía, Toribio
    1969   *Historia de los Indios de la Nueva España*. Mexico City: Porrúa.
Nash, June
    1978   "The Aztecs and the Ideology of Male Dominance." *Signs* 4:349–62.
Nazareo de Xaltocan, Don Pablo
    1940   "Carta al Rey Don Felipe II." In *Epistolario de Nueva España*, edited by F. del Paso y Troncoso, 10:109–29. Mexico City: Antigua Librería Robredo.
Offner, Jerome A.
    1983   *Law and Politics in Aztec Texcoco*. Cambridge: Cambridge University Press.
Otis Charlton, Cynthia L.
    1994   "Plebeians and Patricians: Contrasting Patterns of Production and Distribution in the Aztec Figurine and Lapidary Industries." In *Economies and Polities in the Aztec Realm*, edited by M. G. Hodge and

M. E. Smith, 195–219. Albany: State University of New York at Albany, Institute for Mesoamerican Studies.

1995 "Las figurillas prehispánicas y coloniales de Tlatelelco." Unpublished report submitted to the Subdirección Arqueológica, Instituto Nacional de Antropología e Historia, Mexico City.

Parsons, Mary H.
1972 "Aztec Figurines from the Teotihuacan Valley, Mexico." In *Miscellaneous Studies in Mexican Prehistory*, by M. W. Spence, J. R. Parsons, and M. H. Parsons, 81–164. Ann Arbor: University of Michigan Museum of Anthropology, Anthropological Papers, 45.

Pasztory, Esther
1983 *Aztec Art.* New York: Abrams.

Pollock, Susan
1991 "Women in a Men's World: Images of Sumerian Women." In *Engendering Archaeology: Women and Prehistory*, edited by Joan M. Gero and Margaret W. Conkey, 366–87. Oxford: Basil Blackwell.

Preuss, K. Th.
1901 "Mexikanische Thonfiguren." *Globus* 79, no. 6:87–91. Brunswick.

Rapp, Rayna
1978 "The Search for Origins: Unraveling the Threads of Gender Hierarchy." *Critique of Anthropology* 3:5–24.

Robertson, Donald
1964 "Los manuscritos religiosos mixtecos." In *Thirty-fifth International Congress of Americanists, Mexico, 1962. Actas*, 1:425–35.

Rodríguez, María J.
1988 *La Mujer Azteca.* Toluca: Universidad Autónoma del Estado de México.
1989 "La condición femenina en Tlaxcala según las fuentes." *Mesoamérica* 17:1–23.

Sahagún, Bernardino de
1950–69 *Florentine Codex: General History of the Things of New Spain.* Translated by A. Anderson and C. Dibble. 11 vols. Santa Fe, N.M., and Salt Lake City: School of American Research and the University of Utah Press.

Scott, James C.
1985 *The Weapons of the Weak: Everyday Forms of Peasant Resistance.* New Haven, Conn.: Yale University Press.

Seler, Eduard
1902–23 *Gesammelte Abhandlungen zur Amerikanischen Sprach- und Altertumskunde.* 4 vols. Berlin. Reprinted, 1960–61. Graz, Austria.

Silverblatt, Irene
1987 *Moon, Sun, and Witches: Gender Ideologies and Class in Inca and Colonial Peru.* Princeton, N.J.: Princeton University Press.

Smith, Michael E.
1979 "The Aztec Marketing System and Settlement Pattern in the Valley of Mexico: A Central-Place Analysis." *American Antiquity* 44:110–25.

Sullivan, Thelma D.
1982 "Tlazolteotl-Ixcuina: The Great Spinner and Weaver." In *The Art and Iconography of Late Post-Classic Central Mexico*, edited by E. H. Boone, 7–35. Washington, D.C.: Dumbarton Oaks.

Chapter 6
The Construction of Gender in Classic Maya Monuments

Rosemary A. Joyce

Introduction

In 1960, Tatiana Proskouriakoff began a revolution in English-language scholarship of Classic Maya societies of Mexico and Guatemala with her demonstration that texts on monuments from this civilization recorded events in the lives of men and women, not the religious and calendrical esoterica previously supposed to be their topics. Subsequent research on the Classic period (maximally A.D. 250–1000) Maya archaeological culture has focused on the delineation of specific sequences of rulers. The identification of events discussed in texts, including birth, death and burial, warfare, personal blood sacrifice, ritual execution of captives, ritual dancing, and the experience of visions, have been treated as the material of a Classic Maya history, in which women figure in very peripheral ways, as parts of the biographies of ruling men.

In contrast to this recent historical scholarship, the approach I adopt is anthropological, and the media I use for my inquiry are visual. Like other studies of the status of women in stratified societies, I assume that the writing-out of women from one medium does not necessarily reflect the actual range of their involvement in political process. I argue that the images on monuments in Classic Maya sites served as a medium for the development of particular gender constructs, not necessarily entirely congruent with those represented by texts found on the same monuments or with everyday practice. The term monument, as used here, refers to large-scale architectural elaborations (carved stone, carved wood, and modeled stucco wall panels, lintels, benches and the like, and murals painted on walls) and freestanding carved stone sculptures that served to create formal exterior spaces. The gender discourse embodied in Classic Maya monuments is that of a single social stratum or class, the elite, and particularly ruling elites, who were the patrons and subjects of these monuments. I assume that the ideological dimensions of Classic Maya monuments pertain primarily to the negotiation of political power among elites, and between ruling elites and the kinship groups that made up Maya society.

The production of representational images is a cultural means to respond to and shape the conditions of social existence. The selection of features to be incorporated in human images promulgates stereotypes of natural or essential human behavior. Such "iconic" images, suggesting aspects of human appearance and behavior through resemblance, "because they either 'look natural' or can be 'naturalized' . . . lend themselves with particular ease to totalizing cultural ideologies" (Herzfeld 1992:68–69). Naturalizing of ideologies of gender may thus be especially susceptible to archaeological evaluation, as material media of representation change over time (compare Brumfiel, this volume).

In this chapter, I approach gender as a culturally constructed "set of categories which we can give the same label cross-linguistically, or cross-culturally, because they have some connection to sex differences," where the connections are "conventional and arbitrary insofar as they are not reducible to, or directly derivative of, natural, biological facts" (Shapiro 1981:449). I distinguish between gender and biological identity, described here as "reproductive sexuality" (following Shore 1981:194). The terms "male" and "female" here refer to gender categories that can be conceived of as the strongly marked dichotomous poles of a continuum of gender. In different circumstances, the gender continuum could be represented as a more fluid set of multiple intermediate possibilities, reflecting a more realistic concept of gender as performance (Butler 1990:112). In the translation from lived reality to fixed representation, however, the real freedom possible in action was conventionalized, in the case of the Classic Maya in ways related to the circumstances of political centralization. I argue that constructions of gender in Classic Maya monuments embodied elite interests, as part of state formation, in deemphasizing women's contributions to the potential economic independence of nonruling households (compare Silverblatt 1988; Gailey 1987a, 1987b; Muller 1987). Representing select moments in ritual, monumental images presented only those aspects of action that reinforced the formation of an elite class, stereotyping all women (and men) in extremely limited ways.

The male and female images I discuss conform to a small set of patterns regardless of arguments, based on accompanying texts, about the historical identity or reproductive sexuality of the person depicted. The relationship between texts and images on Maya monuments has received considerable attention in recent years, as ability to paraphrase and even read Maya texts has progressed. Clearly text and image are not always parallel in content (compare Barthes 1977c). It is likely that not all members of Maya society were literate, and because of the allowable variation in writing, not all texts are equally accessible to the reader. Crucial for my purpose, text and image on monuments provide different information and would be perceived in different ways by viewers whether literate or not. Maya images stress conventionalization of features, allowing even total outsiders to immediately characterize the representational content of the image. Text, in contrast, calls for an analytic attention to reading order, clause structure, and mathematics of chronological sequence. The conventionalization of human images in Classic Maya sculpture represents an enduring depiction of distinct social personae, and it is this information that is immediately available to the viewer.

In the pages that follow, I will demonstrate that Classic Maya monuments create a gender dichotomy expressed through distinctive costume. I will show that images with female costume are typically presented in conjunction with male images and are placed in regular spatial relationships to them: on the reverse, left, or south side, or in a lower position. Differences in reproductive sexuality are systematically deemphasized. Instead, the details of the paired costumes relate the individuals wearing them to the geographic landscape. The complementary male-female pair represented through spatial and geographic imagery is presented engaged in identical or complementary ritual action, with women's distinctive activities in Maya society subordinated to their activities as elites. The deemphasis of sexual characteristics and the embodiment of gender in costume aided the expression, as part of elite strategies of power construction, of a claimed comprehensive gender identity signaled by combined costume elements.

Gender Imagery in Classic Maya Public Monuments

Classic Maya public monuments do not generally distinguish gender through overt sexual characteristics, as is the case in other media. Contemporary cave paintings (Stone 1988) and pottery depict exposed breasts to mark female figures, a convention also found in late stone relief sculpture at Terminal Classic Chichén Itzá and in Postclassic pictorial manuscripts (Joyce 1993b). The absence of overt sexual characteristics in Classic Maya public sculpture is thus clearly deliberate. The basic body and facial type on Classic Maya monuments is essentially sexless, and it is only by distinctive costumes and distinct signs modifying the names of females in texts that male and female actors have been identified (Proskouriakoff 1961; Miller 1974; Marcus 1976:157–79, 1987; Schele 1979; Bruhns 1988).

Costume carries most of the burden of establishing distinctions in Classic Maya monuments. Only three kinds of dress have been taken to indicate female gender (Proskouriakoff 1961; Bruhns 1988; Joyce 1992b). Simple wrapped garments covering the breasts but leaving bare the arms, typical of painted ceramics, are rare in monuments. Elaborately woven huipils, which cover the entire body, appear on sculptured lintels and stelae. These garments are typical of images in less visible locations: on lintels inside temples at Yaxchilan and Tikal, on the rear of stelae facing temples at Piedras Negras and Bonampak, and in the murals inside a small building on a raised platform at Bonampak. The third female costume, typical of public monuments, is a latticework skirt and cape, usually interpreted as composed of interlocking jade beads (Figure 6.1). The cape is occasionally absent or replaced by a bead collar. A belt with a pendant, the frontal head of a fish monster (*xoc*) with open mouth above a bivalve shell, is usual (Miller 1974). The most visible images of women in Classic Maya centers, carved on stone monuments set facing central plazas, are those of figures wearing this beaded net costume.

Proskouriakoff (1961) initially identified the latticework beaded garment as a female costume through comparison with texts naming women that seemed to act as captions for the depicted individuals, but others have challenged this conclusion. Sometimes, the same costume occurs on monuments with texts featuring only the names of men, prompting debate about the identification of this as a female costume. Andrea Stone (1991:201–2) argues that named women wearing this costume are "impersonating a male image of power" because the costume is not exclusively associated with women's names. She suggests that the symbolism of component elements is more strongly tied to two male supernaturals, a maize god and a primordial deity, whose birth is recorded in texts at Palenque, who wears shell ear ornaments and has catfish barbels on his cheeks. Stone proposes a series of specific historical explanations for the use of this costume by individual women who had enough power or status to claim a male prerogative. The separation of gender as a category distinct from reproductive sexuality allows an analysis of the net-skirt costume as typical of a gender identity not tied to specific reproductive sexuality, but commonly associated with women and an important part of the cultural construction of elite female gender (Joyce 1992b). Because its symbolism is not linked to reproductive sexuality, the costume may be assumed by human men and male supernaturals who share the characteristics that constitute this female identity, combining them with male reproductive sexuality signaled by bare chests lacking breasts.

Figures wearing the net skirt are commonly paired with others wear-

Figure 6.1. A person wearing the net skirt with fish-
monster belt ornament holds a bowl. Naranjo Stela
24, paired with Stela 22 illustrated in Figure 6.2.
(From the *Corpus of Maya Hieroglyphic Inscriptions*
2:63; courtesy of the Peabody Museum)

ing a short kilt and loincloth (Figure 6.2). This costume marks a complementary, elite male gender identity. From the belt hangs an ornament composed of a jade maskette with three pendant celts and a loincloth that is a collapsed image of a tree with jeweled serpent branches and trunk marked with a deity face (Schele and Miller 1986:77). I compare the maskette with the decapitated heads depicted as corncobs in Classic Maya iconography (Schele and Miller 1986:53) and the decapitated head of the hero Hun Hunahpu hung from a tree in the underworld in the Postclassic Quiché Maya text, the *Popol Vuh* (Joyce 1992b:35). The distinctive elements of this male costume refer to the central world tree, the vertical axis of the universe.

The net-skirt costume has complementary spatial symbolism. The pendant belt ornament of the female costume incorporates bivalve shells and the head of a fish monster based on the shark. However, the net skirt itself is not a marine icon. It is worn in Postclassic codices both by young female deities and earth-associated male deities, the young maize god and the gods who support the earth's surface. It has been identified as a component of the costume of the Classic period young maize god (Taube 1985). Its associations with the surface of the earth are strengthened by imagery at Chichén Itzá (Joyce 1993b). There, figures with exposed female breasts, wearing the net skirt, are depicted in the same positions and engaged in the same gestures as male deities wearing turtle or conch shells, long recognized as supporting the earth's surface. One set of images shows these male and female figures supporting an image of the mountainous earth with ancestors holding corn plants emerging from caves. In another sculpture, the network pattern itself is depicted with sprouting plants emerging from it. As an image of the horizontal surface of the earth bounded by ocean waters, the net skirt and fish-monster belt ornament form a costume spatially complementary to the vertical axis represented by the male world-tree loincloth.

Gender in the Space of the Classic Maya Center

The placement of monuments with paired figures wearing the net skirt and the world-tree loincloth divides space within Classic Maya centers into gendered settings along a variety of axes consistent with the spatial symbolism of male and female costume as vertical axis and horizontal plane. Up and down, front and back, outer and inner, right and left, and north and south each are associated with paired dichotomous gender imagery at different sites. Variation between sites is the rule, rather than the exception, suggesting that gender imagery was being constructed independently in site-specific processes. Despite this, the association of gender with space corresponds generally to patterns recorded in mod-

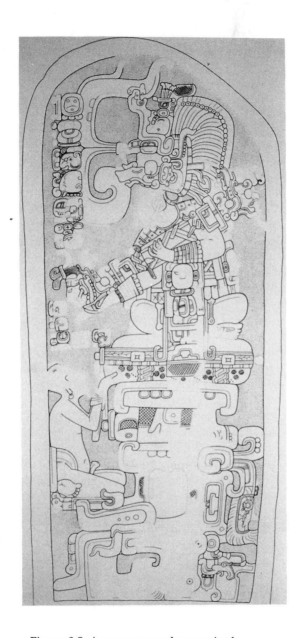

Figure 6.2. A person seated on a raised
throne, wearing the world-tree loincloth,
holds a double-headed serpent bar. Naranjo
Stela 22, paired with Stela 24 illustrated
in Figure 6.2. (From the *Corpus* 2:55;
courtesy of the Peabody Museum)

ern Maya ethnographies, sources that provide possible guidance in understanding those situations where regularities appear to be violated.

Ethnographic sources associate female gender with the left and lower elevation, and male gender with the right and higher elevation. These two kinds of directionality, right/left and up/down, appear to override cardinal orientations. This in turn may reflect the fact that cardinal directions in Maya cosmology primarily reflect orientations derived from the sun's daily path through the sky and seasonal movement north and south along the eastern and western horizons. Rather than being an absolute system of reference to fixed directions, cardinal orientations represent relative direction from a point of reference, the position of the sun. Gary Gossen (1974:32) notes that right-left orientation is crucial in ritual circuits in Chamula, with north and south defined in practice as the right- and left-hand directions with respect to the rising sun on the eastern horizon. The importance of the sun as a point of reference in ordering spatial relationships in Chamula also leads to an emphasis on the direction up, associated with the sun's rising path from east to the right, or north. The sun is conceived of as moving down in the west, and the earth's surface is spoken of as tilted, the eastern horizon higher than the western horizon (Gossen 1974:35–36).

The association of the sun with Classic Maya rulers thus provides a culturally specific logic for the positions occupied by males in Classic Maya paired representations. And like the relative positioning with respect to the sun in modern Chamula, Classic Maya directional orientations can only be understood in terms of a particular point of orientation provided by these male figures, or more generally by the sun's path. The simplest spatial association of paired male and female images in Classic Maya centers is placement on opposite sides of a single stela (Table 6.1). In most cases, double-sided stelae were set so that the side with female imagery faced away from the open plaza, toward a nearby building. The frontality of the stela was consequently associated with the male position. Here neither right-left nor up-down orientations can be relevant.

When paired figures are not on opposite sides of a single monument, right-left orientation becomes salient (Table 6.2), with the female figure more often on viewer's left and the male figure on viewer's right. Paired male and female figures could be separated on two stelae, usually set side-by-side with faces in profile gazing at each other. Such paired stelae were placed in no regular relation to cardinal directions. Instead, they establish local distinctions between right-hand and left-hand positions from a point of orientation. While this point of orientation is often assumed to be that of a viewer in front of the monuments, it can also be a point internal to the composition. Such shifting points of observation may be responsible for cases of apparent reversal, with the left-hand

TABLE 6.1. Images paired on opposite sides of stela.

Monument	Front	Back
Calakmul Stela 9	Male	Female
Calakmul Stela 88	Male	Female
Coba Stela 1	Female	Male
Pechal Stela 1	Male	Female
El Zapote Stela 5	Male	Female
Tulum Stela 1	Male	Female
Cancuen Stela 1	Female	Male

TABLE 6.2. Paired images placed right and left.

Monuments	Viewer's left	Viewer's right
Tikal Stela 25, sides	Female	Male
Tikal Stelae 1 and 2	Female	Male
Calakmul Stelae 28 and 29	Female	Male
Calakmul Stelae 52 and 54	Female	Male
Calakmul Stelae 23 and 24	Female	Male
Naranjo Stelae 28 and 29	Male	Female
Naranjo Stelae 1 and 3	Male	Female
Cleveland and Kimball stelae	Male	Female
Copan Stelae A and H	Male	Female
Yaxchilan Stela 1 (main figure faces south)	Female	Male
Yaxchilan Stela 4 (main figure faces north)	Male	Female

position of the female figure preserved with respect to an actor within the composition rather than outside it.

These two aspects of paired representations, the possibility of separation on independent monuments, and the importance of orientation relative to an observation point that cannot be presumed, are amply illustrated by examination of more complex spatial arrangements evident at some Classic Maya sites, including Naranjo, Xultun, and Copan (Table 6.3). Examination of such complex spatial layouts emphasizes the primacy of right and left over other organizing principles, closely following by pairing of up and down. Stelae from Piedras Negras (Proskouriakoff 1960) embody the same associations in single monuments, with a male ruler seated in an elevated niche or on an elevated throne and a woman standing at ground level drawn either on the front or side of the stela (e.g., Stelae 14 and 33). These two spatial dimensions most concretely embody complementarity as a relation, since each exists only by pairing and distinction from the other. Other spatial axes do not have this inherent quality of pairing, with the notable exception of

TABLE 6.3. Complex spatial relationships of paired images.

Location	Viewpoint	Left	Right
Naranjo Group C	East terrace	Female Stela 24	Male Stelae 21, 22, 23
Copan Great Plaza	North terrace, Stela D	Female Stela H	Male Stelae A, 4, B
Xultun	Sacbe or central platform, facing west	Female Stelae 23, 24, 25	Male Stelae 14, 15, 16, 17
Xultun	North plaza	Female Stelae 23, 24, 25	Male Stelae 1, 3, 22, 4, 5, 7, 8, 9, 10

the front/back pairing that is the major format found on single monuments. Rather than defining some spaces as inherently male and others as inherently female, the spatial associations created by monument placement serve to reinforce the complementarity of each of these two gendered representations to the other, a point I consider further below.

The spatial relationships of paired costumes persist despite the reproductive sexual identity implied by associated texts. At Xultun, figures with net skirts also wear the world-tree loincloth (Figure 6.3), and caption texts give these individuals male names. On Tikal Stelae 1 and 2, both figures have bare legs, short kilts, and bare chests, suggesting male reproductive sexuality, but the left-hand figure wears as his kilt a short net skirt combined with the maskette and three celts belt ornament. The spatially constituted gender identities of the paired male and female costumes are reinforced by their symbolism, incorporating references to the landscape as horizontal surface (net skirt) and vertical axis (world-tree loincloth), together representing the totality of the spatial setting of Classic Maya society.

Narrative and Gender in Classic Maya Sculpture

Human images on Maya sculpture are generally static, but imply particular action through specific costumes worn and implements held. Roland Barthes (1977b:79) discusses narrative as a communicative mode, expressed both in language and image, with certain distinctive features. Among these are symbolic codes based on metaphor, analogy, or paradigm, combined with the sequential denotative code based on metonym or syntagmatic sequence (Barthes 1977b:92–101; 1977c:48–51). Single still images composed by the selection of representative elements (as in Classic Maya painting, drawing, and low relief carvings) distill narrative

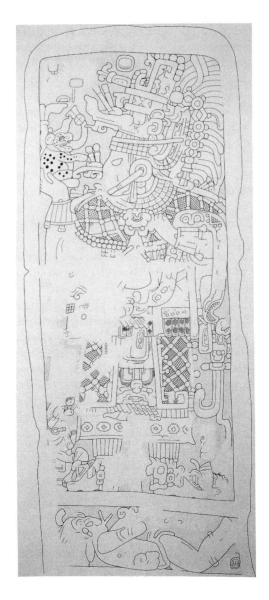

Figure 6.3. A person wearing the net skirt
costume combined with world-tree loincloth
holds a serpent and jaguar cub. Xultun Stela
24. (From the *Corpus* 5:85; courtesy of the
Peabody Museum)

into a "pregnant moment": "In order to tell a story, the painter possesses only one moment . . . [the image] will be a hieroglyph in which can be read at a glance . . . the present, the past, and the future, i.e. the historical meaning of the represented gesture" (Barthes 1977a:73). Because of this condensation of a narrative sequence in a single image, "all images are polysemous; they imply, underlying their signifiers, a 'floating chain' of signifieds, the reader able to choose some and ignore others" (Barthes 1977c:38–39). The signs united in a narrative are bound in a relationship of "double implication: two terms presuppose one another," transforming chronological order to a logical binding "capable of integrating backwards and forwards movements" through the narrative (Barthes 1977b:101, 120–22). To understand the images on Classic Maya monuments, the chains of connected implications that radiate temporally and logically from the represented moment must be explored through a reading of their narratives.

What narratives can be associated with the net-skirt costume? Initially, the wide range of items held by these figures would seem to negate any particular significance other than to identify a preexisting category through connotation. But gender is not a preexisting category; the images associating the net skirt with particular actions themselves actively constitute the identity represented. The items held by figures wearing the net skirt include many that can also be held by figures wearing typical male costume: the double-headed bar, shields, spears, staffs, and manikin scepters. A ceramic bowl is the only item that is not also held by figures in male costume in these paired compositions (see Figure 6.1).

Holding and offering ceramic bowls as receptacles in ritual is a common gesture of female figures in Maya monumental images, regardless of the costume of the figure or the location of the image. Figures wearing huipils hold bowls containing paper and bloodletting instruments. Figures in huipils are also shown holding and offering cloth bundles (Figure 6.4). I argue that the gestures of holding cloth bundles and ceramic vessels are references through these products to women's labor in cloth and food production as one of the causes underlying the narrative (Joyce 1992a, 1993a). Classic Maya figurines and painted vessels show women actively weaving and preparing maize, the two stereotyped activities of women's labor in ethnohistoric and ethnographic discussions of the Maya. The cloth bundles held by figures in female dress on monuments were a product of this labor, while bowls metonymically suggest the food they commonly contain, another product of women's work.

In Classic Maya monuments this reading is muted: the context of the presentation of bowls and bundles is ritual action and the consequences implied by these actions are cosmological. In these narratives, female figures sometimes reiterate and sometimes complement the ac-

Figure 6.4. A person wearing the world-tree loincloth holds manikin scepter and round shield, accompanied by a huipil-clad person holding a textile bundle. Yaxchilan Lintel 32. (From the *Corpus* 3:73; courtesy of the Peabody Museum)

tions of male figures. Duality of gender identity of participants in a single action is stressed, whether there are two separate people involved or a single person in two gendered roles. Variation in gesture between paired images places the emphasis on the action, and suggests the necessary interdependence of individuals of distinct gender. Paired figures with different gestures illuminate complementary gendered actions. Female figures hold bowls or the double-headed serpent bar, while their male counterparts hold the double-headed bar, the manikin scepter and shield, or weapons. While either of the paired figures can hold the double-headed bar, only the male figures in pairs hold icons that refer to warfare and human sacrifice: weapons, the shield, and the manikin scepter, which personifies a hafted ax (see Table 6.4). The complement to women's gendered labor implied by bowls and bundles may be men's labor as warriors producing sacrificial victims.

Gender Complementarity: A Comparative Perspective

Gender complementarity, as an alternative to gender opposition, has received less ethnographic attention, but suggestive analyses exist for Hopi (Schlegel 1977), Aymara (Harris 1978, 1980) and Tzotzil Maya (Devereaux 1987). The presence of ideas of gender complementarity in these widely separated areas suggests that it may be an important part of wider native American traditions. Alice Schlegel (1977:246) characterizes Hopi gender ideology as one of "sexual interdependence — between male and female actors in the social scene and between principles of maleness and femaleness in ideology." Women have crucial roles in ritual, particularly in grinding "the sacred cornmeal, the symbol of natural and spiritual life, that is a necessary ingredient in almost all ceremonies" (Schlegel 1977:255). Specialized women's ceremonies are conducted by women's societies conceived of as siblings to men's ceremonial societies. "Through the women's ceremonies, the necessary interdependence of male and female is expressed" (Schlegel 1977:260).

Hopi gender complementarity is based on distinctive contributions to both household labor and ritual. The same principles underlie gender complementarity in the Andean Aymara community of Laymi, Bolivia (Harris 1978). Here, men and women become full social actors only as a couple, *chachawarmi*, a word composed of the separate terms for husband/man and wife/woman. Sexual pairing is pervasive in cosmology, with gods, aspects of nature, and sacred stones conceived of as part of male-female pairs. Duality is reinforced within the household through strict division of certain stereotyped tasks: male plowing and female planting; male weaving on the foot loom, female weaving on the backstrap loom. Duality is perhaps most crucial in ritual, where the basic ritual action, pouring libations, ideally calls for a couple, each pouring with both hands. The gender complementarity in ritual is projected onto the individual as well: the two hands are conceived of as male (right) and female (left), and the ritual libation involves expression of a gender totality by each person.

Olivia Harris (1978:38) questions "the common assumption that the symbolic representation of woman and man can be derived solely from the biological basis to their relationship." She relates gender complementarity to economic and ritual roles. Rejecting a universal association of the male/female dichotomy with a culture/nature distinction, Harris (1978:28) identifies an association of the *couple* with culture in Laymi: "It is the fruitful cooperation of woman and man as a unity that produces culture, and this is counterposed to an unmarried person as non-cultural; culture is based on duality, and contrasted with what has remained single when it should be paired."

Complementarity is also the basic theme of gender ideology discerned for the Tzotzil Maya of Zinacantan by Leslie Devereaux (1987: 92): social "goals can only be achieved (perhaps one should say can best, or most appropriately be achieved) by couples, acting in concert through their complementary work skills." Complementary roles, not essential biological features, are the core of Zinacantec gender ideology, which Devereaux (1987:89) describes as "action-based or role oriented"; male and female are conceived of as "different, without emphasizing essence or substance as the source of difference so much as stressing action and appearance as appropriately displaying difference." Similar statements of gender complementarity have been made for other Maya communities. Nathaniel Tarn and Martin Prechtel (1986:173) note that "Atiteco thought conceives of male and female as aspects of one original unit," where "no unit can be other than both male and female. Certainly, nothing complete, nothing fully fulfilling its function in the world, can be other than this. Thus, a man cannot take office before marriage and all offices have complementary tasks for the husband/wife pair, whether they function together on any given occasion or not."

Common to these groups are conceptions of a male-female pair, not men and women separately, as socially significant, recalling Marilyn Strathern's (1981:167–69) cautions about the culture-bound nature of assumptions of the individual as a natural analytic unit. Complementarity in each case is constructed by and expressed in distinctive productive and ritual roles. These gender codes rely not on biological features, but on the actions of men and women as culturally constituted within these societies.

Gender complementarity places an emphasis on the relations between men and women, not simply their presumed essential character. Male and female in Zinacantan are at a most basic level conceived of as mother and father, daughter and son. "The most productive gender terms in Tzotzil are *me'*, mother, and *tot*, father. . . . *Me'*, extended, carries a causative element of meaning, which has to do with the origins of things. . . . *Tot*, on the other hand, is used in metaphoric extension to convey the notion of authority, overlordship" (Devereaux 1987:92). Together, *totilme'il* means parents, ritual advisers, and the collective, ancestral gods. The gender totality in Zinacantan embodies notions both of origin and of authority.

The importance of a gender dichotomy subsumed in a single encompassing being is a characteristic feature of many Mesoamerican systems. The Aztec creator god, Ometeotl, was a single entity with male and female aspects, Ometecuhtli and Omecihuatl (Leon-Portilla 1963:99–111). Aztec governance embodied this creative duality in the offices of *tlatoani* and *cihuacoatl*, both held by men, but gendered male and female (Gillespie 1989:62–63, 133). While scholars debate the actual status of women in Aztec society and the degree to which Aztec state religion expressed violent subordination of women (see Brumfiel, this volume), what is remarkable here is the resilience of this basic Mesoamerican concept even in the face of extreme centralization and a state ideology that may have disparaged female gender.

Such concepts are not limited to Mesoamerican or other native American cultures. The Kodi of Indonesia, for example, stress a "complementary dualism that makes the participation of both male and female elements a requirement for all creative production and a characteristic of overarching power" (Hoskins 1990:275) and embody this in double-gendered deities similar to Ometeotl. Although all Kodi are conceived to initially have both male and female attributes, adult gender identity is produced by the elimination of the attributes of the opposite gender through ritual. Only Kodi deities are fully and permanently double-gendered, while some ritual practitioners are required to cross gender lines to temporarily reconstitute the dual-gendered status. The presentation of complementary gender imagery in Classic Maya centers is similarly related to the assertion of power like that of primordial beings.

Comprehensive Gender Identity and Power

Classic Maya images that incorporate aspects of both male and female costumes simultaneously convey gender difference and encompass it. Because the gender identities constructed in monumental images in Classic Maya centers deemphasize sexual characteristics, they are independent of reproductive sexuality. The gender identities could be assumed with the costume elements that embodied them. Male and female costumes could be combined in ways that blurred the boundary between the dichotomous gender poles they represented, creating a costume reflecting other genders encompassing maleness and femaleness. Because of the association of gender combination in Mesoamerica with creator gods, these combined gender costumes embodied great cosmological power. The combined costumes themselves represented images of the total natural universe: the horizontal plane of the earth's surface and the vertical axis of the central world tree.

Distinct modes of incorporating the paired costume in a single image are found (Table 6.4). A short kilt of bead lattice may take the place of the skirt, but the fish-monster-and-shell belt ornament is used. Com-

TABLE 6.4. Actions associated with net-skirt costume variants.

Monument location	Costume variant*	Action	Object held
INSIDE BUILDINGS			
Palenque sarcopha-gus lid	Short kilt	Falls into under-world	
Palenque oval tablet			Drum-major head-dress
Palenque palace tablet			Unwrapped bundle with flint and shield in bowl
Palenque Temple 14			Unwrapped bundle with God K mani-kin
Palenque Temple of the Foliated Cross	Short kilt		Unwrapped bundle with manikin
Palenque Bodega 186			Throne bar
Xupa, Chiapas			Throne bar and bundle
IN PUBLIC VIEW			
Paired images			
Naranjo Stela 3	Loincloth		Bloodletter?
Naranjo Stela 24			Bowl
Naranjo Stela 29			Bowl
Calakmul Stela 28			Double-headed bar
Calakmul Stela 88, back			Double-headed bar
Cancuen Stela 1			Double-headed bar
Yaxchilan Stela 1			Double-headed bar
Yaxchilan Stela 4			Double-headed bar
Copan Stela H	Jaguar skin kilt		Double-headed bar
Coba Stela 1, front	Loincloth		Double-headed bar
Tikal Stela 1	Short kilt and Loincloth		Double-headed bar
El Zapote Stela 5			Glyph
Xultun Stela 24	Loincloth		Jaguar cub in right hand, serpent on left arm
Xultun Stela 25	Loincloth		Jaguar cub in right hand, serpent on left arm
Xultun Stela 23	Loincloth		Manikin in right hand, serpent on left arm

TABLE 6.4. Continued.

Monument location	Costume variant*	Action	Object held
IN PUBLIC VIEW			
Paired images			
Calakmul Stela 54			Manikin scepter and water lily
Palenque Temple of the Inscriptions, east pier	Loincloth		Manikin scepter personified as baby
Palenque Temple of the Inscriptions, west pier	Short kilt and Loincloth		Manikin scepter personified as baby
Cleveland stela			Shield and flapstaff
Unpaired images			
Yaxchilan Structure 33 Hieroglyphic Stairway, Step VII	Short kilt	Plays ballgame accompanied by dwarfs with Venus signs	
Copan Altar T		Sits in rows with animal monsters	
Dos Pilas Stela 6			Double-headed bar
Altar Stela 1			Double-headed bar
Caracol Stela 1	Short kilt		Double-headed bar
Caracol Stela 3	Short kilt		Double-headed bar
Naranjo Stela 31			Double-headed bar
Naranjo Stela 37	Loincloth		Double-headed bar
Piedras Negras Stela 8	Short kilt and Loincloth		Spear and rectangular shield

*Costume includes beaded skirt and belt with fish monster and shell unless noted as a variant.

bined with a bare chest without breasts this variant identifies the reproductive sexual status of the person as not-female, while otherwise
presenting a female gender image. The short kilt is sometimes combined with a male loincloth, in images where the chest is not completely
visible. At Piedras Negras, this costume marks the portrait of a warrior.
The similarly dressed figure on Tikal Stela 1 holds the double-headed
serpent bar. A ballplayer from the central step of the Hieroglyphic Stair-
way of Yaxchilan Structure 33 combines a short beaded kilt with a variant loincloth. The short beaded kilt and world-tree loincloth contrast
with another mixed costume, the long beaded skirt and loincloth. That
these are different combined costumes is suggested by their pairing on

figures on the piers of the Temple of the Inscriptions at Palenque. The long net skirt with world-tree loincloth is a combination commonly worn by figures identified in texts as men, for example at Xultun (Figure 6.3).

More generally, Classic Maya texts, like Classic Maya sculptural images, suggest that complementary contributions of male and female were emphasized as part of the construction of political power. Three-figure compositions at Palenque show rulers receiving regalia from mother and father (Schele 1979). Even when no female image is depicted, parentage statements are a common element in Classic Maya texts. Following the personal name and titles of the ruler, the paired names of mother and father are presented, linked by signs that have been glossed as "child of woman" and "child of man." Paired men and women in texts are primarily represented in relation to an individual who is the product of their collaboration. The general rarity of references to husbands and wives in Classic Maya inscriptions is notable in contrast. Culturally constructed male and female roles and images are the background for the power of individual rulers who assert claims to represent in themselves the split and complementary totality that they would like to control.

Discussion

The Classic Maya images considered in this chapter represent sequences of ritual action consistent with an emphasis on cosmological gender complementarity in spatial and symbolic elements of the compositions. As media for the construction of gender, these images are ideological propositions. They provide a beginning point for a consideration of practice, particularly as it relates to gender relations in ritual, and extending by implication to questions of diversity of practice by individuals in different social positions.

The major sixteenth-century account of Maya ritual in Yucatan describes complementary ritual roles for males and females both in the temples and in households (Joyce 1992a:66–68). In the ritual *cargo* systems of the contemporary Maya, gender complementarity is evident in practice. In cargo systems, selected individuals spend a year providing services and performing ceremonies necessary for the public celebration of the feast of a saint important to the community. Through cargo service, status is earned at the cost of the expenditure of substantial economic resources. Only married men can assume a cargo position, which calls for the gender-specific work of both man and woman (Vogt 1969:241). The labor of the wife is indispensable in the preparation of meals, a constant part of cargo rituals, while the economic burdens of the cargo are partly financed through aid from kin of both husband

and wife (Devereaux 1987:94–95). Women act as *named* ritual assistants (Vogt 1969:266–68), including postmenopausal women who tend burning censers used in purification ceremonies (*Hchik' pometik*), old women who "direct the work in the kitchen which will serve special foods on certain ritual occasions" and are "responsible for knowing the requirements of food and of etiquette in serving for various fiestas" (*Hpachvaneh ve'elil*), a woman who presides over certain ritual feasts (*Hk'el ve'elil*), and a drink measurer who pours rum from a storage vessel into individual bottles (*Hch'ol vo'*). The use of a special garment called the *chilil*, worn by the *Hchik' pometik* and by the women who serve the ritual meal during the consecration of new cargo holders (Vogt 1969:98–101, 511) is another indication of the formalization of their ritual status. The common requirement that female ritual assistants be old, often postmenopausal, suggests an association of higher status with older women. Regardless of her actual age, similar status is accorded the wife of the cargo holder, who receives the title "Mother" of the man's named position (Gossen 1974:40–41).

Descriptions of the ceremonies undertaken by the Mayordomos of Zinacantan provide an example of the interdependence of male and female action in ritual (Vogt 1969:485–88, 498–99, 501–2, 508–9). Female Incense Bearers tend censers during ceremonies in the house of the cargo holder. During construction of decorated house altars, the male Mayordomos bow to these women and wait to be released in the gesture that embodies recognition of seniority in Zinacantan (Vogt 1969:239–40). Kneeling on a mat, the Incense Bearers make bouquets of flowers and leaves that the Mayordomos use to decorate the altar, and later both the Mayordomos and the Incense Bearers burn candles as food for the saints. On other occasions, the Incense Bearers kneel on the mat while the saints' necklaces, stored in cloth bundles in special chests, are counted and purified in the smoke of their censers. When the Mayordomos dance as part of each of these ceremonies, the Incense Bearers dance in a line behind them. The spatial relationships of the Mayordomos and the Incense Bearers reiterate the contrasts of high and low, front and back, present in Classic Maya monuments. The recognition of seniority embodied in the release gesture suggests that the women's ritual status is high.

Imagery of complementary roles in ritual in Classic Maya monuments may reflect participation by women in ritual like the practices noted among the sixteenth-century and contemporary Maya. While the genders constructed through the depiction of paired costumes in Classic Maya monuments embody the ideology of gender complementarity associated with ritual and cosmological contexts, the muting of biological features in these images stresses a unified elite identity that allowed the assumption of both gender identities by single actors. The complementary costumes, spatial relations, and actions represented as female were open to visible appropriation in ritual practice by the male rulers of individual sites.

Gender and Labor in Practice

Connections between gender and labor are intimately related to social status derived from work. In the two-spirit phenomenon of North America, in which a person takes on cross-sex gender identity, gender was defined primarily by dress and occupation and "of the two attributes, occupational preference and dress, it is the first that is most often mentioned and commented on, inclining us to believe that it was the most central of the social attributes definitive of gender" (Whitehead 1981:88). In these societies, the association of gender and occupational specialization was related to an ethic "centered largely upon individual variation in prestige-relevant occupations. The reason this ideology bore upon gender-anomalous behavior at all is that gender itself was heavily defined in terms of prestige-relevant occupations" where a woman's production of valued goods "redounded to her own credit officially, and not simply informally" (Whitehead 1981:102, 104). As part of a general emphasis on personal achievement, the male two-spirit could practice a prestigious activity otherwise not open to men.

In the sociopolitical context of stratified societies typical of Mesoamerica, a native American association of gender with craft and craft with prestige might have been played out differently than in North American cultures. Harriet Whitehead (1981:112–13) found a general association of two-spirits with cultures in which women practiced prestigious crafts. Although she suggested that in Mesoamerica a lack of prestigious production activities carried out by women may have limited the development of similar cross-gender statuses, textiles were crucial prestige goods produced by women. Evidence of production of textiles within nonruling elite households has been documented for the Classic Maya site of Copan (Hendon 1992). Among the Aztec, elaborate textiles were a primary tribute good and women's labor in producing them was important in negotiation of sociopolitical status (Brumfiel 1991:226, 229, 245). Instead of accruing to the craftsperson, however, the products and prestige associated with textile production were subject to appropriation by the household group, its leaders, and ultimately political authorities.

The assumption of female costume by male rulers in Classic Maya society may have reflected not only the symbolic assertion of totalizing ability, but also a claim to the control of the products of female labor.

This rhetorical strategy was not uncontested. Images in more abundant and widely distributed Classic Maya media, painted pottery and ceramic figurines, represent women's activities more explicitly than monumental images, while men are depicted in the same range and type of action (Joyce 1993a:260–63). Women appear as sexual beings with explicitly marked breasts, their reproductive role marked by the presence of children. These female figures weave, grind corn and cook, and offer food in ceramic vessels. In her analysis of shifts in frequencies and subjects of figurines in provincial Aztec sites, Elizabeth Brumfiel (this volume) demonstrates a similar divergence in official and popular imagery of women, citing imagery of reproduction in particular as present in popular images and absent from official images.

The muting of references to women's labor in Maya public monuments may represent elite interests in deemphasizing the potential economic independence of individual households as part of state formation. In her analyses of historic Tonga, Christine Ward Gailey (1987a, 1987b) demonstrates that control of women's labor became a subject of contention between men attempting to create centralized power and other men resisting efforts at centralization that would erode their own status, in part by increasing their control over women of their kin group (compare Muller 1987). While the political contention involved is actually between socioeconomic kin groups that attempt and resist centralization, women's independent action becomes the symbol and site of attempted control and resistance. By representing female figures in ritual action, Classic Maya monumental images presented women as part of an elite class and subordinated their distinctive abilities and crucial contributions to socioeconomic survival to the goals of that class.

Conclusion

The Classic Maya imagery discussed in this chapter represents rhetorical constructions of gender. I have argued that there were diverse gender constructions in monumental and small-scale images reflecting distinct interests. The emphasis in monumental imagery on costume created gender identities divorced from biological characteristics, allowing the assumption of these by male rulers. The deemphasis of biological characteristics and the narrowing of action to ritual action stressed the role of the ruling elite and the cohesion of this group. Small-scale images on ceramics and figurines used by nonruling elites highlight the productive labor and reproductive status of women in ways that suggest a tension between ruling elites and potentially independent residential groups. In this contest of ideologies, the narratives implied in images seek to naturalize history; as Barthes notes, narrative "seems to found in nature the signs of culture" (1977c:45–46; see also 1977b:116). By reference to implicit narrative chains the symbolic content of the connotative code gains a historical reality: "the discontinuous connotators are connected, actualized, 'spoken' through the syntagm of the denotation, the discontinuous world of symbols plunges into the story of the denoted scene as though into a lustral bath of innocence" (Barthes 1977c:51).

None of the representations of gender discussed here can be assumed to mirror the actual status of women within Classic Maya society. Despite an ideology of ritual interdependence, Laymi women are largely absent from community-level ritual and political process and are subject to considerable violent treatment by men (Harris 1978:32–37). In Zinacantan, differential access for men and women to public roles and resources leads to inequalities in the realization of interests despite a gender ideology of complementarity (Devereaux 1987:102–10). Some implications of the imagery of gender in Classic Maya society for actual status and role of women may be inferred, however, from the conflict between images of gender and the areas of practice they implicate.

Annette Weiner's (1976, 1989) descriptions of how women's control over their production of goods necessary for ritual results in power and status in Oceania has particular relevance for the Classic Maya. Women's production of textiles and food necessary for ritual in sixteenth-century Yucatan created a similar opportunity for Maya women, and Classic Maya antecedents are suggested by the imagery of women's production in small-scale ceramic figurines and painted pots. But Gailey (1987b) argues that in political centralization, the separation of control of production from kinship groups erodes the status of female producers, particularly when potential independence of kinship groups based on women's production is perceived as a threat to centralized political authority. This kind of conflict seems evident in the contrast between Classic Maya monumental and small-scale images of gender. The recognition of women's production recorded in small-scale images may reflect greater status of women in nonruling elite residential groups as a result of their labor.

While Gailey's analysis would suggest that successful centralization of Classic Maya society inevitably produced an erosion of women's status, the example of Inka expansion shows the importance of considering internal differentiation within complex societies (Silverblatt 1987, 1988:439–44). The Inka transformed indigenous concepts of gender complementarity in cosmology into an ideology of gender hierarchy. They extracted textiles produced by nonelite women through a tribute system, and even exercised direct control over women weavers moved to administrative centers as *aqlla*, ritual virgins (see Murra 1989). Yet Irene Silverblatt (1988:440–42) stresses the continuation of the ideology and practice of gender parallelism outside the narrow confines of the Inka administrative structure, under which Andean women's status and power were maintained. Brumfiel's analysis of shifts in figurines in Mexican sites brought under different degrees of Aztec political control (this volume) makes a similar point. Despite an official gender ideology that includes disturbing imagery of the mutilation of women, Brumfiel finds increases in the presentation of female subjects in the popular media of figurines, in particular of women in reproductive roles that might be of special concern to the survival of their kin groups.

The data on Maya women's participation in ritual in sixteenth-century Yucatan also suggest a bifurcation in the experience of women, with restrictions on their participation in centralized ritual in the temples contrasting with their necessary cooperation in household level ritual. The experience of women in Classic Maya society undoubtedly varied in similar ways. Even in ideologically constrained monumental images, women of the ruling elite are represented as differing in experience. Joyce Marcus (1976:150–82) has discussed the high visibility of women in secondary centers of the Classic Maya world, relating their prominence to the possibilities they represent of affiliation with more powerful centers. In secondary centers, the status of individual elite women might have been higher and their opportunities to exercise power greater than in primary centers.

Monumental images incorporated in the architecture of Classic Maya centers attempted to "naturalize" and represent as permanent particular gender constructions that served the purposes of certain segments of society. Complementary action in ritual acted as a metaphor of elite comprehension of the natural world symbolized in costume and the social world represented through gender. Monumental images muted other constructions of gender, including the diverse contributions to production and reproduction celebrated in contemporary small-scale images. Conflicting representations of gender highlight its cultural construction and recall the diversity of experience that Irene Silverblatt (1988:453, 454) urges us to reclaim:

Beware of bogus identifications, that, in the name of Woman, have buried women and their conflicting experiences and future goals. . . . Now aware of gender's social construction, we can ask about its double direction: how it can carry the mystique of state power into the very marrow of human identity; while confused with biological attributes of sex, it can bring feelings of "naturalness" to the machinations of state power.

Acknowledgments

This is a revised version of a paper presented at the annual meeting of the American Anthropological Association in New Orleans (1990) in the session "The Engendered Subject: Practice and Representation in Mesoamerica," organized by Geoffrey McCafferty and Veronica Kann. I owe both of these scholars my thanks for the invitation and for the stimulation provided by their work. My discussion is based on inspection of photographs and drawings published in the *Corpus of Maya Hieroglyphic Inscriptions*, Robertson, Rands, and Graham (1972), Beetz and Satterthwaite (1981), Jones and Satterthwaite (1982), Schele and Mathews (1979), Tate (1991), other published sources cited in the text, and unpublished images from my own slide collection and the photographic collections of the Peabody Museum. I would like to acknowledge the contribution to the development of this essay made by conversations with Chris Fung, who as a student in my graduate seminar prompted me to begin a thorough review of the associations of figures wearing the beaded lattice costume. I would also like to acknowledge the generosity of Lea McChesney in allowing me to read her unpublished review of the literature on gender and hierarchy. The ideas presented here are part of work in progress in collaboration with Susan Gillespie. The comments of James Taggart, Lynn Stephens, Rita Wright, and an anonymous reviewer on earlier versions of this essay were of great value in my revision. Of course, none of these individuals is responsible for the specific conclusions I have drawn, or for errors and omissions in this work.

References

Barthes, Roland
  1977a "Diderot, Brecht, Eisenstein." In *Image-Music-Text*, translated by Stephen Heath, 69–78. New York: Noonday Press.
  1977b "Introduction to the Structural Analysis of Narratives." In *Image-Music-Text*, translated by Stephen Heath, 79–124. New York: Noonday Press.
  1977c "Rhetoric of the Image." In *Image-Music-Text*, translated by Stephen Heath, 32–51. New York: Noonday Press.
Beetz, Carl, and Linton Satterthwaite
  1981 *The Monuments and Inscriptions of Caracol, Belize*. Philadelphia: University Museum Monograph 45, University Museum, University of Pennsylvania.
Bruhns, Karen
  1988 "Yesterday the Queen Wore . . . An Analysis of Women and Costume in Public Art of the Late Classic Maya." In *The Role of Gender in Precolumbian Art and Architecture*, edited by Virginia Miller, 105–34. Lanham, Md.: University Press of America.
Brumfiel, Elizabeth
  1991 "Weaving and Cooking: Women's Production in Aztec Mexico." In *Engendering Archaeology: Women and Prehistory*, edited by Joan M. Gero and Margaret W. Conkey, 224–51. Oxford: Basil Blackwell.
Butler, Judith
  1990 *Gender Trouble: Feminism and the Subversion of Identity*. New York: Routledge.

Devereaux, Leslie
 1987   "Gender Difference and Relations of Inequality in Zinacantan." In
         Dealing with Inequality: Analysing Gender Relations in Melanesia and Be-
         yond, edited by Marilyn Strathern, 89–111. Cambridge: Cambridge
         University Press.
Gailey, Christine Ward
 1987a   "Culture Wars: Resistance to State Formation." In *Power Relations and*
         State Formation, edited by Thomas C. Patterson and Christine Ward
         Gailey, 35–56. Washington, D.C.: Archaeology Section/American
         Anthropological Association.
 1987b   *Kinship to Kingship: Gender Hierarchy and State Formation in the Tongan*
         Islands. Austin: University of Texas Press.
Gillespie, Susan D.
 1989   *The Aztec Kings: The Construction of Rulership in Mexica History*. Tucson:
         University of Arizona Press.
Gossen, Gary
 1974   *Chamulas in the World of the Sun*. Cambridge, Mass.: Harvard Univer-
         sity Press.
Graham, Ian
 1970   "The Ruins of La Florida, Peten, Guatemala." In *Monographs and*
         Papers on Maya Archaeology, edited by William Bullard, 425–55. Papers
         of the Peabody Museum of Archaeology and Ethnology, Harvard
         University, vol. 61, Cambridge, Mass.
Harris, Olivia
 1978   "Complementarity and Conflict: An Andean View of Women and
         Men." In *Sex and Age as Principles of Social Differentiation*, edited by
         J. S. LaFontaine, 21–40. Association of Social Anthropologists Mono-
         graph 17. London: Academic Press.
 1980   "The Power of Signs: Gender, Culture, and the Wild in the Bolivian
         Andes." In *Nature, Culture, and Gender*, edited by Carol MacCor-
         mack and Marilyn Strathern, 70–94. Cambridge: Cambridge Univer-
         sity Press.
Hendon, Julia A.
 1992   "Hilado y tejido en la epoca prehispanica: Tecnología y relaciones
         sociales de la produccion textil." In *La indumentaria y el tejido Mayas a*
         traves del tiempo, edited by Linda Asturias and Dina Fernandez, 7–16.
         Monograph 8 of the Museo Ixchel del Traje Indígena, Guatemala.
Herzfeld, Michael
 1992   "Metapatterns: Archaeology and the Uses of Evidential Scarcity." In
         Representations in Archaeology, edited by Jean Gardin and Christopher
         Peebles, 66–86. Bloomington: Indiana University Press.
Hoskins, Janet
 1990   "Doubling Deities, Descent, and Personhood: An Exploration of
         Kodi Gender Categories." In *Power and Difference: Gender in Island*
         Southeast Asia, edited by Jane Monnig Atkinson and Shelly Errington,
         273–306. Stanford, Calif.: Stanford University Press.
Jones, Christopher, and Linton Satterthwaite
 1982   *The Monuments and Inscriptions at Tikal: The Carved Monuments*. Tikal
         Report, vol. 33 (A). Philadelphia: University Museum, University of
         Pennsylvania.

Joyce, Rosemary
    1992a   "Images of Gender and Labor Organization in Classic Maya Society."
            In *Exploring Gender through Archaeology: Selected Papers from the 1991
            Boone Conference*, edited by Cheryl Claassen, 63–70. Monographs in
            World Archaeology, no. 11. Madison, Wis.: Prehistory Press.
    1992b   "Dimensiones simbolicas del traje en monumentos clasicos Mayas:
            La construccion del genero a traves del vestido." In *La indumentaria
            y el tejido Mayas a traves del tiempo*, edited by Linda Asturias and Dina
            Fernandez, 29–38. Monograph 8 of the Museo Ixchel del Traje Indí-
            gena, Guatemala.
    1993a   "Women's Work: Images of Production and Reproduction in Prehis-
            panic Southern Central America." *Current Anthropology* 34(3):255–74.
    1993b   "Work, Ritual, Politics, and Status: The Changing Position of Women
            in Prehispanic Maya States." In the symposium "Women and the
            State," organized by Rita Wright. American Anthropological Asso-
            ciation, Washington, D.C.
Leon-Portilla, Miguel
    1963   *Aztec Thought and Culture.* Norman: University of Oklahoma Press.
Marcus, Joyce
    1976   *Emblem and State in the Classic Maya Lowlands.* Washington, D.C.: Dum-
            barton Oaks.
    1987   *The Inscriptions of Calakmul: Royal Marriage at a Maya City in Campeche,
            Mexico.* Ann Arbor: University of Michigan Museum of Anthropology
            Technical Report 21.
Miller, Jeffrey
    1974   "Notes on a Stela Pair Probably from Calakmul, Campeche, Mexico."
            In *Primera Mesa Redonda de Palenque, Part 1*, edited by Merle Greene
            Robertson, 149–61. Pebble Beach, Calif.: Robert Louis Stevenson
            School.
Muller, Viana
    1987   "Kin Reproduction and Elite Accumulation in the Archaic States of
            Northwest Europe." In *Power Relations and State Formation*, edited by
            Thomas C. Patterson and Christine Ward Gailey, 81–97. Washington,
            D.C.: Archaeology Section/American Anthropological Association.
Murra, John V.
    1989   "Cloth and Its Function in the Inca State." In *Cloth and Human Experi-
            ence*, edited by Annette Weiner and Jane Schneider, 275–302. Wash-
            ington, D.C.: Smithsonian Institution Press.
Proskouriakoff, Tatiana
    1960   "Historical Implications of a Pattern of Dates at Piedras Negras,
            Guatemala." *American Antiquity* 25 (4):454–75.
    1961   "Portraits of Women in Maya Art." In *Essays in Pre-Columbian Art and
            Archaeology*, edited by Samuel K. Lothrop et al., 81–99. Cambridge,
            Mass.: Harvard University Press.
Robertson, Merle Greene, Robert Rands, and John Graham
    1972   *Maya Sculpture from the Southern Lowlands, the Highlands, and the Pacific
            Piedmont.* Berkeley, Calif.: Lederer, Street and Zeus.
Schele, Linda
    1979   "Genealogical Documentation on the Tri-Figure Panels at Palenque."
            In *Tercera Mesa Redonda de Palenque*, vol. 4, edited by Merle Greene

Robertson and Donnan Call Jeffers, 41–70. San Francisco: Pre-Columbian Art Research Institute.

Schele, Linda, and Peter Mathews
1979   *The Bodega of Palenque, Chiapas, Mexico.* Washington, D.C.: Dumbarton Oaks.

Schele, Linda, and Mary Ellen Miller
1986   *The Blood of Kings: Dynasty and Ritual in Maya Art.* Fort Worth, Texas: Kimball Art Museum.

Schlegel, Alice
1977   "Male and Female in Hopi Thought and Action." In *Sexual Stratification: A Cross-cultural view,* edited by Alice Schlegel, 245–69. New York: Columbia University Press.

Shapiro, Judith
1981   "Anthropology and the Study of Gender." *Soundings: An Interdisciplinary Journal* 64 (4):446–65.

Shore, Bradd
1981   "Sexuality and Gender in Samoa: Conceptions and Missed Conceptions." In *Sexual Meanings: The Cultural Construction of Gender and Sexuality,* edited by Sherry Ortner and Harriet Whitehead, 192–215. Cambridge: Cambridge University Press.

Silverblatt, Irene
1987   *Moon, Sun and Witches: Gender Ideologies and Class in Inca and Colonial Peru.* Princeton, N.J.: Princeton University Press.
1988   "Women in States." *Annual Reviews in Anthropology* 17:427–60.

Stone, Andrea
1988   "Sacrifice and Sexuality: Some Structural Relationships in Classic Maya Art." In *The Role of Gender in Pre-Columbian Art and Architecture,* edited by Virginia Miller, 75–104. Lanham, Md.: University Press of America.
1991   "Aspects of Impersonation in Classic Maya Art." In *Sixth Palenque Round Table, 1986,* edited by Merle Greene Robertson and Virginia Fields, 194–202. Norman: University of Oklahoma Press.

Strathern, Marilyn
1981   "Self-interest and the Social Good: Some Implications of Hagen Gender Imagery." In *Sexual Meanings: The Cultural Construction of Gender and Sexuality,* edited by Sherry Ortner and Harriet Whitehead, 166–91. Cambridge: Cambridge University Press.

Tarn, Nathaniel, and Martin Prechtel
1986   "Constant Inconstancy: The Feminine Principle in Atiteco Mythology." In *Symbol and Meaning beyond the Closed Community,* edited by Gary Gossen, 173–84. Albany: Institute for Mesoamerican Studies, State University of New York at Albany.

Tate, Carolyn
1991   "The Period-Ending Stelae of Yaxchilan." In *Sixth Palenque Round Table, 1986,* edited by Merle Greene Robertson and Virginia Fields, 102–9. Norman: University of Oklahoma Press.

Taube, Karl
1985   "The Classic Maya Maize God: A Reappraisal." In *Fifth Palenque Round Table, 1983,* edited by Merle Greene Robertson and Virginia Fields, 171–81. San Francisco: Pre-Columbian Art Research Institute.

Vogt, Evon Z.
  1969   *Zinacantan: A Maya Community in the Highlands of Chiapas.* Cambridge,
          Mass.: Harvard University Press.
Weiner, Annette B.
  1976   *Women of Value, Men of Renown: New Perspectives in Trobriand Exchange.*
          Austin: University of Texas Press.
  1989   "Why Cloth? Wealth, Gender, and Power in Oceania." In *Cloth and
          Human Experience,* edited by Annette Weiner and Jane Schneider, 33–
          72. Washington, D.C.: Smithsonian Institution Press.
Whitehead, Harriet
  1981   "The Bow and the Burden Strap: A New Look at Institutionalized
          Homosexuality in Native North America." In *Sexual Meanings: The
          Cultural Construction of Gender and Sexuality,* edited by Sherry Ortner
          and Harriet Whitehead, 80–115. Cambridge: Cambridge University
          Press.

Part IV
Gender and Practice

Chapter 7
Gendered Perspectives in the Classroom

Janet V. Romanowicz
Rita P. Wright

In the preceding chapters, several examples of the ways in which gender issues may be addressed in archaeological contexts have been presented. Each has demonstrated how particular theoretical and methodological perspectives can be applied to issues that have been central to archaeological research agendas—demography, osteology, sexual division of labor, social identity and status, and ideological domination in states— as well as new considerations—reproductive ecology and reproductive status, gender attribution, and gender and technology. Although the perspectives of the individual scholars vary, they share a common interest in establishing feminist initiatives for understanding the role gender may play in structuring human societies, ideologies, economic systems, and political forms.

The three chapters in this section focus on gender issues in the teaching and practice of archaeology, activities which are integral to the archaeological enterprise. In Chapter 8, Margaret Conkey and Ruth Tringham explore the practice of teaching, in which they implement an interactive class format, conceived as coaching archaeology through panels. The courses they discuss, informed and motivated by aspects of feminist thought, are Archaeology and the Goddess, European and Mediterranean Archaeology, and Prehistoric Art. In the final chapter (9), Joan Gero examines assumptions about accepted field practices in archaeology and the "cognitive values that shape and guide" its inquiry.

In this chapter, we begin with our thoughts on why gender issues should be included in course offerings. Next, we discuss two levels of courses that incorporate gender issues into archaeology programs. First, we address the undergraduate or introductory level course and focus on incorporating gender into existing archaeology syllabi and established course offerings. This section is followed by a more formal outline of an upper-division undergraduate/graduate course dedicated to gender issues in archaeology. Finally, we consider ways to include engendered archaeology courses in campus-wide curricula, such as core curricula or women's studies. Our suggestions are based on our own experiences in the classroom and informal discussions with graduate students and faculty held at New York University with several contributors to this volume. Their varying personal experiences at colleges and universities of very different sizes and their diverse research interests provide alternative perspectives and ways to address gender issues in the classroom. Still, our suggestions by no means exhaust the available literature on this topic, and we encourage readers to consult other sources.[1]

Why Gender in Archaeology?

The biases and assumptions about gender that archaeologists bring to their research and practice are embedded in the general archaeological literature, such as in textbooks and review articles, and they must be directly challenged in the classroom. First, as Margaret Conkey and Janet Spector (1984) noted a decade ago, while archaeologists rarely mention the words "gender" or "sex," their analyses contain assumptions about them. Recent research on gender in archaeology generally has substantiated this claim as the contributions to this volume attest. Second, it is not that women are more visible in ethnography or history than they are in the archaeological record nor that they are inaccessible; rather, archaeologists have tended to project twentieth-century Euroamerican gender structures onto the past, thus making gender roles unchanging, uninteresting, and irrelevant to a study of cultural dynamics (Wylie 1991a, 1991b, 1992). For example, Alison Wylie notes that while an ecosystem paradigm or the study of large-scale culture processes should not necessarily exclude gender research, for much of "New Archaeology," which appeared on the scene at the same time as feminist research in other disciplines, gender is an ethnographic variable and thus not causal or worthy of study. She also argues that archaeologists must be prepared to bring women into view as subjects of research, and to do that we must develop a "conceptual framework that raises the relevant questions, directing attention to gender and providing the impetus to study women's activities and experiences" (1991a:32; see also Conkey and Gero 1991:23).

Given the above, a second rationale is that raising questions about gender in archaeology can be a focal point for the development of critical skills and evaluation of archaeological interpretations. In most archaeology courses, the topics traditionally covered have gender implications, although often these implications are not acknowledged in the lecture or assigned text. For example, can you (or should you) discuss resource procurement and use without considering who is obtaining and using these resources? While it is possible to talk about the development of hierarchy in the abstract, when we get down to specific case studies, we have to people these hierarchies and gender may be a significant factor in them.

A third rationale is that for too long archaeologists have ignored gender research in the discipline of anthropology as a whole. For example, until recently little research *explicitly* and *critically* evaluated prehistoric gender relations or women's social, economic, and political roles and contributions based on the archaeological record. Although there were some notable exceptions who examined the contribution of "woman the gatherer" to human evolution (Slocum 1975; Tanner and Zihlman 1976; Zihlman 1978, 1981), these authors were not archaeologists. A similar case could be made for state formation, if one considers the many discussions by social/cultural anthropologists about changes in gender relations in which they document the division of labor and loss of status by women (Leacock 1972; Silverblatt 1987; Gailey 1985) and raise many important questions about gender and early states (Rapp 1977). According to Rayna Rapp, in many historically documented states, colonizing powers subsume parallel forms of gender-linked relations of production and distribution under male activities so that "leadership and authority are assigned to activities which are male, while female tasks and roles are devalued, or obliterated" (Rapp 1977:313). A contribution that may be made by archaeology is to question whether the pattern known from these historically documented cases occurred in earlier states. While there may not be ready answers to these questions, this research, known to our students from other courses and readings, must be addressed.

Fourth, all archaeologists must be concerned about the public presentation of our discipline and the volumes of misinformation available in many bookstores, journalistic accounts, television programs, or films. Archaeology is a favorite topic in popular literature, and it comes in many forms, including children's books (see Burtt 1987 for a discussion of bias in children's literature). Archaeology courses that explicitly address these inaccurate accounts can be effective in laying to rest many erroneous myths about gender roles, such as mother goddesses, that both distort our results and serve as major ideological deterrents in the discussion of gender inequalities and other differences today. Courses that address gender issues in archaeology will provide a more realistic appraisal of the realities of women's lives in the earliest stages of human social and cultural development. Further, both in introductory and advanced level courses, directing students' attention to gender as a viable topic will enable them to develop the critical skills with which to evaluate presentations of ancient and contemporary women and men in both the scholarly literature and the more popular media. Addressing gender in these courses, therefore, is essential to informing students of many of the distortions in popular literature, which may have a ripple effect on the public perception of the past. In more advanced courses, discussions of gender issues in the popular media will sharpen students' critical skills and alert them to the ways in which the images that we create of the past affect the present.

Finally, in the suggestions that follow, our goal, as in the other chapters in this volume, is not merely "finding" women or attributing activities to different genders. Although determining female and male activities may be one part of the research, gender studies involve broader objectives such as the investigation of "gender ideologies, gender roles, gender relations, and all of the ways in which gender intersects and is influenced by other aspects of social life" (Conkey and Gero 1991:12).

Introductory Level Courses in Archaeology

Many of our students come to archaeology courses with a very limited understanding of both archaeology and gender-related issues, and an introductory course will be their only experience with the archaeological literature. As discussed above, in introductory level courses, students can be exposed to the questioning of many of the unexamined assumptions made by archaeologists in our research and technical reports and also those carried into the public domain through the media and even museum exhibitions.

The topics that we suggest for introducing gender issues into introductory courses provide general information and are selected from three standard types of archaeological evidence—architecture, artifacts, and ecofacts—in addition to gender bias. Here, we do not provide a syllabus for a particular course, but rather suggest topics that can be introduced into a variety of introductory courses, such as surveys of prehistory, human origins, method and theory. We also consider textbook selection and supplemental, source readings and offer some suggestions for related practical exercises (see also Spector and Whelan 1989:82–89).

Our suggestions for the introductory course can be implemented in classes with large or small enrollments organized around a standard lecture format, those in which discussion sections are employed, or those in which the coaching model discussed by Conkey and Tringham in this volume (Chapter 8) is employed. As we have indicated, our goal in this chapter is to provide suggestions that may be incorporated into preexisting course syllabi. Still, we are not suggesting that instructors simply "add women and stir," since each of our suggestions requires thoughtful implementation and a commitment to the idea that gender analysis is integral to archaeological interpretation.

Textbooks

The choice of a textbook often is one of the more frustrating aspects of designing a course. It is not that there are no good textbooks available, but that none exactly speaks to the intentions of an individual course or instructor. Courses in which gender issues are incorporated are particularly problematic since there has been little attention to gender in most texts. Still, in many courses, particularly introductory ones, textbooks serve as the major source for discussions of scientific dating methods, stone tool typologies, techniques for pollen analysis, and other aspects of archaeological knowledge that students fear they must memorize and then reproduce on exams (see Conkey and Tringham in Chapter 8 of this volume for comments on the "banking method" of teaching). Yet textbooks also interpret and synthesize research results for presentation to nonspecialists. Where bias exists in the scholarly literature, it may be reproduced and reflected in textbooks. For example, Sarah Nelson, in a discussion of the treatment of Upper Paleolithic female figurines, found that texts ignored the rich literature that explores variation in the form of the figurines and their possible meanings and functions, as well as the great range of time and geographic space involved in their distribution (Nelson 1990:11–12). She attributes this homogenization to the underlying interpretation that figurines were made by men and served erotic or reproductive purposes for men, which she argues derives from a "masculist construction of the world," where "females are assumed to exist primarily for the use of males, sexually or reproductively" (Nelson 1990:16). These generalities then are picked up and reflected in archaeology textbooks.

Given the potential for bias that Nelson's article cogently illustrates and the tremendous influence textbooks have as disseminators of "facts," the choice of a textbook is crucial. We consider that, in seeking out a good textbook for courses in which gender issues are introduced, an important consideration is whether it bridges the gaps between scholarly research, potential bias, and popular conceptions. Since students regard the textbook as the "authority" in a given field, even subtle issues of gender difference are more easily conveyed and accepted as serious ones if they are directly addressed by a major archaeologist (Conkey in Wright and Romanowicz 1994). Unfortunately, there is no textbook that deals comprehensively with gender issues.[2] Two books that have been recommended to us by colleagues are David Hurst Thomas's *Archaeology* (1989), a text that explicitly addresses gender issues in some sections, and Thomas Patterson's *Archaeology: The Historical Development of Civilizations* (1993). While others such as *The Emergence of Humankind* by John Pfeiffer (1985) have adopted some gender-neutral language, there continues to be significant gender bias in interpretation. Of course, biases of this kind can serve instructors as points for discussions.

Supplemental Source Readings

Whether a suitable textbook can or cannot be found, courses can include supplementary readings that specifically address gender issues. Here we suggest both scholarly and popular articles as aids to expanding upon issues raised in texts or to introducing questions not addressed in them.

There currently are a number of sources from which to select supplemental readings on gender. In 1989, when the American Anthropological Association put together the volume *Gender and Anthropology* (Morgen 1989) to serve as a guide to incorporating gender in undergraduate courses, a search of the literature for books or articles by anthropological archaeologists yielded few sources (Spector and Whelan 1989).[3] Janet Spector and Mary Whelan's annotated bibliography remains useful, but two others now are more up-to-date. A bibliography in *A Gendered Past* (Bacus et al. 1993) includes 197 references of published works on gender in archaeology, and Cheryl Claassen's *Exploring Gender through Archaeology* (1992) refers to papers delivered at archaeological conferences between 1964 and 1992. The latter is available on disk. Some books published after these bibliographies were prepared include *Women in Archaeology* (Claassen 1994), *Women in Archaeology: A Feminist Critique* (du Cros and Smith 1993), *The Archaeology of Gender: Separating the Spheres in Urban America* (Wall 1994), and *Equity Issues for Women in Archeology* (Nelson, Nelson, and Wylie 1994).

Topics

Our suggestions begin with a discussion of gender bias drawn from popular literature; we then concentrate on architecture, artifacts, and ecofacts. With respect to architecture, our focus is household archaeology; with artifacts, material culture studies; and with ecofacts, floral and faunal analyses. Each topic is flexible and should easily fit into any introductory level course and format (see Table 7.1).

TABLE 7.1. Selected gender topics for introductory level undergraduate courses.*

I. Gender Bias

This topic relies on popular literature to focus student awareness on gender bias. Instructors can draw on reports from *National Geographic, Discover, Time, Newsweek,* or *U.S. News and World Report.* The underlying racism and Eurocentrism, as well as the invisibility of women in many of these reports can be perceived easily by students.

II. Architecture and Household Archaeology

This topic focuses on household archaeology as a logical place to begin to draw attention to gendered spaces in the archaeological record, not because women are always to be associated with domestic labor (housework) but because households are places where we can reasonably assume that both males and females are present.

III. Artifacts and Material Culture

This topic examines the role of material culture in human life. We use examples from American popular culture and from archaeological case studies in three different research contexts. One study relies on archaeological and ethnographic evidence, a second complements archaeological evidence with ethnohistoric accounts and a third uses historical documents and archaeological evidence.

IV. Ecofacts—Archaeobotanical/Zooarchaeological Remains

This topic concentrates on animal and plant remains in developing a gendered perspective. Several case studies are introduced in which gender-related issues are discussed; other published case studies are engendered by examining them for gender assumptions.

*For implementation with existing syllabi.

Gender Bias

In introductory courses, popular literature can serve as a useful tool to create student awareness of gender issues. Virtually all illustrated articles in the popular press on human evolution provide discussion-provoking text and imagery that drive home the way that unexamined assumptions about gender pervade our culture, are transposed onto the past, and result in our cultural stereotypes becoming biological givens, part of being "human"—a tautology that reinforces the notion that Western culture's "traditional" gender roles are both natural and inescapable.

As we have indicated, popular discussions of archaeological topics, although often grossly distorted, have their origins in scholarly literature. Scientific findings are reported in *National Geographic* (see both

Lutz and Collins 1993 and Gero and Root 1987 for critiques). *Discover* magazine also interprets science for the nonspecialist, and reports in newspapers and national magazines, such as *Time, Newsweek*, or *U.S. News and World Report*, are widely read. The underlying racism and Eurocentrism, as well as the invisibility of women in many of these articles, should be easily perceived by students. We provide a brief summary of the gender treatment in two popular magazines that we have used in courses, although we also recommend the discussion of this topic by Margaret Conkey with Sarah Williams (1991:116–20). A feminist perspective need not confine itself to gender bias alone; indeed engendering the past can only be enriched by considering, as Henrietta Moore has suggested for ethnography, "the complex ways in which gender, race and class intersect and cross-cut each other" (1990:10).

A pervasive bias is the representation of human evolution by only male figures. Students can easily perceive the bias in illustrations in which "human" is synonymous with "male." In *Discover* (May 1989), an article entitled "The Great Leap Forward" shows "our family tree" peopled only with males, and the illustration also gives the incorrect impression that Cro-Magnon represents an evolutionary advance over anatomically modern Africans. The cover of *U.S. News and World Report* (September 16, 1991) shows a bearded man (labeled as Cro-Magnon man, 36,000 years ago), and the title of the article reads "Early Man: The Radical New View of Where We Came From." All the illustrations in the article are of men, despite a section called "Eve's genes." This cover drawing at least manages to avoid the blatant racism in the *Newsweek* (November 10, 1986) cover article entitled "The Way We Were," which depicts a single white male. The "we" obviously ignores and excludes anyone who is not of Western European ancestry and places the emphasis on males as the inventors of "Our Ice Age Heritage: Language, Art, Fashion, and the Family." As Conkey and Williams point out, these topics are prominent features in media directed at upper/middle-class white America and prompt the reader to ask "What do you mean by 'WE'?" (1991:119–20).

A related exercise would be for students to scan magazines, newspapers, novels, or films such as *The Clan of the Cave Bear* (see Pollak 1991), advertisements, cartoons, television commercials, and any other forms of popular media for depictions of prehistory. Students can discuss whether these examples project middle-class American values onto the past. These caricatures of prehistory can provide useful and humorous illustrations of gender stereotypes and may lighten the tension when the topic of gender is introduced in class discussion. To emphasize the subtle ways in which gender and other differences are conveyed through imagery, the chapter "The Photograph as an Intersection of

Gazes" in Catherine Lutz and Jane Collins's *Reading National Geographic* (1993:187–216) and Adrienne Zihlman's discussion of "images of women and men in prehistory" (1989:39) provide useful descriptions. Students also could test some of the findings reported by Lutz and Collins, especially their provocative discussion of race, age, and gender differences with respect to perspectives on the camera gaze (1993:199) against their own sample of photographs.

Finally, in conjunction with a class discussion of popular science and gender bias, it may be a useful exercise to have students visit the local natural history or art museum and look at the way prehistory is "engendered" for public consumption. Students could comment both in written and oral discussion on the exhibit in response to questions such as: What are your thoughts on the entire exhibit (both positive and negative)? Can you detect any biases related to gender? Any other biases? What kinds of archaeological evidence are being used to reconstruct the past? How do you think the general public will perceive prehistoric gender roles? Do you think the depictions of females and males in the past are accurate? Can you think of any additional ways to depict females and males in the past? Would you have chosen the same activities and/or the same locales as most significant?[4]

Architecture and Household Archaeology

Household archaeology is a logical place to begin to draw attention to gendered spaces in the archaeological record. This is not because women are always to be associated with domestic labor (housework), but because households are places where we can reasonably assume that both males and females are present. Here, we follow Richard Blanton's definition of household as "a group of people coresiding in a dwelling or residential compound, and who, to some degree, share householding activities and decision making" (1994:5).

In her course in Mesoamerican archaeology, Rosemary Joyce introduces gender issues to undergraduate classes through discussions of the basic residential unit in Mesoamerica, the patio group. After providing a background to some well-documented cases, she asks students to discuss *who* is living in the household groups (both in terms of sex and age groups) and *who* is farming, toolmaking, or taking care of the children. Her point is not to arrive at an attribution of specific activities to specific genders, but rather to get at the notion that there can be a cluster of activities represented by the materials that come into the household, and that these activities are carried out by a diverse body of people who are not necessarily all doing the same things (Joyce in Wright and Romanowicz 1994:142–43; see also Joyce's comments in Claassen 1992:140–41).

These kinds of questions help students move into the lives of people in other cultures. They can be assisted in this endeavor through the use of ethnographic material and they may begin to question the imposition of our Western conceptions of gender roles on archaeological data. More importantly, however, students can begin to understand the social, political, and economic relations within household contexts and the relationship of these factors to other households and institutions outside of the household.

Household archaeology also can be useful in introducing students to the concept of macro- and microscales of analyses and the types of questions that can be addressed at different scales. Whereas it may be difficult to discuss gender in the context of macroscale analyses—trade and regional systems, for example (but see Zagarell 1986)—analyses on the microscale lend themselves to task-related activities. Clearly, household analyses bring archaeologists and students closer to understanding what people were actually doing and the relative value attached to certain activities. Just as archaeologists have made calculations of time allocated to craft production (for example, Feinman, Upham, and Lightfoot 1981), the same types of analyses can be applied to other household activities, which may represent group or individual male or female activities. With respect to gender attribution (Conkey and Gero 1991; Conkey 1991; Wylie 1991a, 1991b), even if we cannot "find" women or men in these contexts, the questions produce a "visibility of gender" (Tringham 1994:181) that has been missing from our constructions of the past.

Finally, the household as a unit of analysis and its relation to the macroscale, such as the community, region, or interregional "system," can establish a useful dialogue within the classroom. Ruth Tringham's discussion of the history of archaeology's general disregard of household archaeology is very important. Her basic argument is that archaeologists have ignored household production and relations, while in other social science disciplines the household (whether defined as co-residential group or family or in some other way) has been considered essential to the understanding of the social relations of production in the society as a whole (Tringham 1991, 1994). She believes the rationale for this neglect is that in archaeology "this scale of interpretation is thought to make no difference in the big picture of cultural evolution, being a constant rather than a variable in human social behavior" (Tringham 1994:171). Her central point is that, because in our own society households have been equated with housework, they have been considered irrelevant. In fact, nothing could be more central to social process than the social relations within households.

Artifacts and Material Culture

The role of material culture in human life, and specifically in re-inforcing gender roles in American society, is another aspect of popular culture that may help undergraduates to understand how archaeologists work. One example is from Elizabeth Brumfiel's course at Albion College in which she discusses how children's toys and video games can be used to explore with students the way the forms of these twentieth-century artifacts are determined by, yet continue to shape, our culture (Brumfiel in Wright and Romanowicz 1994:113). A related exercise would be to ask students to consider the material culture of some aspect of their own lives (for example, a dormitory room, fraternity or sorority house, department store, office) and discuss how a future archaeologist might interpret this "site," including what, if anything, the artifacts and their spatial organization could tell a researcher about gender roles and relations in our culture.

To bring the discussion back to archaeological evidence, we recommend two studies, each of which combines artifact analysis with other evidence. The studies vary in their ability, and even their attempt, to define the material correlates of gender roles in a specific culture. Joan Gero (1991:163ff.) combines ethnographic and other data with evidence for stone tool production in an archaeological context in north central highland Peru, and Elizabeth Brumfiel (1991:224ff.) utilizes archaeological and ethnohistoric data in a discussion of Aztec weaving and cooking.[5]

The article by Gero (1991) is an excellent example of the study of material culture in contexts for which written sources are not available. Gero relies principally on archaeological evidence, which she complements with investigations of biological, sociological, historical, ethnographic, ethnohistorical, and experimental data to counter the strong bias that assigns stone tool production to men. Since stone tool making often is a standard by which human intellectual evolution is measured, her study serves as a valuable introduction to the ways in which gender can be made visible in the archaeological record. It would be interesting to consider in class discussion how different our typologies might be if from the outset this male bias had been eliminated from lithic analysis (Conkey and Gero 1991:21). Discussion could challenge the initial linkage of male with stone tools and consider the implications for bias in the traditional research focus on elaborately finished stone tools and tool typologies at the expense of "unretouched" or "utilized" flakes.

Brumfiel's (1991) article on weaving and cooking in Aztec Mexico combines ethnohistoric sources with archaeological evidence. In it the points she raises about weaving and cooking that can serve as a basis for discussion include the variability of women's work (such as differences in types of work carried out by elite and commoner women), the political significance of women's activities, and the idealization of women's roles. Further, Brumfiel links her argument to the more general issues of political economy and anthropological literature on states.

In addition to these two studies, Judith McGaw's contribution to this volume (Chapter 2), although not archaeological, would provide a good introduction to the concept of "material culture." Chapters 3 through 6 of this volume provide additional research topics in which material culture is a primary focus.

Ecofacts—Archaeobotanical and Zooarchaeological Remains

Animal and plant remains are particularly well suited to a gendered perspective. Animal and plant domestication must have involved not only changes in land use, but also changes in the organization of labor. Domestic animals must be cared for year round, while plants must be sown, maintained, harvested, and stored for use during the fallow season and for replanting. Any discussion of this pivotal development should include a conscious consideration of changes in social organization, including potential shifts in gender-specific activities.

A number of recent studies deal with plant remains from a gendered perspective. Two readily accessible articles are those by Christine Hastorf (1991), who looks at evidence for the production and consumption of food to explore changing gender relations among the pre-Hispanic Sausa of Peru, and Patty Jo Watson and Mary Kennedy (1991), who reconsider the development of horticulture in the Eastern Woodlands. These articles combine analyses of the sexual division of labor, women's contributions to food production, and, in the case of Hastorf, the simultaneous intensification of women's roles in processing foods and their exclusion from consumption of foods associated with nonhousehold, sociopolitical activities.

Considering the implications of faunal evidence for social organization is standard practice in archaeology, although few researchers critically address gender issues. One example of a gendered analysis is Pamela Crabtree's (1991) review of Natufian evidence, which relies on what Richard Klein and Kathryn Cruz-Uribe (1984:56–57) have termed "catastrophic" age profiles. Crabtree contests the adoption for the Natufians of an unexamined division of labor (women gathering, fishing, and trapping small game while the men hunted large ungulates), including Donald Henry's suggestion, based on this proposed division of labor, that the society was both matrilineal and matrilocal (Henry 1989:51). She argues that since Natufian food resources were highly seasonal and required the coordinated labor of many people, both women and men would have participated in hunting gazelle and wild birds and gathering cereals.

A related class exercise could be to "engender" a published archaeological report. In a roundtable discussion at the 1991 Boone Conference, Rosemary Joyce suggested that Kent Flannery's 1968 article would be a good choice for this type of exercise (Claassen 1992:140). Flannery's article is thoughtful and informative, and its style and language make it accessible and interesting to undergraduates. Flannery's ecosystem approach was an early exploration of seasonality and scheduling in prehistoric Mesoamerica that avoided a simplistic division of labor into male hunters and female gatherers. Flannery makes no gender assumptions in this work, yet he provides a detailed description of seasonal resource availability, including a division of resources into those resources that must be procured rapidly due to short availability and competition from other animals and those that are available year round and more suited to solitary or small group procurement. Flannery's article easily lends itself to the inclusion of gender as a major analytic variable, which then allows the students themselves to work with the material to develop a richer and more detailed picture of the past.

Flannery's article can be juxtaposed with Crabtree's recent critique of interpretations of Natufian evidence (1991:384–90) discussed above. The goal of this comparative exercise, which addresses the viability and variability of a gendered division of labor in different cultures, would be to have students realize, as Judith McGaw has noted, that there is no single or simple "truth" out there (in Wright and Romanowicz 1994:180), but rather that gender roles and relations are important concepts with which archaeologists must grapple and that they are integral elements (even when it is unconscious) of most interpretations of prehistory. Students should come to realize that gender research involves more than a critique of existing bias in the literature; it can draw on the positive elements of earlier work and reinterpret the evidence by placing women and men, and the social and economic implications of their interrelationship, at the forefront of the analytic process.

Finally, the reproductive role of women and related issues raised by Gillian Bentley in Chapter 1 would serve as a good counterpoint to those raised by archaeologists with regard to population increase and reproductive fertility. In particular, differences among foragers and agriculturalists are discussed at some length in her chapter and elsewhere (Bentley, Goldberg, and Jasienska 1993; Bentley, Jasienska, and Goldberg 1993). Her discussions of nutritional needs and weaning foods for infants also are relevant to early cereal production.

TABLE 7.2. Selected topics for an advanced undergraduate/graduate level course on gender issues in archaeology.

I. Reflections on science and archaeology
  A. Feminist critiques of science
  B. Archaeology and the other subfields
  C. Archaeology at a cross-roads of knowledge production
II. Biological and social bases of gender differences
  A. Males and females in human evolution
  B. Primate behavior and human society
  C. Biological and social bases of gender roles and status
  D. Female reproductive ecology
III. Gender, power, and social life
  A. Mobile societies
  B. Sedentary communities
  C. Household archaeology
  D. Agriculture, demography and paleodemography
  E. Craft production and occupational specialization
  F. State level societies
IV. Gender and long-term historical processes
  A. Women's religious responses: example, from the twelfth to sixteenth centuries in medieval western Europe
  B. Women, economy, and society: examples from the third to second millennia B.C., Mesopotamia

An Advanced Undergraduate/Graduate Course

A course dedicated to gender issues in archaeology views gender as a historical problematic and a central category in the major historical transformations known from the archaeological record. Through the discussion of basic epistemological questions and examination of archaeologically grounded case studies, it promotes an understanding of, as Judith McGaw has phrased it, "those ideologies that have attributed certain characteristics to men and others to women . . . and the ways in which our gender notions shape the way we write . . . history" (1989:173) or, in this case, archaeology.

In designing the course outlined in Table 7.2,[6] our principal emphases are on examining many of the assumptions brought to the interpretation of archaeological materials about gender and to introduce students to as much of the developing body of literature in archaeology on this topic as practical. We have recommended some readings from this literature, but others can be drawn from bibliographic and supplemental source readings referred to in earlier sections of this chapter and in this volume.

The course is divided into four topical areas: reflections on science and archaeology; biological and social bases of gender difference; gender, power, and social life; and gender and long-term processes.

In the first topical area, reflections on science and archaeology, our intention is to familiarize students with feminist critiques of science. Our objective is not to indoctrinate them into these critiques (that is, to "convert" them), but we hope to promote an awareness of the very embeddedness of gender bias underlying much of scientific thought. An accessible and effective way to get into this discussion is through the writings of Evelyn Fox Keller (1985) and especially her PBS interview with Bill Moyers available on video. Using these discussions as a base, then, similar questions can be raised in the context of archaeology and the other subfields in anthropology, along with archaeology's place at a kind of crossroads of knowledge production.[7] Recommended source reading for these discussions are Conkey and Spector (1984), Gero and Conkey (1991), diLeonardo (1991, esp. chap. 1), Moore (1990), Wylie (1992, 1993) and Conkey and Tringham in Chapter 8 and Gero in Chapter 9 of this volume.[8] Readings from the recently published *Equity Issues for Women in Archaeology* (Nelson, Nelson, and Wylie 1994) by the American Anthropological Association and *Women in Archaeology* (Claassen 1994) also would be relevant to this segment of the course.

The second topical area, biological and social bases of gender differences, primarily focuses on the effects of biological determinants on the division of labor and on the roles and status of males and females. Feminist scholars differ in their perspectives on the relative impacts of biology and culture, and here, we introduce only some of the literature outside of anthropology. Some useful readings in related disciplines take the position of what sometimes is referred to as "difference feminism," for example, Nancy Chodorow (1978) on the reproduction of mothering and Carol Gilligan (1982) on differences between men and women in moral decision making.[9] These readings can be contrasted with others that emphasize the social construction of gender difference (for example, Fausto-Sterling 1985; Pollitt 1994, esp. 42ff.; and McGaw in this volume). To bring the topic back to anthropology and archaeology, some classic articles are Susan Rogers's (1978) critique of male-female interaction in peasant societies; Judith Brown's (1970) cross-cultural analysis of the division of labor by sex; Linda Fedigan's (1982) work on sex roles and social bonds among primates; Michelle Rosaldo and Louise Lamphere (1974); and the recent contributions of Anne Fausto-Sterling (1985) and Gillian Bentley (Chapter 1, this volume).

The third topical area, gender, power, and social relations, addresses these issues in a variety of contexts. Earlier in this chapter, we recommended several topics that could be included in this section (for example, see our discussion of Crabtree 1991). Here, we recommend an explicit focus on the concept of power, gender studies, and evolutionary comparative analysis. A selection of recommended readings on these topics are Wylie (1992), Gailey (1987), Silverblatt (1987, 1988), Leacock (1983), McGaw (1989), Nash (1978), and Sacks (1979). For archaeological case studies we recommend Brumfiel (1991), Wright (1991), Pollock (1991), and contributions in this volume by Costin (Chapter 4), Wright (Chapter 3), Brumfiel (Chapter 5), and Joyce (Chapter 6) for an examination of state level societies. Further, we recommend discussions of gender, power, and multiscalar analyses, especially Ruth Tringham's comments on the general lack of interest in households among archaeologists, which she attributes to the explicit focus on ". . . what goes on beyond the household: for example, the corporate production of surplus goods, exchange and alliances on a regional and interregional scale, the struggle of humans to control the environment, the hierarchies and dominance structures between settlements" (Tringham 1991:99). Ironically, this disregard for household level analyses runs counter to much recent research that views the labor and social relations of the household as crucial to production at larger scales (Tringham 1991:102; 1994).

The fourth topical area, gender and long-term historical processes is designed to develop methodologies for drawing out long-term historical processes and to introduce works by feminist scholars in related disciplines. As Wylie has suggested there is a "rich and sophisticated feminist literature on 'sex/gender systems' . . . in closely aligned fields" (1993:x) from which archaeologists can draw. Here, we have selected the research of Carolyn Bynum, a historian of medieval history and religious women in western Europe between the twelfth and sixteenth centuries. Of particular relevance to archaeology is Bynum's focus on long-term historical processes that may provide a useful model for archaeologists. Because Bynum (1986, 1987) emphasizes historical contexts and compares male and female differences in symbol-using, her work provides a historically documented and uniquely long-term example that complements archaeological methodologies. With Bynum's study as a base, case studies involving long-term perspectives based upon archaeological or documentary evidence can provide a point of discussion for employing her methodology. One set of articles we find useful in this context is from the third and second millennia B.C. in Mesopotamia, in which there is a body of published literature on women craft producers and others attached to temple organizations (Stone 1977; Zagarell 1986; and Wright in Chapter 3, this volume).

We have no specific recommendation for how this course should be structured, for it lends itself to a number of different formats. Each topic provides a strong basis for formal lectures. At the same time, the topics, either singly or combined, can be employed as a focus of seminar discussions. A format that one of us has used is to combine an initial series of formal lectures with student-led critiques and discussions for the remainder of the semester. One method is to have each student select a topic from the list, conduct extensive research in consultation with the instructor, and submit a paper to each student in the class one week before its critique and discussion. The paper is not read during the class period, but all students read it in advance of the following week's class, when the paper forms the basis of a class discussion of the topic. Two other members of the class lead the discussion and in consultation with the instructor draw out relevant points to build the discussion; since the writers of the paper are asked to defend some points and expand on others, they are supplied with questions well in advance of the discussion section. This format has two advantages. First, it fosters the students' deep involvement in the research and helps them develop critical skills with which they can articulate strengths and weaknesses of the materials early in the semester. Second, it provides a basis on which to establish a set of ground rules for the critiques and discussion that will promote a nonadversarial, productive exchange. This form of discourse is just as effective (perhaps more so) in conveying incisive criticism as the more common confrontational model and is another way in which many feminists envision changing archaeological agendas.

Broadening a Departmental or University Curriculum

The incorporation of gender issues into archaeology courses can contribute to departmental and university-wide curricula. Here, we suggest three ways in which this can be accomplished. For other suggestions and strategies for implementation, we recommend works by Betty Schmitz (1985) for guidance and bibliographic references, and Margo Culley and Catherine Portuges (1985) on feminist pedagogy and teaching gender-related courses.

One way departmental offerings can be broadened is through the implementation of faculty development seminars. Sponsored by a grant from the Humanities Council at New York University, we instituted a three-part program as an informational resource for faculty and graduate students. Our funds, first, were utilized to bring several scholars to our campus to consult with students and faculty on recent research on gender in archaeology and to suggest ways in which to incorporate gender in research and teaching. Subsequent to these meetings, some faculty members incorporated gender-related topics into the department's undergraduate offerings. For example, in a course in human evolution and prehistory, some of the issues raised in our section on undergraduate introductory courses were introduced. Since this course has a laboratory component, gender-related exercises were included in lab problems. In recent upper-division courses taught at New York University and Hunter College, we were surprised to find broad interest in gender issues among both male and female undergraduate students. Finally, since graduate students work with the undergraduates in introductory and lower level courses and will be designing their own syllabi in the future, a noncredit discussion group was organized around readings from the literature in feminist archaeology.

A second suggestion involves more substantial curricular reform at the undergraduate level. At Albion College, students are required to select one course from a series of offerings approved for meeting a gender requirement and an ethnic requirement. Approval of courses is not based on subject matter, but on the extent to which scholarship generated by a "feminist initiative" or "minority critiques of the canon in a given field" are included (Brumfiel in Wright and Romanowicz 1994:112). In many of the courses offered, the emphasis is on an intellectual critique and philosophy of knowledge. In that context, Brumfiel teaches an introductory course in anthropology in which she introduces topics traditionally discussed in archaeology courses, some of which have a gender component (for example, material culture studies) and others that do not (for example, site formation processes).

Finally, a course dedicated to gender issues in archaeology, such as the advanced undergraduate/graduate course proposed in this chapter can be cross-listed or become integral to a women's studies program. As we have said, there is considerable discussion in the popular literature, in the scholarship on women in other disciplines, and in anthropology itself that touches on archaeological evidence. A women's studies program is an ideal setting in which to introduce the most recent research in archaeology.

Conclusion

This chapter has provided a number of suggestions for incorporating gender into mainstream archaeology courses and for the development of courses dedicated to gender issues in archaeology. We also have presented some of the reasons why it is essential for archaeologists to explicitly address gender issues in the classroom as well as in our own research.

In putting together these suggestions, we have been struck by the advances that already have occurred in gender studies in archaeology. Still, the proposals we have made for introducing gender issues into the classroom are modest and should accommodate archaeologists of various theoretical persuasions. Obviously, it won't be enough just to "add women and stir"; teaching such a course requires a commitment to integrating gender into the analysis of social process. As we have said earlier, in peopling the past, the topic of gender should stand alongside discussions of stratification and the development of hierarchies, divisions of labor, and social status.

Finally, after several decades of constructing an essentially unpeopled past, archaeology stands ready to initiate new programs of research and new ways of thinking about human social life. We now have an opportunity to make important contributions to articulating those (pre)histories of gender constructed by others and to redressing some erroneous perceptions about them, both within anthropology itself and in the public domain. One very important place to begin disseminating this knowledge is in the classroom.

Acknowledgments

We would like to thank the feminist scholars who spoke at New York University during the fall of 1991. Their talks and the informal discussions with graduate students and faculty on incorporating gender in the classroom provided us with many ideas and insights. Their participation in and the development of a graduate course on gender issues in archaeology were supported by a New York University Curriculum Enrichment Grant awarded to Rita Wright. Janet Romanowicz would like to thank Greg Johnson for giving her the opportunity to teach a gender course at Hunter College (CUNY). Her contribution to this chapter is based upon work supported under a National Science Foundation Graduate Research Fellowship. We also would like to thank reviewers of an earlier version of this chapter for their invaluable comments.

Notes

1. Our suggestions are not the first to be made. For other examples, see the chapter by Janet Spector and Mary Whelan (1989), especially on textbooks, material culture, and ethnoarchaeology, some bibliographic references, practical exercises, and videos. Other contributions in the same volume on special topics and geographical regions may be relevant. Also see Claassen (1992:137ff.).

2. One way to remedy this situation may be to write to publishers suggesting that gender issues be included in future publications. For example, Margaret Conkey proposed that assigning textbooks to large introductory courses gives archaeologists power to influence content and that rather than simply waiting for a better book to come along, it is our responsibility to write to publishers with both positive and negative feedback (Wright and Romanowicz 1994:25).

3. Significantly, most of the articles available at the time were written by socio/cultural anthropologists. We were able to identify only twelve archaeologists among the authors cited in their proposed teaching bibliographies.

4. Two books, *Gendered Perspectives* (Glaser and Zenetou 1994) and *Museums and Communities* (Karp, Kreamer, and Lavine 1992), especially the chapter by Appadurai and Breckenridge, examine museum displays and the ideas and images they express.

5. Another example of the use of ethnographic data and archaeological evidence for a culture in which written documents or ethnohistoric data are not

available is Rita Wright's discussion of craft production in periods related to the Harappan civilization (1991:194ff.). In it, she argues that, while women craft producers cannot necessarily be "found," many types of craft production, when viewed in cross-cultural context, are carried out within household units and that there is no reason to exclude women from this production. In addition, Diana Wall's (1994) historical study of eighteenth- and nineteenth-century New York City combines archaeology with documents from American history. This work could be used to provide a second type of study that utilizes documentary, in addition to archaeological, evidence.

6. Our suggestions for a course dedicated to gender issues in archaeology is just one example of the many ways in which one can be organized (for other examples, see Claassen 1992:155ff.). Here, we have designed a course that reflects our own research interests and perspectives.

7. The phrase "crossroads of knowledge production" is borrowed from Micaela diLeonardo (1991). As she states it: "anthropology stands at the crossroads of knowledge production, embracing scientific, social-scientific, and humanistic modes of interpretation" (1991:1). To this comment we would add that of the four subfields in anthropology, archaeology is at the intersection of the other subfields.

8. The introduction to Gero and Conkey (1991) is particularly relevant to this discussion.

9. For a critique of this view, see Wylie (1991b:40).

References

Allman, William F.
  1991   "The Origins of Modern Humans: Who We Were." *U.S. News & World Report* (September 16):53–60.
Appadurai, Arjun, and Carol A. Breckenridge
  1992   "Museums Are Good to Think: Heritage on View in India." In *Museums and Communities: The Politics of Public Culture,* edited by Ivan Karp, Christine Mullen Kreamer, and Steven D. Lavine, 34–35. Washington, D.C.: Smithsonian Institution Press.
Bacus, Elisabeth A., Alex W. Barker, Jeffrey D. Bonevich, Sandra L. Dunavan, J. Benjamin Fitzhugh, Debra L. Gold, Nurit S. Goldman-Finn, William Griffin, Karen M. Mudar, Editors
  1993   *A Gendered Past.* Ann Arbor: University of Michigan Museum of Anthropology, Technical Report 25.
Begley, Sharon, with Louise Lief
  1986   "The Way We Were." *Newsweek* (November 10):62–72.
Bentley, Gillian R.
  1988   "Population Increase and the Secondary Products Revolution." Ms. on file, Department of Anthropology, Harvard University, Cambridge, Mass.
Bentley, Gillian R., Tony Goldberg, and Grazyna Jasienska
  1993   "The Fertility of Agricultural and Non-agricultural Traditional Societies." *Population Studies* 47:269–81.
Bentley, Gillian R., Grazyna Jasienska, and Tony Goldberg
  1993   "Is the Fertility of Agriculturalists Higher Than That of Non-agriculturalists?" *Current Anthropology*:778–85.

Blanton, Richard E.
1994   *Houses and Households: A Comparative Study*. New York: Plenum Press.
Brown, Judith K.
1970   "A Note on the Division of Labor by Sex." *American Anthropologist* 72(5):1073–78.
Brumfiel, Elizabeth M.
1991   "Weaving and Cooking: Women's Production in Aztec Mexico." In *Engendering Archaeology: Women and Prehistory*, edited by Joan M. Gero and Margaret W. Conkey, 224–51. Oxford: Basil Blackwell.
Burtt, Fiona
1987   " 'Man the Hunter': Gender Bias in Children's Archaeology Books." *Archaeological Review from Cambridge* 6(2):157–74.
Bynum, Caroline
1986   *Gender and Religion: On the Complexity of Symbols*. Boston: Beacon Press.
1987   *Holy Feast and Holy Fast: The Religious Significance of Food*. Berkeley: University of California Press.
Chodorow, Nancy
1978   *The Reproduction of Mothering: Psychoanalysis and the Sociology of Gender*. Berkeley: University of California Press.
Claassen, Cheryl, ed.
1992   *Exploring Gender through Archaeology*. Madison, Wis.: Prehistory Press.
1994   *Women in Archaeology*. Philadelphia: University of Pennsylvania Press.
Conkey, Margaret W.
1991   "Does It Make a Difference? Feminist Thinking and Archaeologies of Gender." In *The Archaeology of Gender*, edited by Dale Walde and Noreen Willows, 24–33. Calgary: Archaeological Association of the University of Calgary.
Conkey, Margaret W., and Joan M. Gero
1991   "Tensions, Pluralities, and Engendering Archaeology: An Introduction to Women and Prehistory." In *Engendering Archaeology: Women and Prehistory*, edited by Joan M. Gero and Margaret W. Conkey, 3–30. Oxford: Basil Blackwell.
Conkey, Margaret, and Janet D. Spector
1984   "Archaeology and the Study of Gender." In *Advances in Archaeological Method and Theory*, edited by M. Schiffer, 7:1–38. New York: Academic Press.
Conkey, Margaret W., with Sarah H. Williams
1991   "Original Narratives: The Political Economy of Gender in Archaeology." In *Gender at the Crossroads of Knowledge: Feminist Anthropology in the Postmodern Era*, edited by Micaela diLeonardo, 102–39. Berkeley: University of California Press.
Crabtree, Pamela J.
1991   "Gender Hierarchies and the Sexual Division of Labor in the Natufian Culture of the Southern Levant." In *The Archaeology of Gender*, edited by Dale Walde and Noreen D. Willows, 384–91. Calgary: Archaeological Association of the University of Calgary.
Culley, Margo, and Catherine Portuges, eds.
1985   *Gendered Subjects: The Dynamics of Feminist Teaching*. Boston: Routledge and Kegan Paul.
Diamond, Jared
1989   "The Great Leap Forward." *Discover* (May):50–60.

diLeonardo, Micaela, ed.
1991   *Gender at the Crossroads of Knowledge: Feminist Anthropology in the Postmodern Era.* Berkeley: University of California Press.
du Cros, Hilary, and Laurajane Smith, eds.
1993   *Women in Archaeology: A Feminist Critique.* Canberra, Australia: Occasional Papers in Prehistory, No. 23, Australian National University.
Fausto-Sterling, Anne
1985   *Myths of Gender: Biological Theories about Women and Men.* New York: Basic Books.
Fedigan, Linda
1982   *Primate Paradigms: Sex Roles and Social Bonds.* Montreal: Eden Press.
Feinman, Gary M., Steadman Upham, and Kent G. Lightfoot
1981   "The Production Step-Measure: An Ordinal Index of Labor Input in Ceramic Analysis." *American Antiquity* 46:871–84.
Flannery, Kent V.
1968   "Archeological Systems Theory and Early Mesoamerica." In *Anthropological Archaeology in the Americas,* edited by Betty Meggers, 67–87. Washington, D.C.: Anthropological Society of Washington, D.C.
Gailey, Christine Ward
1985   "The State of the State in Anthropology." *Dialectical Anthropology* 9 (1–4):65–89.
1987   *Kinship to Kingship: Gender Hierarchy and State Formation in the Tongan Islands.* Austin: University of Texas Press.
Gero, Joan M.
1991   "Genderlithics: Women's Roles in Stone Tool Production." In *Engendering Archaeology: Women and Prehistory,* edited by Joan M. Gero and Margaret W. Conkey, 163–93. Oxford: Basil Blackwell.
Gero, Joan M., and Margaret W. Conkey, eds.
1991   *Engendering Archaeology: Women and Prehistory.* Oxford: Basil Blackwell.
Gero, Joan M., and Dolores Root
1987   "Public Presentations and Private Concerns: Archaeology in the Pages of *National Geographic.*" In *The Politics of the Past,* edited by Peter Gathercole and David Lowenthals, 19–37. Proceedings of the World Archaeological Congress, Southampton, England, September 1986. London: Allen and Unwin.
Gilligan, Carol
1982   *In a Different Voice: Psychological Theory and Women's Development.* Cambridge, Mass.: Harvard University Press.
Glaser, Jane R., and Artemis A. Zenetou, eds.
1994   *Gendered Perspectives: Essays on Women in Museums.* Washington, D.C.: Smithsonian Institution Press.
Hastorf, Christine A.
1991   "Gender, Space and Food in Prehistory." In *Engendering Archaeology: Women and Prehistory,* edited by Joan M. Gero and Margaret W. Conkey, 132–59. Oxford: Basil Blackwell.
Henry, Donald O.
1989   *From Foraging to Agriculture: The Levant at the End of the Ice Age.* Philadelphia: University of Pennsylvania Press.
Karp, Ivan, Christine Mullen Kreamer, Steven D. Lavine, eds.
1992   *Museums and Communities: The Politics of Public Culture.* Washington, D.C.: Smithsonian Institution Press.

Keller, Evelyn Fox
  1985   *Reflections on Gender and Science.* New Haven, Conn.: Yale University Press.
Klein, Richard G., and Kathryn Cruz-Uribe
  1984   *The Analysis of Animal Bones from Archaeological Sites.* Chicago: University of Chicago Press.
Leacock, Eleanor
  1972   Introduction. In *Origin of the Family, Private Property and the State*, by F. Engels, 7–67. New York: International Publishers.
  1983   "Interpreting the Origins of Gender Inequality: Conceptual and Historical Problems." *Dialectical Anthropology* 7:263–84.
Lutz, Catherine A., and Jane L. Collins
  1993   *Reading National Geographic.* Chicago: University of Chicago Press.
McGaw, Judith
  1989   "No Passive Victims, No Separate Spheres: A Feminist Perspective on Technology's History." In *In Context: History and the History of Technology*, edited by S. H. Cutcliffe and R. C. Post, 172–91. Bethlehem, Pa.: Lehigh University Press.
Moore, Henrietta
  1990   *Feminism and Anthropology.* Minneapolis: University of Minnesota Press.
Morgen, Sandra, ed.
  1989   *Gender and Anthropology: Critical Reviews for Research and Teaching.* Washington, D.C.: American Anthropological Association.
Nash, June
  1978   "The Aztecs and the Ideology of Male Dominance." *Signs* 4(2):349–62.
Nelson, Margaret C., Sarah M. Nelson, and Alison Wylie, eds.
  1994   *Equity Issues for Women in Archaeology.* Washington, D.C.: Archeological Papers of the American Anthropological Association, no. 5.
Nelson, Sarah M.
  1990   "Diversity of the Upper Paleolithic 'Venus' Figurines and Archeological Mythology." In *Powers of Observation: Alternative Views in Archeology*, edited by Sarah M. Nelson and Alice B. Kehoe, 11–22. Washington, D.C.: Archeological Papers of the American Anthropological Association, no. 2.
Patterson, Thomas
  1993   *Archaeology: The Historical Development of Civilizations.* 2d ed. Englewood Cliffs, N.J.: Prentice-Hall.
Pfeiffer, John E.
  1985   *The Emergence of Humankind.* New York: Harper and Row.
Pollak, Janet S.
  1991   "Excavating Auel: The Gender Roles of Earth's Children." In *The Archaeology of Gender*, edited by Dale Walde and Noreen D. Willows, 297–301. Calgary: Archaeological Association of the University of Calgary.
Pollitt, Katha
  1994   *Reasonable Creatures: Essays on Women and Feminism.* New York: Alfred Knopf.
Pollock, Susan
  1991   "Women in a Men's World: Images of Sumerian Women." In *Engen-

dering Archaeology: Women and Prehistory, edited by Joan M. Gero and Margaret W. Conkey, 366–87. Oxford: Basil Blackwell.

Rapp, Rayna
    1977   "Gender and Class: An Archaeology of Knowledge Concerning the Origin of the State." *Dialectical Anthropology* 2:309–15.

Rogers, Susan C.
    1978   "Women's Place: A Critical Review of Anthropological Theory." *Comparative Studies in Society and History* 20(1):123–62.

Rosaldo, Michelle Z., and Louise Lamphere, eds.
    1974   *Women, Culture and Society.* Stanford, Calif.: Stanford University Press.

Sacks, Karen
    1979   "State Bias and Women's Status." *American Anthropologist* 78 (3): 565–69.

Schmitz, Betty
    1985   *Integrating Women's Studies into the Curriculum: A Guide and Bibliography.* New York: Feminist Press.

Silverblatt, Irene
    1987   *Moon, Sun, and Witches: Gender Ideologies and Class in Inca and Colonial Peru.* Princeton, N.J.: Princeton University Press.
    1988   "Women in States." *Annual Review of Anthropology* 17:427–60.

Slocum, Sally
    1975   "Woman the Gatherer: Male Bias in Anthropology." In *Toward an Anthropology of Women,* edited by Rayna R. Reiter, 36–50. New York: Monthly Review Press.

Spector, Janet D., and Mary K. Whelan
    1989   "Incorporating Gender into Archaeology Courses." In *Gender and Anthropology: Critical Reviews for Research and Teaching,* edited by Sandra Morgen, 65–94. Washington, D.C.: American Anthropological Association.

Stone, Elizabeth
    1977   "Economic Crisis and Social Upheaval in Old Babylonian Nippur." In L. D. Levine and T. C. Young, *Essays in the Archaeology of Greater Mesopotamia,* edited by Louis Levine and T. Cuyler Young. Malibu, Calif.: Undena Publications.

Tanner, Nancy and Adrienne Zihlman
    1976   "Women in Evolution, Part I: Innovation and Selection in Human Origins." *Signs* 1(3):585–608.

Thomas, David Hurst
    1989   *Archaeology.* Fort Worth: Holt, Rinehart, and Winston.

Tringham, Ruth
    1991   "Households with Faces: The Challenges of Gender in Prehistoric Architectural Remains." In *Engendering Archaeology: Women and Prehistory,* edited by Joan M. Gero and Margaret W. Conkey, 93–131. Oxford: Basil Blackwell.
    1994   "Engendered Places in Prehistory." *Gender, Place and Culture* 1(2):169–203.

Wall, Diana diZerega
    1994   *The Archaeology of Gender: Separating the Spheres in Urban America.* New York: Plenum Press.

Watson, Patty Jo, and Mary C. Kennedy
    1991   "The Development of Horticulture in the Eastern Woodlands of

North America." In *Engendering Archaeology: Women and Prehistory*, edited by Joan M. Gero and Margaret W. Conkey, 255–75. Oxford: Basil Blackwell.

Wright, Rita P.
1991   "Women's Labor and Pottery Production in Prehistory." In *Engendering Archaeology: Women and Prehistory*, edited by Joan M. Gero and Margaret W. Conkey, 194–223. Oxford: Basil Blackwell.
N.d.   "Temple, Family and State: The *Naditu* in Old Babylonian Sippar."

Wright, Rita P., and Janet V. Romanowicz
1994   "Gender Issues in Archaeology: Informal Discussions with Feminist Scholars." Ms. on file, Department of Anthropology, New York University.

Wylie, Alison
1991a   "Feminist Critiques and Archaeological Challenges." In *The Archaeology of Gender*, edited by Dale Walde and Noreen D. Willows, 17–23. Calgary: Archaeological Association of the University of Calgary.
1991b   "Gender Theory and the Archaeological Record: Why Is There No Archaeology of Gender?" In *Engendering Archaeology: Women and Prehistory*, edited by Joan M. Gero and Margaret W. Conkey, 31–54. Oxford: Basil Blackwell.
1992   "The Interplay of Evidential Constraints and Political Interests: Recent Archaeological Research on Gender." *American Antiquity* 57 (1): 15–35.
1993   Foreword. "Gender Archaeology/Feminist Archaeology." In *A Gendered Past*, edited by Elisabeth A. Bacus, Alex W. Barker, Jeffrey D. Bonevich, Sandra L. Dunavan, J. Benjamin Fitzhugh, Debra L. Gold, Nurit S. Goldman-Finn, William Griffin, Karen M. Mudar, vii–xiii. Ann Arbor: University of Michigan Museum of Anthropology, Technical Report 25:15–17.

Zagarell, Allen
1986   "Trade, Women, Class and Society in Ancient Western Asia." *Current Anthropology* 27:415–30.

Zihlman, Adrienne L.
1978   "Women in Evolution, Part II. Subsistence and Social Organization among Early Hominids." *Signs* 4(1):4–20.
1981   "Women as Shapers of the Human Adaptation." In *Woman the Gatherer*, edited by Frances Dahlberg, 75–120. New Haven, Conn.: Yale University Press.
1989   "Woman the Gatherer: The Role of Women in Early Hominid Evolution." In *Gender and Anthropology: Critical Reviews for Research and Teaching*, edited by Sandra Morgen, 21–40. Washington, D.C.: American Anthropological Association.

Chapter 8
Cultivating Thinking/Challenging Authority: Some Experiments in Feminist Pedagogy in Archaeology

Margaret W. Conkey
Ruth E. Tringham

This chapter is primarily about practice, and about a practice—teaching—that necessarily derives from and contributes to our theories about archaeology, about teaching, about pedagogy, and about how to think about "the past." While there is an increasing literature that directly addresses issues of feminism and pedagogy (Luke and Gore 1992, Maher and Tetreault 1994, Middleton 1988, Rosser 1986, Rothschild 1988), and while pedagogical issues have been taken up within anthropology as they relate to gender, race, and ethnicity (e.g., Maxwell and Buck 1992), this chapter is not an attempt to lay out an explicit philosophical or conceptual framework for feminist pedagogy in archaeology nor to integrate various discussions and issues from this wider literature into a synopsis of the field, valuable as this might be. Rather, while we certainly hope that our essay will make a contribution to thinking about feminist pedagogies—especially in anthropology and archaeology—we are primarily interested here in discussing our own recent experiments in the teaching of archaeology, experiments that have been motivated and informed by various aspects of feminist thought.

It is not possible to identify any one cause of our evolving experiments, but it is certain that, once we began with them, there was an increasing interest and engagement on our parts, and now there can be no turning back. A significant influence and stimulus for both of us emerged from our team-teaching, which began with an upper-division course on archaeological history and theory. Here we found ourselves face-to-face with the fact that we were not only mediating more than reporting knowledge, but also that each of us had to find a path through the authority format that comes all too easily when teaching on one's own but which was immediately diffused in our team-teaching collaboration.

Both of us were inspired to engage substantively with the idea that there are different ways to present archaeology—whether in publications or in the classroom—by our experiences at the conference "Women and Production in Prehistory" (1988), which formed the basis for the edited volume *Engendering Archaeology* (Gero and Conkey 1991).

For each of us, there were some separate influences as well. For one of us (Ruth Tringham), the experimentation with alternative presentations and with an explicit focus on the alternative and multiple interpretations of the same data began with the revised paper from the "Women and Production in Prehistory" conference. The radio show format for presenting the different interpreters (and their interpretations) of early Neolithic life was tried out in the paper "Household with Faces" (Tringham 1991a) and was even presented (with many different actors) as part of what are usually single-speaker lectures in our departmental Faculty Seminar series. In writing the paper "Men and Women in Prehistoric Architecture" (Tringham 1991b), Tringham found many ideas to be crystallized in her reading of Jean-Paul Bourdier, who articulated the idea that to ignore ambiguity and to work within the illusion that there are "proven facts" (in archaeology) is to claim that one's interpretation of knowledge *is* knowledge rather than a "mode of transmitting knowledge" (Bourdier 1989).

And if any one published paper or article can be credited with stimulating Conkey, it would be the brief essay reprinted in *Lingua Franca*, written by Jane Tompkins: "Teaching Like It Matters: A Modest Proposal for Revolutionizing the Classroom" (Tompkins 1991). In this article, Tompkins makes many provocative points, and a few of them were instrumental in reshaping our teaching and in encouraging us to scrutinize explicitly the links between our feminist thinking and scholarship and our classroom practices. We will discuss some of these points below, in that they influenced some of the specific formats we took up in order to address our converging ideas about teaching, archaeology, knowledge, and feminist thinking.

In the end, we both see quite clearly that these influences—from conferences, some team-teaching, some readings—were all catapulted into action by the 1991 publication of a book by Marija Gimbutas, *The Civilization of the Goddess.* Even more so than for her book *The Language of the Goddess* (Gimbutas 1989), it was the prepublication announcements, the synopses on the book jacket, and the first summaries of the book—all of which declared it to be "the definitive answer to European prehistory"— that provided the proverbial last straw in our self-critiques of teaching and of the presentation of archaeology. We were thoroughly enmeshed in one of the major enterprises of feminist thinking, that is, to question history, authority, and language, and from that vantage point, the claims for the 1991 Gimbutas book struck a raw chord. We had already team taught a graduate seminar entitled "Archaeology and the Goddess" and were preparing to teach an upper-division undergraduate course on the same topic. And it was in the context of that class (fall 1991) that we most self-consciously began to experiment with our teaching in ways that drew on what we had come to embrace as feminist principles.

Some of the pedagogical background for what we developed can be found in the Tompkins article. Tompkins critiques what she sees as the primary model for pedagogy in the classrooms of American higher education: the performance model.[1] To her, this is a model that is no "less coercive and destructive of creativity and self-motivated learning" than the "banking model" (Freire 1973), which emphasizes the deposition of knowledge, in which students are depositories and the teacher is the depositor. Simply put, what Tompkins advocates, and what she has tried and reports on, is more of a "coaching" model. And, as she says, "what this boils down to is this: The students are responsible for presenting the material to the class" (Tompkins 1991:26).

While Tompkins presents numerous other ideas that are both inspirational and provocative, we took up her challenge to replace performance with coaching, and we confronted her observation that "what really matters as far as our own beliefs and projects for (social) change are concerned is not so much what we talk about in class as what we do" (Tompkins 1991:26). With all these ideas and influences in hand, we have embarked on a series of teaching experiments that have been self-consciously about the intersection of feminist thinking, archaeology, and pedagogy. While we have been fortunate to have departmental and university support for the opportunity to team teach frequently, we have also applied our ever-expanding insights in classes that we have taught individually. As Tompkins reports for her own experience, it will be difficult, if not impossible, for us to teach in the same way again. And while we feel that there has been a good measure—both quantitatively and qualitatively—of success, this does not mean there is no room for improvement or change, and this does not mean our efforts and attempts were ever received unanimously or without question or concern.

However, while we thought we were trying to "liberate" our classrooms, we have—perhaps in a self-centered sort of way—also liberated ourselves. The teaching of archaeology—and all that refers to, from theory to method, to data, to interpretation—has, for us, become not only a context within which we can think about the impact of feminist thinking on how we "do" archaeology and what the human past might have been like; it has itself become a feminist practice. We would argue that, despite the late arrival of feminist thinking in archaeological literature and archaeological circles, the very nature of archaeology—its subject matter and its crucial (if not largely yet unrecognized) position in contemporary cultural politics—is particularly conducive to feminist pedagogy. Despite the resistance of many of its practitioners, the field of archaeology may inherently be one of the most feminist of enterprises!

The following essay will begin by addressing some of the themes or features of what we consider to be included within "feminist pedagogy." Most of the essay, however, will provide the specifics of our experiments in teaching archaeology, in the hope that others may find in them useful or applicable ideas and that we will receive suggestions, critiques, and ideas to develop further or improve these approaches.

What Is Feminist Pedagogy?

A most important point to begin with is that it is not at all necessary to consider feminist pedagogy *only* for those courses that are explicitly feminist or gender-oriented. While we would agree with the feminist tenet that taking sex/gender seriously is indeed an integral part of what contemporary feminism is all about, feminist pedagogy in archaeology is not limited to courses such as "Archaeology and Gender," "Women in Archaeology," or to sections of courses that deal with the more explicitly gendered categories or topics, such as household analysis, craft production, and so on. While we began our feminist teaching in a team-taught upper-division undergraduate course that *was* explicitly gender-oriented and feminist—"Archaeology and the Goddess"—we saw immediately how our various pedagogical experiments were completely appropriate to what might be considered more mainstream courses, such as regional, topical, or evolutionary courses. In our own case, for example, this has meant applying our ideas as much to our course "Archaeology and Prehistory of Europe" as to the course "Archaeology and the Goddess."

Our primary pedagogical device, which served as the core of our "coaching" in each class, was the use of panels. We describe some of these in detail, as well as note both the strengths and weaknesses of such a format. We note this "device" at this point so that, as we discuss our feminist pedagogy a bit more, the reader can imagine how a panel format might be a viable means to approximate and achieve our feminist goals.

We envision that a major part of our role as teachers is to mediate information between the literature (texts, articles, and so forth) and our own experience/knowledge, on the one hand, and an active participating class, on the other hand. This active participating class is not a transitional group of faceless students, but comprises diverse individuals, each of whom is in the class not to be "filled" with knowledge, but, to use a current but not inappropriate phrase, to find their own voice through the interaction of experience and knowledge. We strive to break down the barriers between knowledge and experience. We no longer view the classroom as a place where we—the instructors—should "polish" our skills (as Tompkins says).

Rather, we aim to stimulate critical awareness and to provide students with some of the ways through which they can express their critical thoughts and observations. We encourage students to question—not passively accept—authors as authority. In archaeology, we are particularly concerned with encouraging the exploration of the legitimacy of multiple interpretations. In classroom dynamics, we sought to find ways to encourage open expression of opinion among peers, if not an outright theater of discourse. We hoped to be able to foster their engagement with nonestablished ways of expression, such as multimedia or truly collaborative presentations, and through these vehicles, to recognize the power of the media themselves. We sought ways to put the feminist critique of science into practice; what other field is as well suited as archaeology to question history, authority, language, and symbol? We see the questioning of such things as central to the feminist critique and to the feminist enterprise.

Coaching Archaeology through Panels

While the above heading may strike you as strange in contrast to the more familiar "Teaching Archaeology through Lectures," this is the essence of our approach. The panels, as described below, took on varying forms and content. The basic idea here is that during seven to fourteen class meetings (in a fifteen-week semester), the class would basically be "taught" by a group of students composed as a panel. We experimented with optimal sizes for the panels, with ways to prepare and provide guidelines, and with kinds of topics to assign to each panel in advance. We inevitably left the format—a debate, a skit, a set of presentations, use of slides or props, handouts, and so on—up to the student panelists. While many were at first overwhelmed by the very idea of getting together with some four to seven other (usually previously unacquainted) students to work out an entire presentation, there is no doubt that almost all rose to the occasion. In some courses, all students enrolled were panelists; in other courses, there were too many for all to participate and so the class had to be divided, and alternative modes of expression for nonpanelists were devised (such as a five-to-seven page research paper).

The panels were more successful when the material to be addressed by them was already somehow familiar in the personal experiences of the panelists, whether from previous reading, coursework, media, or through general life experiences of travel, household dynamics, power relations, and so on. We thus had to think through which of the many potential panel topics would work best. The panels were also more successful when one or two of the panelists were strong leaders. And they were more successful when the guidelines from us (oral or written) were specific and detailed. Panel participants inevitably went from an initial fear that they would have nothing to say to taking too long in their presentations, so that an important part of the panel idea — open discussion and debate in the classroom — was often minimized or had to be (due to time constraints of the 50-minute lecture period) cut off in the middle just as it was getting interesting.

Of course, the panels were only one part of the course learning. There were always readings, and we did have lectures by each of us and by visitors. The panels did not replace exams or even papers, though we found that the kinds of exams we gave, especially as a final exam, had to be more open-ended, such as essay exams that could be prepared in advance. We also found that when writing course papers (which were to be interpretive critiques), those that built on the topic they took up as a panelist were often the most effective. For example, if an individual had been involved in the panel on the Terra Amata "hut" (in the European archaeology course), for that panelist, writing a critique on the interpretation of architecture and structures in the European Paleolithic would encourage the growth and consolidation of knowledge within a particular archaeological domain.

In many courses, we had a panel every week; in others, we had only seven panels out of the fifteen weeks. In one course ("Archaeology and the Goddess") we had a quite explicit schedule, with a "data" lecture on Monday, a "theory" lecture on Wednesday, and a panel on Friday. We tried varying ways to involve the nonpanelists each week in the critical assessment of the panels. Perhaps the most extensive attempt was in Conkey's "Prehistoric Art" course, in which some one hundred students each wrote a one-paragraph critique of any six of the seven panels, thus generating some six hundred paragraphs to be read and annotated by the instructor!

The following three-part description of the panels takes up the different course sets: (1) the inaugural course — one that was topically an explicitly feminist/gender-oriented course, entitled "Archaeology and the

Goddess"; (2) the conventional area courses, "Archaeology and Prehistory of Europe" (team-taught, but taught two different times and with intentional differences in format) and "Mediterranean Archaeology" (taught by Tringham alone); and (3) a conventional topical course, "Prehistoric Art" (taught by Conkey alone).

Archaeology and the Goddess

The "Archaeology and the Goddess" course (fall 1991) was designed to look at the ways in which a contemporary theme in popular culture—"The Goddess Movement"—uses archaeology.[2] Just a few of the questions that motivated this course were: What is the relationship of archaeology to popular culture? How is archaeology used in the construction of contemporary belief systems? What archaeological evidence is there and what is claimed in support of certain prehistoric belief systems? The course was designed to be a critical evaluation of the recently accumulated work that has drawn substantially on the archaeology of the Paleolithic and Neolithic to underwrite and sustain a particular gendered interpretation of the human past.

The topics for discussion in the panels, which were held almost every week, focused on theoretical issues (Table 8.1). The aim of these panels was to draw out different viewpoints for debate. The course in general used "The Goddess Movement" as a podium to prompt consideration of what the feminist critique of archaeology is all about and what difference it makes to consider gender issues in past human societies from a critical perspective, including a critique of the archaeologist-as-authority. For this reason, the panels ranged over some very important theoretical debates about the construction of knowledge about the past. These debates, however, were placed in a context in which the issues were quite explicit, clearly observed, and critiqued. At the same time, the topical focus of the course—"the goddess"—is one that has been discussed quite a bit in the popular media and in differing contexts. All of this contributed to the generally stimulating effect that the course content had on the class (more than fifty students).

About five of the students were what one might describe as "goddess activists," as goddess-inspired artists and dancers, as members of a coven, or as self-proclaimed "witches," which certainly enhanced the experiential basis for the class discussions! Other students had backgrounds in religious studies, as well as in anthropology, archaeology, and other fields.

The second meeting of the course, while not a panel, was intended to set the stage for the understanding and simultaneous critique of

TABLE 8.1. "Archaeology and the Goddess" panels.

I. Is the goddess literature feminist?
The topic of the first panel actually turned out to be the most important one discussed. This panel worked because the panelists had had previous exposure to the feminist critique. All panelists pointed out in their own way that a consideration of women is not the same thing as feminism.

II. Does a discovery of the "origins" of the goddess in deep prehistory give the movement a greater legitimacy?
The "no" side of the debate team brought up the important point that, in seeking for origins and roots and continuous evolution, the only legitimacy that the Goddess Movement gains is in the eyes of conventional presentism in the construction of "prehistory."

III. The place and role of speculation in archaeology.
The panel came to the consensus that speculation is an essential part of the scientific enterprise. It also noted, however, that in the Goddess Movement literature speculation often poses as an authoritative statement about "true facts." The panel noted a further problem: when speculation is presented in an authoritative statement, the ambiguity and possible multiple interpretations of the archaeological data are lost because the process by which the speculation was conceived has been mystified and is never stated.

IV. Plausibility, reality and ambiguity in the goddess literature.
This panel focused explicitly on the writing of Marija Gimbutas and reconstructed how she would construct her arguments by assertion and make inferences from the archaeological data. The panel did not give Gimbutas much of a chance. Obviously, we were not impartial enough in our suggestions.

V. The meaning and treatment of material culture in archaeology.
The point here was to try to understand the theories of material culture used by archaeologists. The panel addressed a very core issue that there is variable perception and meaningfulness of symbols.

VI. The megalithic "mystery"—does it have to be unraveled?
This panel focused on the megalithic monuments of prehistoric western Europe and their incorporation into the Goddess Movement "repertoire." The panel put the presentation of "megaliths" as a mystery into the context of conventional science, which demands closure and resolution, that is, a single "truth."

VII. Archaeologists' demise when dealing with things spiritual.
This panel inquired into why archaeologists seem to have real difficulty in dealing with the symbolic or spiritual. It had the most vigorous debate over archaeological epistemology and "how we know what we know."

VIII. Archaeology and the history of religion.
The idea here was to explore other ways in which archaeology has been used in the construction of belief systems and how the archaeologically grounded goddess accounts of religion in deep prehistory have been received and considered by scholars in religious history and religious studies.

TABLE 8.1. Continued.

IX. Christa Wolf's *Cassandra* and the creation and power of myths.

The theme was to consider the creation and power of myths in human life and culture. *Cassandra* was presented as an example of this. We asked the panel to examine the idea that myths reside in our consciousness in many places and that they affect our everyday lives in ways that we are not aware of (including the academic construction of prehistory). We asked each panel member to tell the class how myth had affected his or her everyday life or is affecting it right now. The panel responded wonderfully to these suggestions and told parts of their own life story as myth. One student related how she had been ordained as a witch. In many ways, this was the most stimulating panel, but it was obviously building on much of the coursework that had preceded it. The students in this panel were all, as it turned out, serious feminists, which helped. The only problem was that the telling of the myths took a very long time and left little time for participation from the rest of the class.

X. What is the point of a critique of the Goddess Movement's use of archaeological sources?

Do archaeologists weaken the power of the Goddess Movement by their critique of its use of archaeological sources? Does archaeological data strengthen or legitimize the Goddess Movement? The panel came up with a wide range of reasons as to why we should engage in such critiques. We were also pleased that somehow enough of a balance had been achieved so that the power of the critique did not seriously undermine the very enterprise of "doing archaeology," although, as we discuss below, this balance is always precarious.

---

the way in which archaeological narratives are constructed, and, more specifically, of the way in which the narrative of "The Goddess" in prehistory was being presented. While we chose to do this by means of a media presentation—a video of the film "The Goddess Remembered" (Read 1988)—this very medium reinforced for us and the class the fact that the media representations of archaeology, of the human past, and of gender relations are potent and rich pedagogical sources (see also Maxwell and Buck 1992).

Tringham selected and showed certain sections of the video. At each point where an "authoritative" statement was made, the film was stopped and the class members were invited to make their own interpretation, to think how such statements were constructed (such as questioning what the path of inference from data to interpretation was), and to offer other commentary, questions, or critique. For example, in the film Charlene Spretnak states:

I would say a matrifocal culture is one in which the female has a place of honor and respect and that doesn't mean domination. The men and women in these cultures in Old Europe were buried in almost equal ways. The women had a little more "stuff." But nothing like the patriarchal chieftain system later, where one man owned women and other men and horses and objects. So it was really pretty much an egalitarian society. There was not a putting down of men in order to elevate women. There was just a natural reverence of the bountiful powers of Mother Earth and the bountiful powers of the female. (Read 1988)

This quote was a wonderful demonstration of argument by assertion using archaeological data: how people lived, what they owned (and what "ownership" is), who ruled over whom, and so on. It provided a starting point for a discussion of the use of burial goods to infer the status and ownership of the living person; of evolutionary terms such as egalitarian, chieftain system, matrifocal, patriarchal; and of the problems of essentializing what must have been a very complex set of people into a single category: "the female" or "the male," as well as the gendering of the Earth, which provokes discussion of the dualistic nature/culture concepts, their intellectual history and the gendering (female) of Nature and its own intellectual history (e.g., Keller 1985, Merchant 1980).

While this video may seem like an easy "target" for critique precisely because it was intended for a popular audience, this only reinforces for us the need to expand our analytical scope—as archaeologists within contemporary societies—to include and even focus on the popular media rather than to ignore them (in the hopes they will go away, which they won't!) because we may think they are not scholarly archaeology. It is *precisely* because the media are controlled and in the service of the very same controlling agents that have fostered patriarchal, essentialist, authoritative thinking that an explicit engagement with the media is even more crucial to a feminist pedagogy.

As the first course in which we used panels, the students were given less explicit guidance than we later came to adopt. For each panel, we provided students with some lead questions and some—but not too much—additional literature, as well as explicit reference to the assigned readings that would be most relevant to the panel topic. (In addition to the panels [ten panels of five students], each student wrote an independent research paper, and there was an essay final exam, for which a set of possible essay questions was distributed in advance of the exam. We held at least one large [optional, but well-attended] review session to go over issues related to those questions before the exam.)

Area Courses: European and Mediterranean Archaeology

In many ways, it is more of a challenge to teach "mainstream" courses such as the prehistory or archaeology of a specific area from a feminist perspective than a course like the one described above, which focused more obviously on feminist or gender issues. We have some specific lessons learned from a feminist teaching of the archaeology of the European continent and that of the Mediterranean Basin.

Textbooks on the archaeology of these regions abound with authoritative statements about macroscale evolutionary and regionwide changes from the first human colonization to the beginnings of art and then agriculture, on through to the development of complex chiefdoms and exchange systems and so on. As practitioners within these research areas, we know that few things about the past are quite that definitive. We found, however, that we wanted to use some of these textbooks to provide much of the needed informational background against which a variety of issues could be developed. So, while we did not at all dismiss the generations of archaeological research and what they have yielded, we were equally interested in discussing in class the uses to which these data and these "facts" have been put.

As with "Archaeology and the Goddess," our aim was to break down the mystification of these authoritative "facts" by exposing the ways in which multiple interpretations may be made of the same data by archaeologists, often with different sociopolitical backgrounds or who come from different archaeological "schools." That we ourselves were trained in two countries and at slightly different periods in Anglo-American archaeology also made for an ongoing dialogue in the classroom, as we each often queried the other on how the other's intellectual heritage was showing!

Another important way in which the feminist critique was put into practice was in trying to observe and interpret the data at multiple scales. Whereas the evolutionary scale was one that was the basis for the textbooks—*is* the scale for much of the established academic literature—we aimed instead, following much of the feminist critique in literature, geography, art, and history, to focus more attention on microscale interpretation: on individual intentional action, on life in the household, on the specific meaningfulness of single objects, on single events, and on the specifics of human social action, against and within a background of the more macroscale changes. This is actually very hard to put into practice in teaching, because it demands more time to talk about it. But more importantly it demands a greater familiarity of the instructor with the archaeological materials. Finally, it demands a greater effort in familiarization and imagination by the students.

The panels for the area courses—"Archaeology and the Prehistory of Europe" (taught jointly, spring 1992 and spring 1994) and "Mediterranean Archaeology" (taught by Tringham, spring 1993)—used as a starting point a site, a feature, a set of artifacts, or sometimes a cultural "group" or period (Table 8.2). In the first teaching of an area course (European archaeology) in which such panels were organized,

TABLE 8.2. European and Mediterranean archaeology panels.

Egolzwil, Switzerland: lake dwelling

Lepenski Vir, Yugoslavia: Mesolithic village

Oetzi the Iceman, Austria/Italy: Frozen body dated to 3300 B.C.

New Grange, Ireland: Neolithic megalithic tomb

Maiden Castle, England: Iron Age hill fort

Terra Amata, France: Lower Paleolithic "hut"

La Solutré, France: Upper Paleolithic "kill site"

Mas d'Azil, France: Epipaleolithic site with painted pebbles as the focus

Opovo, Yugoslavia: Eneolithic village with a well as the focus

The Cursus, Dorset, England: Neolithic earthen monument

Dereivka, Ukraine: Kurgan (Neolithic) settlement

Stonehenge and Silbury Hill, England: Early Bronze Age monumental architecture

Vix, France: Iron Age princess's grave

The "end" of Paleolithic art

Varna, Bulgaria: Eneolithic cemetery

The Natufian culture

Maltese "temples": Stone-cut buildings, dated to 5000–2000 B.C.

The Nuraghi, Sardinia: Stone towers, dated ca. 2000–1000 B.C.

Carthage, Tunisia: Phoenician colonial-Roman city

we provided background information rather informally, mostly verbally, although a relevant bibliography (often including the books and articles themselves) was provided. But otherwise, after a short initial meeting, the students were left to themselves. There were nine panels offered in the first teaching of this course with approximately forty-five students, so each student was expected to participate in at least one panel, and might have had a chance at being in a second.

In the course "Mediterranean Archaeology" and in the second attempt at teaching European archaeology with these panels, each panel was provided with a more formal (written) set of background information that included the details of the archaeological data, the broad prehistoric context of the topic, background and specific literature, and some indication as to the kind of variable interpretations that would be plausible. This was an important advance on the earlier attempts at panels and dealt with the problem of wild, less-than-plausible theories (e.g., astronauts at Stonehenge, beer-making in the Maltese "temples").

An example of the kind of background information that the panel received is that for the Lepenski Vir panel, shown in Table 8.3. At the

TABLE 8.3. The Mesolithic Village at Lepenski Vir, Yugoslavia.

Place: Lepenski Vir, right bank of Danube, Danube Gorges, Yugoslavia. Discovered during survey for Danube Dam. Excavated in the late 1960s by Dragoslav Srejovic. Post-Pleistocene (Mesolithic) hunter-gatherers. Excavator believes the site is basically pre-agricultural. Others (e.g., Tringham) believe it represents hunter-gatherer/agriculturalist (Neolithic) interaction.

General context: Mesolithic-Neolithic transition in southeast Europe. Hunter-gatherer/agriculturalist interaction in Europe.

Interesting finds at the site: Trapezoid houses with unusual shaped hearths in terraces; carved stone heads; burials; rich bone and stone tools; fishbones.

Interpretations: Symbolic (including Jungian); domus; structuralism; gender division of labor; goddess; art; the demise of hunter-gatherers when agriculturalists come on the scene; the result of sedentary living; the first domestication of humans in Europe.

Relevant literature: [Some references were provided in the reader, and three to four extra readings were recommended.]

same time that we were encouraging the interpretive challenges and grounded storytelling, using specific sites or artifacts as the focus, we—as feminists—wanted to explore with the students the demystification of authority of scientific facts and the challenges involved in writing prehistory at a microscale. We felt one vehicle for this would be this investigation into the alternative ways in which prehistory can be presented. It was for this reason that we suggested early on that it was okay for students to bring themselves into the interpretation of archaeological materials by the use of strategies such as narratives, personal experience, and perception.

The use of narratives and other alternative media was encouraged. We provided some background in the very first readings by including three articles. The first was by John Terrell (1990), addressing explicitly the issue of "storytelling" in archaeology and anthropology, using the Pacific area as his example. Secondly, we provided the article by Janet Spector (1991), now expanded into a book (Spector 1993), that takes a specific archaeological artifact and presents an empirically grounded "story" about its owner and maker. And finally we provided a chapter from one of the best fictional accounts of Ice Age Europe, *Reindeer Moon* (Thomas 1987).

Thus the panel participants in following our guidelines were encouraged to take up different interpretations and viewpoints, which could be that of the different archaeologists or even that of the prehistoric social actors, basing their constructions in the archaeological literature as well as their imaginations. They did this through various skits (as at Maiden

Castle, Varna, Malta, and Oetzi), wearing costumes and incorporating multimedia effects, such as music. They grounded their interpretations in the empirical archaeological data with slides, overheads, and handouts (Table 8.4).

Students who did not wish to participate in a panel or could not do so (for example, if they had certain disabilities or lived too far away to have group meetings between classes), were given an alternative to the panel assignment: to write a three to five page paper. The students opting to write the paper were to read one of the recommended fictional narratives of prehistoric/protohistoric Europe. Their task was to compare the narrative version with the conventional academic interpretations and reporting of the same general archaeological evidence, in terms of (1) the contribution that the narrative makes to our (re)construction of prehistory, and (2) the contribution that the academic literature has made to the narratives. This assignment, which would be worth following up in a more structured and supervised way, allows the student to examine the interplay of mutual contribution between the public media and the academic (usually more) authoritative view of prehistory.

The other main creative assignment, required of all students in one of the area courses, was the term paper (ten to fifteen pages). The assignment was to take a particular place (a mountain, a valley, an island, an archaeological site, a modern city, a tree) in the Mediterranean or Europe and trace its changing history from 10,000 B.P. (or earlier if they wished) until the present. Obviously this meant talking about the humans for whom the place had been an arena for social action and for whom it had meant something in more than just "space container" terms.

We gave the students some advice such as "Don't worry, we know that your 'histories' will be spotty—empty at some times, very full at others, depending on what you can find out about the archaeological evidence available. In other words, for some periods, you will be passing through time very quickly, for others you will dwell on a particular time in more detail. That is fine, as long as you tell us what you are doing."

We also gave some guidelines for how to proceed, based on our experience from the panels: "To start, choose a place where there seems to be enough archaeological data, for example, a site that we have mentioned in class, such as in the panels. The best of these places to choose would be one that is relatively close to a place that you know from personal experience or is written about in guidebooks, for example, London, Oxford, Rome, Florence, Paris, Vienna, or Athens."

With this paper topic our aims were similar to those for the panels, in that we wanted to focus on the specific place and imagined social actors in their broader sociohistorical-geographical context. At the same time we wanted to draw attention to the fact that places are seen by both pre-

TABLE 8.4. European and Mediterranean archaeology panels: Some detailed comments.

Lepenski Vir, Yugoslavia: Mesolithic village. This was a good site to choose for such a panel discussion since many alternative interpretations have been published in English. This site came up as a topic in every course with panels, including "Archaeology and the Goddess," so that panelists became experienced and their contributions were marked by a much more sophisticated attention as to how the inferences were made and to the multiple interpretations that have been made, as well as to the gender biases of the different archaeologists.

Oetzi the Iceman, Austria/Italy: Frozen body dated to 3300 B.C. This panel had an advantage in that much has been said and written about the "Iceman" in both the scientific and popular media, with many conflicting interpretations. In addition, it zeroed in on the smallest unit or scale of archaeological resolution: the individual person. Tringham considers this panel on the Iceman to have been the most successful panel taught, due in large part to the participants, who included the experienced Andre Tschan, a Swiss student and archaeology major, who had in a previous year organized the Egolzwil (lake dwelling) panel. Each panel member had a double presentation: the first as part of the story of the Iceman's personal demise, from his home to the point of his death on the mountain, tools, clothes, environment, mission, rituals, death, and discovery; the second presentation of each covered the same themes from the point of view of the archaeologist and "objective" science. The contrasts were obvious and thrilling to everyone, especially given the multimedia nature of the presentation.

Maiden Castle, England: Iron Age hill fort, focus on massacre at the gate. This panel topic was personally familiar to several panel members and there was support literature in English. The panel reenacted the 1930s camp of archaeologists excavating the fort, and panelists presented their different interpretations that way, at the same time as introducing the archaeological data and the Roman historians' viewpoints.

Opovo, Yugoslavia: Eneolithic village with a well as the focus. This panel demonstrates that a focus on a specific set of archaeological data that was reported in English—in this case a well—was not always a successful topic for a panel. Opovo was excavated by Tringham, but none of the panelists had participated in the excavations. They had to rely on materials published only by Tringham's team and on the empirical evidence of plans, photographs, diaries, and so on. This meant discussing, even questioning, their instructor's ideas. We had overestimated the daring and confidence of the panelists. It was too much of a challenge for them.

Dereivka, Ukraine, Kurgan settlement: Although there was support literature in English and the Kurgans are featured quite dramatically in all of the narratives of Indo-European origins in Europe and the end of the "Civilization of the Goddess," the panelists were not able to "play" with this topic because the context (Ukrainian prehistory) was just too unfamiliar to them. Perhaps we should have coached them more intensively!

Varna, Bulgaria: Eneolithic cemetery; graves without skeletons, which were assumed to have been male. This was a successful panel, using interpretive support literature in English and multimedia presentations. The panel used multimedia technology to focus on the ambiguity of the gender of the people buried (and not buried) in the graves.

TABLE 8.4. Continued.

Maltese "temples": Stone-cut buildings, dated to 5000–2000 B.C. This panel demonstrates that even though these monuments have been described and variously interpreted in English and are part of the important body of literature concerning archaeology and the goddess, this condition will not necessarily lead to a successful panel. Part of the problem was that this panel had a hard act to follow (Oetzi the Iceman). The panel members tried to outdo their Iceman predecessors. Rather than present the many different interpretations, they tried a strategy that was bound to be taken sooner or later in this kind of teaching. They tried to examine all the empirical data through the eyes of their own alternative single unified model of the interpretation of the "temples," one that had not been suggested by any archaeologist, probably because it was fairly implausible. Their model proposed that the focus of the culture and its rituals was on beermaking and beer-drinking! Another problem was that the focus of the panel— all the monumental architecture of prehistoric Malta—was just too diffuse.

---

historic and modern (e.g., tourists, archaeologists) social actors, all of whom themselves have different life histories and cultural experiences.

On the basis of the papers that were written in this course, we were fairly certain that we were on a "right track" in the construction of prehistory for undergraduates. Many of them threw themselves into the creative business of constructing prehistory in fascinating, inspiring, and enterprising ways. These papers were all required to be based on the empirical and available evidence; these were not to be—nor were they—flights of fancy detached from the archaeology and archaeological record. The best papers took up the suggestion that prehistory cannot be written in a linear fashion but is of necessity discontinuous. Many used the "time-machine" format, but these were by no means the most successful. The best ones were carefully and explicitly aware of the empirical data on which their interpretations were based.

Some of the inspiring examples are cited in Table 8.5.

A Topic Course: Prehistoric Art

This turned out to be a large course (about one hundred students), which met for two one-and-a-half-hour sessions each week. We had not previously had this longer time block for panels, which in this course were allotted half of the week's class time instead of only one-third. This class was taught by Conkey alone and focused primarily on the "arts" of both prehistoric and some ethnographic/ethnohistoric gatherer-hunter small-scale societies. The idea was to try to see how anthropologists and archaeologists have and could study the visual cultures of the past.

Seven panel topics were established and sign-up lists were posted out-

TABLE 8.5. European and Mediterranean archaeology term paper: Examples.

In writing a prehistory of Ain Malaha in Jordan from 10,000 B.P. to the present, **Brent** chose to speak through eight differently gendered and aged voices, ending with a female United Nations peacekeeper ca. A.D. 1978.

Limor wrote about Jericho as the story of a woman 11,993 years old—the oldest woman on earth.

May told the story of Knossos as the song of a magic harper in Minoan times who can see into and sing about the future.

Jenna wrote about the dreams that five women, including the archaeologist Dorothy Garrod, had in a cave in Mount Carmel in modern Israel. It was the explicit discussion of dreams, remembering, and prehistory as a real issue rather than a trick to cover the assignment that was gripping in this paper.

Dora told the story of Tunisia through the "eyes" of the west winds of winter with the idea being that winds are a constant throughout prehistory and yet are responsible for the changes that we call prehistory.

Cheryl used a format of tablets that had been discovered in Cyprus and gave insight into the original inhabitants' views of their times.

In a divergence from the strict requirements of the assignment, **Michael** presented the prehistory of Akrotiri from 1628 B.C. to the present in the form of a screenplay for a video using computer-generated imagery. In this he integrated the archaeologists' observations with dramatized prehistoric actions. A preview of media methods to come?

Claire used a format that was not taken up as frequently as expected—the alien view. This can be a very tedious format, but Claire's use of the prehistory and history of Bologna from one million years ago to A.D. 10,000 as a field assignment for two cadets in an outer space anthropology program was delightful.

Cameron told the story of Avebury through the voices of ten participants in prehistory, instilling emotion and a real "feel" for prehistoric social action. He ended the voices with his own as he visited Avebury himself—a wonderful blend of interpretive microscale archaeology based on empirical archaeological evidence.

In Cassandra's story, **Dejah** revealed the prehistory and early archaeology of the Basel area in Switzerland through the diary of her (fictional?) great-grandmother Cassandra, who had been a vocational archaeologist in the nineteenth century. The paper shows an inspired mix of personal experience, history, and archaeology, and reconstruction of what it was like to be a nineteenth-century archaeologist.

---

side the instructor's office. A handout was given along with the course syllabus, which described the kinds of topics one might take up for each panel and what the idea behind each panel was. The panel groups could decide on their own format. Rather than these being individual monologues or somewhat disconnected summaries of sets of information, alternative and imaginative formats were encouraged. Individual panelists could choose to be certain authors or analysts or to take on the opinions, roles, or positions of different interest groups (e.g., what a "shaman" might say about the relation between shamanism and imagery; what a 1993 Australian aboriginal might say about bark paintings; and so on). The panels were scheduled mostly for the second half of the course. By limiting the panels to no more than eight (preferably six) participants, only half of the class could participate in panels, so the other half was asked to write not only a five-to-seven-page research paper but also a one-paragraph evaluation (not a summary) of six out of the seven panels. Panelists also were asked to critique their own panel and their own contribution to the panel. Students were instructed to evaluate the panels on the basis of both the individual contributions as well as on the integration of the different individual parts of the panel. The panel and the research paper each were 33 percent of the course grade.

Here we shall discuss some of the strengths and weaknesses of teaching with panels by focusing on a few specific panels of the "Prehistoric Art" course listed in Table 8.6. Two of the panels were set up as debates, with two different stances to be taken on an issue. In each instance, the students demonstrated that the issue could not be reduced to a simple for-and-against debate, that the issue was complicated, and that the duelism of the debate format did not do justice to the issue at hand. For some of the students, it was somewhat difficult to accept that there was not a real "one side versus the other side" kind of situation, if only because such dichotomies are easier to understand. However, in terms of critical thinking, grasping that issues are too complex, too ambiguous, and too much the products of specific interested stances was an important pedagogical gain.

Some panel topics were overly ambitious in that they were too abstract and were hard to translate into a panel format in front of a large class. This was particularly the case with Panel 4 (Table 8.6), where there was to be a debate that considered which might be more crucial in understanding image-making, the very making of imagery (techniques, technologies, the praxis, and thus the objects themselves) or the circumstances of imagery (the social and cultural contexts). The debate broke down since everyone wanted to argue that both "sides" were important. Moreover, this topic comes with a huge and long history of theoretical debate within art history and anthropology, which also made it hard for the students to develop their own opinions.

The other ambitious panel was the group that chose to exhibit a selection of native California baskets from the Hearst Museum's collection in the museum's teaching area. Given the museum's staff shortages and the complexities of organizing eight people's schedules to work with

TABLE 8.6. "Prehistoric Art" panels.

1. Gender Issues (Gendered Makers, Gendered Images). This panel considered the issue of gender in image-making. The participants used two case studies in the course reader as a starting point: Ann Solomon's challenge to David Lewis-Williams's idea (see below) by emphasizing the importance of gender ideology in image-making, and the varied interpretations of the Paleolithic "Venus" statuettes. They focused their presentations on questions such as: What can we say about images of males or females from past cultural contexts? How do we avoid "reading" our own gender notions into these images? What do we know about how images might be part of defining gender ideologies or of "negotiating" gender relations? Are there differences and variations in who makes "art" in different cultures and why?

2. Shamanism Debate (two "teams" of four). This panel debated the idea that shamanism is the primary source for image-making in not only the rock art of southern Africa but in other rock art traditions elsewhere, which is a view that has become increasingly popular in recent years, especially under the influence of the research and writings of David Lewis-Williams. In the debate one side argued that it is possible to identify so-called "entoptic" designs even archaeologically based on cross-cultural similarities due to human neuropsychology. They thus argued for the power and widespread applicability of the "grand" view of the shamanism hypothesis. The other side argued against this position.

3. The Science of Art. This panel was for those who are more empirically minded. They presented all the fascinating things that the science of image-making can contribute, including the explosion of recent literature on the microscopic study of pigment composition, fracturing patterns and breakage of objects, the ways in which underlying technical processes (such as the steps of making bronze ear spools or ceramic pots) can be used to infer mental or ideological notions about cosmology, and so on.

4. The Making of Images versus the Circumstances of Images. The topic for this panel was inspired by an interview with Svetlana Alpers, a University of California professor in the history of art, who notes that there is often the tendency to differentiate between the "making of pictures" (concentrating on the objects or images themselves) and the "circumstances of pictures." Traditionally, this has lined up as the difference between art history (object-centered) and anthropology (context-centered), though recent developments in both fields have blurred this distinction. In this debate one "side" was to argue for the study of imagery in terms of the culture around it and the other "side" was to argue against this position, for the study of the "making of pictures." In fact, they tried to find a way *not* to make it an either/or issue.

5. The Art of Aboriginal Australians. This panel focused on artistic traditions and practices that may date back more than twenty thousand years and that are still being carried out under very different cultural, political, and social circumstances. What, in this case, do we mean by "prehistoric" art? What is a "living tradition"? What are the dilemmas raised by the practice of contemporary aboriginals who want to and are painting over ancient rock paintings? What do we mean by "conservation"?

TABLE 8.6. Continued.

6. California Basketry. Even if we weren't in California and did not have available the Hearst Museum collection of California basketry, we would have to say that this basketry is among the finest and most sophisticated in the world. There is a rich repertoire of images and designs, there are specific techniques among some groups for baskets that have different social and symbolic "uses," and there came to be some basket-making specialists—mostly women—who created, defined, and redefined the styles and the forms. This panel presented information about California basketry traditions that was a prelude to the exhibition that they put together in the Hearst Museum Teaching Exhibition area. The panel also considered the whole topic of "exhibitions" and "collections," as political and ethical issues as well as cultural and anthropological activities.

7. Course Summary. This panel presented their views on what this course was all about.

the materials in the museum, the students felt they put in an inordinate amount of preparation time and found themselves more frustrated than inspired by what they came to see as the limitations of museum collections. This was a rather sophisticated group of students who argued a lot over what they should attempt to "say" about the baskets without the voices of the native makers. They, of course, found themselves quickly embroiled in some of the most interesting but difficult issues of museums and anthropology today (see Stocking 1985): Who speaks for the makers? What is "authentic"? How do you display objects without people? While they effectively communicated their differences in their panel, they all were quite pleased to be able to indicate on their résumés that they had actually co-"curated" a mini-exhibit in a major anthropological museum.

The entire class went to see the exhibit for its evaluation of the panel, and we were able to take advantage of some schedule problems. The materials went without labels for a few weeks and people tried to go both before they were labeled—to imagine the themes or the issues or the stories of the baskets—and then after labeling. The no-labels exhibit was greatly enjoyed, given the background reading on the anthropological understandings about material and visual culture in general and on California basketry, specifically.

Because of their courage and imagination, the last panel—the summary panel—was also particularly effective. While some students in the class really wanted this group to give them a straightforward summary of what we studied, this panel chose instead to do an honest and imaginative critique of some of the course materials, including a constructive but pointed critique of the course organization and the topics that were *not* considered. Conkey, as instructor, was both surprised and pleased at this healthy and mature critique, which pointed out topics that were given too much attention, where the instructor's biases showed through too clearly, and why these panels were always an experience like treading on thin ice. Overall, they thought the experience well worth it, but there were indeed a few "feet" (and legs, and torsos?) that fell into icy water!

Always Teaching Fragments

The above descriptions of our panel experiences provide some of the specifics on how we have experimented with what we believe to be feminist-inspired methods for teaching archaeology in a variety of course contexts.

In the "Archaeology and the Goddess" class, we found that *theoretical questions and debates*—about feminist interpretations, material culture, archaeology, and speculation—served to provide the most substance to the class and the panels.

In the course on prehistoric art, we found that the topical approach worked well for panel foci, especially topics with some edge of controversy—gender, museum exhibits, "continuing tradition" in the emergent capitalism of international art markets—or with outright attempts at debates with "sides."

In our area courses, on the other hand, we have found that the panels that focused on the *specifics* of the archaeological record for interpretation—a site, a feature, even just an artifact, or an event or individual (such as the massacre at the entrance to Maiden Castle or Oetzi the Iceman)—were more satisfying and provoked more stimulating discussion than those panels treating a wider topic, such as a cultural group (such as the Natufians), especially with our encouragement for grounded but imaginative alternative interpretations. Not all specific microscale topics were successful, however. Examples of topics that "bombed" were Opovo, Dereivka, and Mas d'Azil.

In all courses, the panels were more successful when the material addressed in the panel was already somehow familiar in the personal experiences of the panelists, whether from previous reading, coursework, media, or through general life experiences of travel, household dynamics, power relations, and so on.

Failing this, the ability to read about the topic for themselves (usually meaning publication in English) helped the success. This is particularly a problem when teaching an "area" course such as European archaeology. Thus, exotic sites such as Lepenski Vir (Yugoslavia) and the cemetery at Varna (Bulgaria) that have extensive, often quite interpretive, publication in English provided more successful "take-off points" for the panels than geographically less exotic sites, such as the princess's grave at Vix in France, that seemed to us equally provocative.

In almost all cases each and every panelist rose to the occasion, but it was again clear that the success of the panel was often directly linked to the enterprise, confidence, and coordinating abilities of at least one or two leaders among the student participants in each panel. Some panels were threatened, though, by very strong leaders who insisted on their own agenda and viewpoint, which took some resisting: a hard lesson for undergraduates but a necessary one should they face group life, as they inevitably will!

It was quite clear that the students who had taken a number of our panel courses developed in their skill at panel organization and discussion. They learned after two or three classes that it is important to start organizing the panels early, to plan the panel as a whole, and to plan the timing of their own presentations. They learned that it's all right to use their imaginations and narratives, as well as multimedia devices and props such as clothes and handouts. They also learned that it was to their advantage if one or two people took it upon themselves to lead the panels. They did get emboldened by the success of their predecessors, so that as the semester went on, the panels were better overall. They *do* learn from their peers! By 1994, the panel presentations were often so ambitious that they left little room for discussion—this is an important aspect of the panel courses that is difficult to accommodate within the fifty-minute classroom time.

In the official instructions to students for evaluating panels for the "Prehistoric Art" class, Conkey asked them to evaluate the effectiveness of each panel to communicate its stated goals and objectives and its abilities to contribute to the understanding and interpretation of prehistoric and anthropological arts. In our own minds we have evaluated "panel success" by the degree to which the participants were able to demonstrate the ambiguity of the archaeological record and a critical appraisal of interpretations of this data, at the same time as drawing out the multiplicity of possible interpretations that may be made of the data as prehistory is written from different vantage points, whether it be vantage points of the interpreters and archaeologists or the vantage points of people in the past.

In trying to be coaches rather than performers in these courses, we encouraged other "voices" from guests: an archaeologist from the classics department for the Mediterranean course; a social anthropologist to talk about the anthropology of art; an author of one of the popular goddess books; a visiting researcher working with contemporary aboriginal arts. In our large introductory archaeology course each semester, we expect that all the archaeology faculty, including those in other departments and traditions, and each of the course teaching assistants will give lectures on their approaches, their research concerns. This view and practice is shared by all of our archaeology faculty.

Other "techniques" have included using a video that presents one strong or controversial view with an article to "balance" it. For example, we used Susan Rogers's article (1975) to balance the film *Kypseli: Women and Men Apart, A Divided Reality*, which claims that Greek gender rigidity "goes back to the origins of Mediterranean societies" (Hoffman et al., 1976). Another technique was to show a set of images or reconstructions of particular periods or events in prehistory, along with an article that raises our consciousness about the powers of the "visual language of archaeology" (Conkey 1992; Gifford-Gonzalez 1993; Moser 1992; Tringham 1992).

We have experimented with using graduate students as intergenerational coaches for specific panels or debates; sometimes the undergraduate students feel they can explore unknown topics more freely with them. This has been especially beneficial for the debates.

We have tried to structure some exam questions for which there are no "true" or absolute answers. For example, using a slide "identification" in the prehistoric art class, we ask the students to identify an image and make a case for *why* the image could be identified as from that group or culture or time; their answers are graded on the case they make not on the absolute veracity of their identification. The identification can be "wrong" but the "reasons" could be right! We find that study questions given in advance promote collaborative learning among groups, and we try to provide a space for such groups to meet for their discussions. At the same time, for the area courses, we insist that students know the geography of Europe and of some site locations, using map quizzes.

We do not advocate these panels as a formula nor as an easy way to substitute for our own lectures. We find that we put in more, not less, time in coaching the students, but the gains have been extraordinary. We have had more meaningful contact with students, and we believe we have been able to foster collaborative peer activities among the students that extend beyond that particular class or panel. In these courses, we have received the strongest teaching evaluations of our careers, with particularly encouraging scores on such aspects as "encourages critical thinking," "defines their viewpoint openly," "explores various perspectives" and that the course was "challenging and stimulating."

There are, of course, student anxieties about any kind of open-endedness in courses, and the panels and what we try to do in them always bring these out: "Why isn't there *an* answer or *an* interpretation?" We find that we always have to be on guard about not letting the creativity that we encourage backslide into intellectual paralysis and nihilism. We have to be much more forthright with examples as to why this is not free-floating and where and how there are parameters and constraints (see Wylie 1992). Students need to be guided somehow through the inherent ambiguity of so much of the archaeological record and of so much of the practice of archaeology. We quickly came to the conclusion that our responsibilities in these kinds of courses are in some ways greater.

We do not envision that we will be able to simply reuse the panel topics and techniques year after year. Rather, the interactive "fields" are always changing: the discipline of archaeology is always changing, the students, of course, are usually new and, in any event, short-term. Each course brings a different constellation of experiences and personalities. From one class to the next we ourselves have new experiences and have done new readings and thinking. We can't rely on "notes from the last time we taught this class" alone; they no longer will do.

We are always teaching fragments. Because we are enmeshed in a momentary historical specificity, all of what we do is provisional and emergent, but the tensions of this can be both creative and productive. We hope that with this kind of experimentation we are working toward accepting and communicating that "knowledge is always provisional, open-ended, and relational" (Luke and Gore 1992:7): this is both its strength and its challenge, and as we move—we hope—*through* the received views, the master narratives, and the authorities, we are inspired through the emancipation of the archaeological imagination to be mobilized to encourage critical thinking as much as to gain greater understandings of the human past.

Acknowledgments

Special thanks go to the large number of undergraduate and graduate students who have passed through our classes and have been wonderful participants in our experiments in feminist pedagogy. Many of you were not so pleased at first to have to go through the "panel" experience or to use a fictional narrative format in writing about archaeological data. We thank you all for staying with us and allowing us to benefit from your patience and creative responses to our challenge.

Special thanks also go to Kristin Luker for sharing the article "Teaching Like It Matters" by Jane Tompkins with Conkey, and thanks as well to all the "Chickens" for ongoing discussions of feminism, pedagogy, and architectural (rather than housekeeping) action in the university.

Notes

1. Tompkins describes herself in the performance mode in her own teaching: "I had been putting on a performance whose goal was not to help the students

learn but to perform before them in such a way that they would have a good opinion of me" (Tompkins 1991:24).

2. In the past fifteen years, a suite of ideas about prehistoric matriarchies, female power and empowerment, harmonious gender relations, spiritual re-definitions, ecological consciousness, and the politics of spirituality have been mobilized by reference to and through imagery of "The Goddess" (Eisler 1987; Gadon 1989; Spretnak 1982; Stone 1976; Gimbutas 1989, 1991; for a detailed critique, see Conkey and Tringham 1995; Tringham 1993). In a December 1992 issue, the Phoenix, Arizona, *Republic* reported that, according to Megatrends, more than five hundred thousand people (mostly, but not exclusively, women) "identify" with various aspects of these ideas and issues.

The hypothesis (or conviction, to some) is, in its most basic form, as follows: There were past societies in Europe and the Near East, especially prior to the so-called "invasion" of Indo-Europeans circa five thousand years ago, that were goddess-worshipping, female-centered, in harmony with their environments, more balanced in male-female relationships, and in which the status of women was high and respected. These "facts" about past societies are based on the existence of artifacts (such as female statuettes) and interpretations of certain decorative motifs (e.g., "spirals") as female and of certain architectural features as "altars," "shrines," or "temples" that are then taken to signify the sacred or religious nature of these features and their associated female characteristics or attributes. These are the archaeological manifestations of "The Goddess" or of goddesses.

References

Bourdier, Jean-Paul
    1989   "Reading tradition." In *Dwellings, Settlements and Traditions: Cross-cultural Perspectives*, edited by J.-P. Bourdier and N. AlSayyad, 35–51. Lanham, Md.: University Press of America.

Conkey, Margaret
    1992   "Mobilizing Ideologies: The Archaeo-logics of Paleolithic "Art." Symposium "Envisioning the Past: Visual Forms and the Structuring of Interpretations" at the 91st annual meeting of the American Anthropological Association, San Francisco, Calif., December 2–6.

Conkey, Margaret W., and Ruth E. Tringham
    1995   "Archaeology and the Goddess: Exploring the Contours of Feminist Archaeology." In *Feminisms in the Academy: Rethinking the Disciplines*, edited by A. Stewart and D. Stanton, 199–247. Ann Arbor: University of Michigan Press.

Eisler, Riane
    1987   *The Chalice and the Blade.* San Francisco: Harper and Row.

Freire, Paul
    1973   *Pedagogy of the Oppressed.* New York: Seabury Press.

Gadon, Elinor
    1989   *The Once and Future Goddess.* San Francisco: Harper and Row.

Gero, Joan M., and Margaret W. Conkey, eds.
    1991   *Engendering Archaeology: Women and Prehistory.* Oxford: Basil Blackwell.

Gifford-Gonzalez, Diane
    1993   "You Can Hide but You Can't Run: Representations of Women's

Work in Illustrations of Paleolithic Life." *Visual Anthropology Review* 9 (1): 23–41.

Gimbutas, Marija
1989   *The Language of the Goddess.* San Francisco: Harper and Row.
1991   *Civilization of the Goddess.* San Francisco: Harper and Row.

Hoffman, Susannah, Richard Cowan, and Paul Aratow
1976   *Kypseli: Women and Men Apart, A Divided Reality.* Film produced by University of California Media Resources.

Keller, Evelyn Fox
1985   *Reflections on Gender and Science.* New Haven, Conn.: Yale University Press.

Luke, Carmen, and Jennifer Gore, eds.
1992   *Feminisms and Critical Pedagogy.* London: Routledge.

Maher, Frances, and Mary Kay Thompson Tetreault
1994   *The Feminist Classroom.* New York: Basic Books.

Maxwell, Andrew H., and Pam Davidson Buck
1992   "Teaching as Praxis: Decolonizing Media Representations of Race, Ethnicity, and Gender in the New World Order." Special issue of *Transforming Anthropology*, vol. 3 no. 1.

Merchant, Carolyn
1980   *The Death of Nature: Women, Ecology and the Scientific Revolution.* San Francisco: Harper and Row.

Middleton, Sue
1988   *Educating Feminists: Life Histories and Pedagogy.* Oxford: Pergamon Press.

Moser, Stephanie
1992   "The Visual Language of Archaeology: A Case Study of the Neanderthals." *Antiquity* 66:831–44.

Read, Donna
1988   "The Goddess Remembered." Film directed by Donna Read; produced by Studio D, National Film Board of Canada.

Rogers, Susan C.
1975   "Female Forms of Power and the Myth of Male Dominance: A Model of Female/Male Interaction in Peasant Society." *American Ethnologist* 2 (4): 727–56.

Rosser, Sue V.
1986   *Teaching Science and Health from a Feminist Perspective: A Practical Guide.* Oxford: Pergamon Press.

Rothschild, Joan
1988   *Teaching Technology from a Feminist Perspective: A Practical Guide.* Oxford: Pergamon Press.

Spector, Janet D.
1991   "What This Awl Means: Toward a Feminist Archaeology." In *Engendering Archaeology: Women and Prehistory*, edited by Joan M. Gero and Margaret W. Conkey, 388–407. Oxford: Basil Blackwell.
1993   *What This Awl Means.* Minneapolis: Minnesota Historical Society Press.

Spretnak, Charlene
1982   "The Politics of Women's Spirituality." In *The Politics of Women's Spirituality*, edited by C. Spretnak, 393–98. Garden City, NY: Doubleday.

Stocking, George, ed.
   1985   *Objects and Others: Essays on Museums and Material Culture.* Madison:
           University of Wisconsin Press.
Stone, Merlin
   1976   *When God Was a Woman.* New York: Dial Press.
Terrell, John
   1990   "Storytelling and Prehistory." *Archaeological Method and Theory* 2:1–29.
Thomas, Elizabeth Marshall
   1987   *Reindeer Moon.* New York: Simon and Schuster.
Tompkins, Jane
   1991   "Teaching Like It Matters: A Modest Proposal for Revolutionizing
           the Classroom." *Lingua Franca* (August): 24–27.
Tringham, Ruth
   1991a   "Households with Faces: The Challenge of Gender in Prehistoric Ar-
           chitectural Remains." In *Engendering Archaeology: Women and Prehistory,*
           edited by Joan M. Gero and Margaret W. Conkey, 93–131. Oxford:
           Basil Blackwell.
   1991b   "Men and Women in Prehistoric Architecture." *Traditional Dwellings
           and Settlements Review* 3 (1): 9–28.
   1992   "Visual Images of Archaeological Architecture: Gender in Space."
           Symposium "Envisioning the Past: Visual Forms and the Structur-
           ing of Interpretations" at the 91st annual meeting of the American
           Anthropological Association, San Francisco, December 2–6.
   1993   Review of Marija Gimbutas, "Civilization of the Goddess." *American
           Anthropologist* 95 (1): 196–97.
Wylie, Alison
   1992   "The Interplay of Evidential Constraints and Political Interests: Re-
           cent Archaeological Research on Gender." *American Antiquity* 57 (1):
           15–35.

Chapter 9
Archaeological Practice and Gendered Encounters with Field Data

Joan M. Gero

Introduction

In many fields of science, the construction and reproduction of disciplinary knowledge have come under inspection. Rejecting an earlier "unambiguous facts of nature" model, the once distinct areas of sociology of science, philosophy of science, and history of science have united as "science studies," which takes as its subject the ways in which science is made to work through a conjuncture of ideological, semantic, cultural, sociological, historic, and technical (craft) conventions. Research in this area typically involves close-up inspections of the practice of science, where the complicated material circumstances and the particular historical sequences that underlie the creation of a "fact" are detailed. Remarkably, science studies have largely neglected gender, although feminist critiques of science have offered a wide range of insights into the relationship between knowledge and knowers, objects and subjects, rationality and engagement. This discussion brings science studies and related constructivist approaches together with feminist cognitive theory to examine archaeological field practice and the production of archaeological field data, ultimately to reveal how the organization of gendered personnel in the field insinuates itself in the creation of archaeological fact.

My argument will proceed as follows. Following this general introduction, I lay out my assumptions about archaeological field practice as a socially organized, historically contingent context that interacts with and thoroughly conditions the data it is designed to collect. I then turn to the Paleo-Indian excavations at Arroyo Seco in Argentina to observe field practice close at hand, ultimately focusing on the intersection of field practice and gender. My conclusion, that accepted practice conforms to a masculinist style of research and produces masculinist data, invites thinking about how to proceed with less gender-exclusive, more embracing cognitive values.

That gender relations and gender hierarchies operate at all levels of archaeological research has begun to be detailed, but the effects of these political arrangements on evidential truth are still incompletely understood; more close-grained work is needed. Perhaps even less studied at this point are the curious, even unique epistemic conditions and the specific internal "cultural" dynamics of archaeological research that articulate directly with the knowledge we produce. Some of these dynamics parallel descriptions of other knowledge-producing fields studied by "science studies," beginning with the obvious fact that "facts" are not simply recorded as they are observed but are crafted out of a welter of confusing and conflicting observations, modified and reformulated out of knowledge of what other researchers are working on, and accepted more readily if their proponent is well credentialed (for instance).

But archaeology is also unlike other fields examined by "science studies," exaggerated in its reliance on internally structured, situated, conventionalized, and contingent (constructivist) inquiry and knowledge claims. Specific practical, disciplinary features of archaeology, more than its status as a "social" science per se, predispose its practitioners to engage more heavily in "constructed" dimensions of practice and to put forward more heavily constructed "facts" than other scientists. For one thing, archaeological sites and depositional sequences are unique occurrences and, despite the claims of "New Archaeology," most fine-grained results cannot be rerun at another site, using the standardized procedures and controls that are said to guide experimental replication in the laboratory sciences. Of course, replicability of research results, a hallmark of conventional science, is itself questioned by science studies as unachievable in practice, accomplished in reality only on the basis of protracted negotiations that define conventions of concept breadth, and predicated on pretaught and widely shared skills and assumptions. All replicated experimentation is thus achieved by standardizing tacit knowledge to lump levels of dissimilarity into predetermined and accepted evidential packages.

But if replicability is in all science a powerfully conflated fiction, in archaeology, where excavation is destruction, results cannot even be reviewed or reinspected once data has been collected. Archaeologists have no second chance and competing researchers no independent review process of fundamental evidential matters: what is to count as "association"? or superimposition? or a semantically grouped entity like "postmold"? Where most scientists can dispute and *refute* facticity on many levels, however internally constructed each level may be, dissension in archaeology cannot be resolved by recollecting primary data but only by reference to reported, represented data. Archaeological discourse can only begin at an already more highly constructed level of foundational precepts.

Related to but exacerbating the nonreplicability of destroyed archaeological evidence is the time-honored tradition that "principal" investigators not only direct data collection but also take charge of knowledge assessments and truth claims; nondissenting, hierarchical research teams carry out research tasks "beneath" them but have no say in interpretive conclusions. While hierarchical organization also characterizes many other scientific endeavors, in archaeology the ramification of this hierarchy is that chains of evidential inference are ultimately constructed by a single unchecked, and *uncheckable*, authority. Just where the destruction of interpreted evidence would most demand multiple perspectives on the unique occurrences of archaeological field data, it is denied by the structure of directorship.

Finally, archaeological pronouncements are culturally weightier than many other scientific truths in that "the nature of man" and "the course of human development" are consumed by a larger and more interested public, and are held relevant to a wider social discourse than, say, the outcomes of peptide research. On the weight of sometimes very ambiguous material evidence, archaeologists are pressed to add interpretive levels to their observations, to offer the public constructed, synthetic overviews from uncheckable data.

Thus models of how "science" works, while compelling and informative in situating science as a social enterprise, cannot be expected to apply in any straightforward manner to archaeological constructions of knowledge. Indeed, from within science studies, there is a consistent critique of the "unity of science" thesis, arguing against the idea that the sciences constitute any kind of bounded and coherent set of practices and demanding focused attention to the local and situated practices that constitute all contexts of knowledge production. Whether or not archaeological research practices, from the recognition of primary data to syntheses of the human past, are less stable and foundational, more situated and independent, than corresponding research practices of laboratory sciences, archaeologists must be accountable for their nonreviewed, noncomparative, nonregulated, and highly consumed scientific practices.

As a start, archaeology has recognized the role that "context" and politics (including dominant gender relations and explicitly feminist perspectives) play in archaeological reconstructions (cf. Gero, Lacy, and Blakey 1983; Gathercole and Lowenthal 1990; Pinsky and Wylie 1989). The last decade of research has successfully shown that community values are reflected in how archaeological work is carried out, what particular work is carried out, and in what we make of that work—our interpretations (Edgeworth 1991). We know that "context" is significant at different (and not easily disentangled) levels of conditioning and structuring of knowledge: that Western industrial and state-level ideologies set up sociopolitical relations that are then reiterated in interpretive understandings: the hierarchical relations of power inherent in the modern state are accepted, looked for, and naturalized in evolutionary archaeological trajectories without corresponding attention to horizontal relations of cooperation and exchange that also characterize the social arrangements of complex groups (Fowler 1987; Handsman and Leone 1989). At this most broadly constituting level as well, modern gender assumptions pervade our reconstructions of the past (Gero and Conkey 1991; Claassen 1992, 1994; Walde and Willows 1991; du Cros and Smith 1993). We recognize, too, that a narrower, changing sociopolitical-intellectual context, such as the decades of the Vietnam War or the eco-environmental movement, has conditioned understandings of the past (Wilk 1985). And we know that the political economy of academic life—the hierarchical prestige attached to specific research institutions, or the pressure to publish results in time frames that correspond to tenure and promotion decisions—affect how research is defined and what counts as a significant knowledge contribution (Latour and Woolgar 1979; Wobst and Keene 1983).

But what is left underspecified in these accounts is precisely where and how practitioners bring such contextual assumptions to the data. Where should we locate the processes through which cultural politics condition archaeological knowledge? The old diagram of THEORY interacting with DATA in a feedback loop is clearly inadequate to model these processes; even adding CONTEXT to make a triangle of THEORY-DATA-CONTEXT misrepresents the complex historical and sociopolitical interactions that condition every stage of archaeological research, from the naming and classifying of archaeological data through the writing of interpretive explanations, and from the sociological/genealogical arrangements of professional relationships through the production of published archaeological reports. To conceptualize contextual assumptions, however schematically, as *interacting* with data recognition and recovery and with theoretical choices and ambitions is a poor metaphor because it suggests "context" as separable from and external to data and theory. Given the degree to which cultural politics seemingly act upon every stage of research, we must square off against a pervasive notion of a "context" of knowledge production as some thick and foggy social miasma that surrounds and encompasses, thoroughly drenches and shapes investigators and their data and theory, and through which we attempt to peer in order to recover "facts." It is the evaluation of such a notion that brings us to the role of everyday archaeological practice and its contribution to knowledge production.

The analysis offered here starts with a science studies framework that emphasizes the ethnomethodology perspective. This approach treats as a topic of empirical study the practical activities, the practical circumstances, and the practical sociological reasoning that underlie and organize everyday social interaction. By making practical activities observable, the decisions made "for practical purposes," "in light of this situation," and "given the nature of these circumstances," Harold Garfinkle (1967:7) argues that one can inspect the "rule governed activities of everyday life, known as the 'natural facts of life'" but which, for participants, are actually complex, shared, taken-for-granted rule structures. Using these related frameworks, my study focuses on the organization of everyday field practice and the routine recovery of "primary data" for several reasons. Fieldwork is the common denominator of all archaeological research, the baseline of production that unifies archaeologists of historic and prehistoric, classical and anthropological, New World and Old World, hunter-gatherer and complex society persuasions. Fieldwork also represents a more organized and socially interactive set of practices and can be more readily observed and evaluated than can the private, solitary, and individual activities of interpreting or writing up archaeological conclusions; fieldwork is not subject to the same public review processes as written texts. Finally, the mundane, assumed, routinized practices of fieldwork constitute a particularly sensitive conjuncture of context, personnel, and data, one that we inspect in the following sections.

By closely observing fieldwork, then, I hope to arrive at answers to questions such as: What is the role of human agency in producing or constructing data, as opposed to "discovering data" in the ground? To what degree are archaeological data timeless and neutral, and the methods used to recover them rational, transparent, and gender neutral? Or we might ask our questions another way: To what degree are archaeological data external to us, and how do archaeological data "act back," or constrain, our excitable imaginations and divergent cultural behaviors? How is archaeological knowledge conditioned by the cultural politics—and the gendered politics—of the world in which such knowledge is accumulated?

Practice as Context

In the view adopted here, our knowledge of the past is entrenched in the mundane, unquestioned procedures and practices, the accepted use of specific tools and instruments, and the carefully inculcated technical abilities that we teach and expect of practitioners. The knowledge we produce arises directly out of and is profoundly structured by the assumed features that we build into, and count on, as "doing archaeology."

Successful archaeological fieldwork, like all managed "witnessed" social settings, is accomplished through the coordinated practices of everyday activities. For the practitioner, the organizational "hows" of working in a coordinated setting are unproblematic and commonplace, known only vaguely and only in the doing, which is skillful, reliable, and uniform, with enormous standardization and as an unaccountable matter (Garfinkle 1967:10); practitioners are "mundane reasoners" (Gilbert and Mulkay 1984:87, citing Pollner 1974). Driven by entirely "practical" concerns ("what to do next"), the work exhibits elaborate temporal and spatial coordination and sequencing of activities, coordinated by the commonly held knowledge about how the setting works.

Following Garfinkle, the features of shared background knowledge needed to maintain the smoothly running organization include nomenclature, production programs (digging sequences), laws of conduct appropriate to the setting, rules of inference, models of causation, and rules for rational decision-making when agreement is negotiated. "All of these, together with an inquirer's 'system' of alternatives, his [*sic*] 'decision' methods, his information, his choices, and the rationality of his accounts and actions are all constituent parts of the same practical circumstances in which inquirers do the work of inquiry—and which inquirers know, require, count on, take for granted, use and gloss" (Garfinkle 1967:13). Again and again, practitioners demonstrate to each other their grasp of the taken-for-granted cognitive rule structures and the practical sequencing of activities that organize the setting.

In this sense, then, standard, assumed scientific practice is an organized context that has been socially *accomplished,* and in it are embodied a socially *accomplished* familiarity, a socially *accomplished* objectivity, a socially *accomplished* accountability. The practical activities used to conduct investigations have a recognizable, routinized, methodic character—or impersonability—or "objectivity"—but one that is fundamentally conditioned by the socially organized purpose of their arrangement (Garfinkle 1967:10). Within this system of shared knowledge, each practical activity is "doubly contextual in being both *context-shaped* and *context-renewing*" (Heritage 1984:242, cited in Goodwin and Goodwin n.d.), and "facts" emerging from such a context are thoroughly situated within its rules and organization.

Because the mundane features of activity are so assumed by custom, they have a *moral* character to them; they are the "right" thing to do, and proceeding as they do without question, they constitute their own kind of rationality. Everyday, assumed activities have, as well, a set of accepted and unexamined *aesthetic* criteria such that they are deemed successful when results are pleasingly displayed. Rendering objects more clearly visible and with greater symmetry and balance carries its own persuasive weight and power; things are "done right" when they "look right," when they conform to pre-erected ideals of arrangements.

Thus, as Charles Goodwin and Marjorie Harness Goodwin (n.d.) have noted in other work settings, the recovery of archaeological data, rather than being a transparent "natural" ability, is recognized as a socially organized element of practice that is embedded within, and sustained by, a community of practice. Rather than being simply recorded as they are observed, data are seen as socially situated and as interactive accomplishments inseparable from the course of inquiry that produced them (Lynch 1985:4).

It must be underscored that a significant gulf separates formal accounts of doing science from actual practice (Gilbert and Mulkay 1984). Formal accounts (including final site reports) deliberately obscure the practical organization of knowledge construction. Once data are "achieved," they are quickly freed from the social and technical circumstances of their production and lose all historical reference to the contextual conditions of their construction (Latour and Woolgar 1979:106). New knowledge is summarized in a form that suggests that results followed rationally and directly out of tightly controlled and entirely impersonal procedures: names of technicians or workers are most notably omitted, and the use of a passive tense further removes human agency. Temporal sequences are ignored or inverted; formal and generalized methodological routines are reported as though anyone would have come to the same conclusions, without reference to the local, heterogeneous, individualized, and contextualized "technical know-how" used to make knowledge visible, to negotiate what *counts* as an adequate record of what was observed, or what counts as "the same thing" or what counts as "agreement." Good science achieves a generalized and impersonal context that never exists in practice.

Let me summarize, then. I am arguing that to answer the question, "how is archaeological knowledge conditioned by the cultural politics of the world in which such knowledge is accumulated?" we have taken a false turn. Too often we have looked for a context apart from and external to the knowledge itself and have tried to see how that context acted upon practitioners of science and upon data. In doing so, we have subscribed to an old dichotomy that tried to show data as "external and constraining" in relation to a group of researchers and interpreters who can in some meaningful way be separated from the data and the methods used to uncover that data.

But here, I want to inspect archaeological practices as themselves constituting a context of rational accountability. That is, I want to insist that the embedded, implicit, shared background assumptions, language use, technical know-how, and practical skills that underpin the social, interactive activity of archaeology are themselves a distorting or at least a constituting context. As practitioners, archaeologists *are* each others' context, embodying and reproducing in their everyday work activities aspects of an "external" set of values that are said to condition them. And these, I will show, include gender assumptions.

Field Practice on a Paleo-Indian Site

I turn now to the pampas of Argentina and the site of Arroyo Seco to observe the practice of archaeology. Located near the city of Tres Arroyos, province of Buenos Aires, Arroyo Seco is an open-air, multicomponent site on a small hill above the right bank of the Primer Brazo (first branch) of the river Tres Arroyos. Since 1977, approximately two hundred square meters of excavations focusing on the Paleo-Indian components of the site have been carried out, representing some 10 to 20 percent of the estimated extent of archaeological remains at Arroyo Seco (Politis 1989:28). This work has produced excellent documentation of early human interaction with a paleoenvironment and with Pleistocene fauna as well as dramatic evidence of some of the earliest burials on the American continent. Numerous important publications (Politis 1984, 1986, 1989; Politis and Salemme 1989) have emerged from this work, and it has provided training for large numbers of Argentinian students of archaeology. I was invited to observe field practice at Arroyo Seco in March 1992, as five new two-by-two-meter excavation units were opened adjacent to earlier excavations that had contained eight-thousand-year-old burials in association with extinct megafauna. Together with Charles Goodwin on the video camera, we participated in and observed excavation routines for nine days at the site.

That archaeological practice is socially situated and contextually conditioned was quickly affirmed at Arroyo Seco as we observed a number of taken-for-granted local procedures unfamiliar to me as a North American researcher: the use of red "twist 'ems" to mark the location of small flakes or bone fragments in situ so they would stand out during mapping; unique and clever ways of folding the identifying labels into flaps of plastic bags containing wet flotation samples to protect the labels from moisture; the hanging of flotation bags from associated excavation unit stakes to dry out before being packed away. Unknown in North America, these routine activities were conventionally accepted as mundane, assumed practice by a local community of practitioners, employed unquestioningly and routinely taught to new initiates.

Other routine procedures at Arroyo Seco conformed closely to North American archaeological practice. It is worth looking more closely at such practices, for example the taking of the "level photograph" at the bottom of each ten-centimeter excavation level, across four contiguous two-by-two-meter excavation units. The objective of taking these photographs was to record associations among artifacts and features revealed in the same level across the entire sixteen-square-meter block of excavated area.[1] At Arroyo Seco, after the bottom of each ten-centimeter level had been reached in all four excavation units, a familiar bustle of coordinated activity was initiated to clean up the contiguous excavated area: the surface was brushed carefully with whisk brooms to remove distracting clods of dirt or extraneous debris; strings were tightened across the excavation block to square off the individual units comprising the block; a chalkboard was prepared to identify the level being photographed; and the block was cleared of all tools, buckets, artifact bags, clipboards, notes, papers, and, importantly, people. In a concerted flurry of activity, flotation sample bags were snatched from the stakes on which they had been drying, implements were stashed outside the block and out of the camera's view, wheelbarrows were backed away from the edges of excavation units, and field crew, flocking around to witness this official closing of the excavation level, had to be coaxed farther and farther back so their feet wouldn't appear in the final photograph.

A picture of the excavation block taken during a lunch break (Figure 9.1) shows it emptied of personnel but littered with the implements used to produce and inscribe archaeological knowledge. Figure 9.1 suggests the profoundly coordinated, accomplished, cultural and technological aspects of transforming what is encountered in an excavation into "data" (cf. Edgeworth 1991). Compare this casually interrupted scene to the formal image represented in the final level photograph (Figure 9.2), now with all tools and evidence of human agency removed; the final level photograph shows a depersonalized and de-instrumented distribution of artifacts and features, a set of objective archaeological "facts" divorced from human agency and social interaction, remote from the array of tools and instruments and the skilled technical know-how used to produce them. The official portrait of the excavation level also screens out the active social dialogue that was taking place along the sidelines while this photograph was being taken; this is a happy, relaxing time to enjoy a common accomplishment, take a break, joke with companions, drink some maté, and shoot some less formal shots of the excavation level, none of which is registered in the final level photograph.

Figure 9.1. Excavation block at sixty-three centimeters' depth with tools used to produce archaeological knowledge. (Courtesy of Joan M. Gero)

Figure 9.2. "Official photograph of record" of excavation block at sixty-five centimeters below datum. (Courtesy of Joan M. Gero)

Most tellingly, we fail to see the elaborate (and hilarious) history underlying the accomplishment of the final image: the director balanced first in a wheelbarrow to gain elevation for the wide-angle shot, supported in his precarious stance by two women field crew members, but ultimately abandoning this strategy to recruit a substitute male photographer (Figure 9.3), lighter in weight and build, to sit atop the shoulders of the tallest, strongest, and most "macho" crew member (known on site as "Rambo") to achieve the level photograph shown in Figure 9.2. Ironically, the objectifying "god's eye" aerial perspective is achieved finally not by ignoring or discounting the social circumstances that produced the object of study but by directly affirming, incorporating, and building upon the established social identities of available personnel!

A second familiar practice at Arroyo Seco is the use of the "pedestal" to isolate a significant find, leaving it in place on an unexcavated block of soil matrix while the rest of the level is taken down around it; the purpose of pedestaling artifacts is to preserve the relational positions of (certain) finds as they are encountered in the stratigraphy for future evaluation. This commonly used excavation technique requires individual judgment in selecting finds to leave "pedestaled" since successful pedestaling depends on the "right" number of pedestals being left in the excavation unit: neither too many (which would clutter and complicate the visual perception of stratigraphic order and leave too much soil unexcavated), nor too few (suggesting that the excavator failed to produce valuable data). Success in this activity also depends on the craft aspect of excavation, using the trowel adroitly not to discover artifacts but to render them more visible, which in turn requires producing pleasing-looking pedestals, reducing visual distraction by creating elegant, straight, vertical cuts around finds. But ironically, the socially situated knowledge and the personal technical skill of how to pedestal finds (like the practice sequence of taking level photographs) are employed in service to the idea of a purely natural discovery of data.

Furthermore, the fact that some excavators are more proficient than others at skills of simplifying, enhancing, and displaying data is itself a social product. Pedestaling is learned through observation, repetition, and correction, and some field crew members enjoy more opportunities to improve their skills through these means than do others. In fact, working with competent colleagues and working on parts of the site with interesting finds to pedestal, or even receiving more and better constructive criticism, are themselves largely social outcomes that often depend on assignments by site supervisors, and it is often necessary to have proven yourself or at least to have shown promise by project supervisors' standards to gain access to rapid knowledge. There is no doubt, too, that

Figure 9.3. Technical circumstances required to take the official
photograph of record at sixty-five centimeters below datum.
(Courtesy of Joan M. Gero)

crew members who are "comfortable to work with" and/or who possess attractive physical or personal traits will more readily be selected for sensitive and interesting work assignments. Thus, acquiring a skill like pedestaling proceeds more effectively for personnel who already participate in the knowledge and value system that organizes the archaeological work rather than occurring at the same rate for all project personnel.

At the same time, once acquired, pedestaling (like other data enhancing tasks) is also a powerful social instrument, effectively demonstrating one's skill to colleagues and supervisors by being able to produce a disproportionate amount of useful data for the project. The calculated judgments and instrument-dependent "know-how" of pedestaling can be used to enhance not only the visibility of the data but also one's own position in the excavation hierarchy as "good digging" is recognized and rewarded with greater responsibility. Far from providing a purely factual basis of stratigraphic interpretation, pedestaling constitutes one aspect of a shared, tacit knowledge context that organizes and reproduces, with each practice episode, what is known and who will know it.

Both the preparing of excavation level photographs and the pedestaling of artifacts during excavation show "objectivity" to be an accomplished rather than a natural or transparent rationality; both practices show "objectivity" to be built on shared, assumed, organized social values and practices. Taken together, the unquestioned routine practices of archaeology produce a bounded, internally consistent, disciplined, collective social structure that creates and sustains the factual basis of the community of knowledge-makers. Obscured at this level, however, are the gendered individuals who organize and are organized by practice, and the forms and conventions of social and gendered relations within the practice of archaeology, to which we now turn.

Gender in Practice

Since gender is the most universal social category, operating both functionally (to organize cultural activities) and symbolically (as a system of meanings and social identities), gender would be expected to be manifest at many levels in archaeological practice. At Arroyo Seco, crew members who knew of my interest in gender self-consciously asked if we would be observing on-site flirtations or overtly sexual interactions, and there was some uncomfortable joking about making women carry heavy buckets and move laden wheelbarrows around the site. But my interests lay at a less self-conscious level where gender and science interact, embedded in and renewing the structure of archaeological practice; I also wanted to see how the purportedly gender-neutral practices of archaeology are linked to assertions of power. To witness at least a small number of specific gendered encounters with actual field data in the context of conventional practice would be to go beyond abstract arguments about whether gender politics in some general sense can (or cannot) radically force new constructions of data, whether evidence is (or is not) sufficiently resistant to constructivist politics (cf. Wylie 1992; comments by Fotiadis 1994; Little 1994; Wylie 1994).

In getting beyond, or beneath, the structuring ideologies of gender that most assuredly pervade practice, I will argue that the gender of practitioners makes a difference in knowledge production (although this difference is far from absolute or universal) on three interacting levels. The most inclusive level at which gender insinuates itself in science is at the level of the overarching feminist critique of modern Western rationality as a fundamentally masculinist mode of inquiry, one that values control, autonomy, and separation, and that insists on its ability to proceed objectively and with neutrality. Feminists argue that Western science, far from being value neutral, reflects the dominant categories of cultural experience (white, male, middle-class) and as such, the scientific veneration of objectivity and neutrality have come to be associated with (white, middle-class) masculinity, as opposed to alternative modes of knowledge that might seek, for instance, intimate knowledge and nuanced, even unique understandings of phenomena (Keller 1985). A second largely anecdotal level at which gender insinuates itself in knowledge accumulation suggests that within Western rational science, women undertake a different, "female" style of research practice from men, involving not only less hierarchical and less competitive research relationships, but actually favoring different research approaches, including less emphasis on high technology strategies and a mode of production closer to what has been called "scientific craft production" (Gero 1994; Keller 1985; Rose 1986; *Science* 1993), marked by deeper immersion in a subject with greater attention to complexity and ambiguity. Finally, gender can be seen to interact with science at the level of idiosyncratic, situated practice, where gendered participants on the same project bring the dominant gender ideology to local task arrangements and encounters with data.

Without reviewing the substantial literature that underpins especially the first of these levels, I continue with the perspective that assumed, mundane practice reproduces the context that organizes it, including the gender assumptions and gender relations established in its conduct. This approach necessarily engages the broader constituting levels of feminist thinking, however, as I provide two ethnographic stories from Arroyo Seco about science, practice and gender, hierarchy and objectivity. The first of these addresses power and gender politics within a framework of scientific epistemology called cognitive autonomy; the second addresses gender politics and credibility in relation to the logic of dichotomous thinking.

Ethnographic Story No. 1: Cognitive Autonomy

In the purportedly gender-neutral epistemology of science, a foundational assumption is that "knowers" are autonomous and self-sufficient, and that the objects of knowledge are independent and separate from them (Code 1991:110). Cognitive autonomy and self-sufficiency support a position that rational persons, with detachment and impartial neutrality, will converge on the same knowledge because they are essentially interchangeable self-conscious agents. Note that the "autonomy of knowledge" position places itself beyond the play of power relations (Butler 1992:6) and certainly outside of gender politics.

In archaeological practice, independent observations of data—by dispersed autonomous "knowers" (field crew)—are to count equally and interchangeably in the final summation. The rationalized and generalized (scientific) equivalency of every encounter with data is underscored by having each excavator fill out unit forms, where personality and individual craftsmanship, competence and context, are erased in favor of producing a record of autonomous reason (Gero n.d.). The assumption of cognitive autonomy doesn't discount the need for new fieldworkers to learn observational skills (Edgeworth 1991; Goodwin 1994), but it insists that independent observations should "match" and, with appropriately self-correcting measures, that such observations will accumulate rationally into bodies of knowledge. Each cognitive agent in archaeology is to account for a spatially discrete portion of data, and each portion of data is to count equally in the final analysis.

Clearly, the framework of constructivist knowledge and organized, situated practice contradicts in fundamental ways the operation of a generalized principle like cognitive autonomy and makes us suspicious of the degree to which archaeological practice actually conforms to and can be accounted for in these terms. The rational independence of cognitive agents is untenable, or at least thoroughly compromised, if indeed observations are structured by locally coordinated sequences of activities and embedded in rule structures, epistemic and social, that are in place prior to field observations. Nevertheless, let's return to the construction of pedestals at Arroyo Seco to evaluate how the central scientific principle of cognitive autonomy interacts, in practice, with gender.

We should not be surprised to find significant differences in how pedestals were crafted at Arroyo Seco; the practice of crafting pedestals has already been understood as a socially situated, context-renewing activity, one that in its organization reproduces the setting of which it

Figure 9.4. Franco's large quadrilateral pedestals. (Courtesy of Joan M. Gero)

is an integral part. Not only did pedestals at Arroyo Seco vary in size, but more important the size of a pedestal did not always correspond to the size of the artifacts being pedestaled, even among equally experienced fieldworkers: Franco tended to make large, vertical-walled pedestals even for small artifacts (Figure 9.4), while Laura left artifacts on the smallest possible pedestal surface that would safely sustain the artifact (Figure 9.5). Franco's large pedestals did not conform to the shape of the artifact but were generously cut as predetermined quadrilaterals; Laura's pedestals were crafted to correspond closely to the shape of the artifact by carefully removing soil in a pattern that duplicated the artifact's shape.

These differences in the styling of pedestals, arguably here relating to gender, would be irrelevant within the practiced assumptions of cognitive autonomy: the final level photographs and the hand-drawn level maps provide a record of artifact distributions in situ, whether these were isolated on small or large pedestals. But here we note that data also "count" in other ways, relying on additional context-renewing procedures, in any excavation project. At Arroyo Seco, the site director entered the excavation block during this specific pedestal-making sequence and immediately noted the impressive group of large pedestals

Figure 9.5. Laura's small contoured pedestals. (Courtesy of Joan M. Gero)

arrayed like skyscrapers in Franco's excavation unit. "Objectively," unquestioningly, he requested a feature photograph be taken to isolate
and record just that group of Franco's pedestaled artifacts (which later
proved to be of considerable interest, given what lay below in Franco's
square). Laura's small pedestals were given no special attention, even-
tually to be recorded in the photographs and maps of the level by un-
enhanced channels, but never identified as a significant cluster.

What are we to make of these stylistic differences in producing pedestals and the differential treatment they received? Are we to write them
off as merely an instance of "bad" (misguided? insufficiently coordinated?) practice? It could be that Franco's elevated "International Visi-
tor" status at the site (and his outgoing personality) encouraged him to
magnify the importance of his finds and to exaggerate the size of his
pedestals; the director may "naturally" (politically!) have been hesitant
to correct him and may even have wanted to give him special recognition by attending especially carefully to his work. But this particular
contrast in digging styles and the differential rewards that followed from
it seem better explained, and even predicted, by the common rules of
practice: rendering data more clearly visible is an expected skill, and
a more ambitious, exaggerated style of identifying, isolating, and high-

lighting data, far from being criticized, is precisely the direction of practice that is conventionally recognized as valuable and is rewarded (Lynch 1988:203–4). It is not unwarranted, then, even in this small ethnographic tale, to argue that ambitious, even competitive heightenings of data relate to assertions of power and, moreover, to a "masculinist" pattern of practice. In this reading of the situation, Franco deliberately (if unconsciously) advances his data, pushing it—and himself as its producer—into the limelight of the excavation block.

Scientific logic, of course, disengages itself from such social practices; the epistemology of autonomous cognition establishes a metapolitical basis for negotiations of power (Butler 1992:6). That is, the logic of autonomous reason appears to transcend mere relations of power through appeals to a prior, implicit, universal agreement on what is legitimately to count as an observation. It is this normative universality, this appeal to an abstract, uncontextualized, and generalized neutrality, that is used to deny power. But in fact, the very notion of an abstracted rationality itself constitutes a powerful conceptual practice, a practice that sublimates, disguises, and extends its own power through appeals to objectivity (Butler 1992:6–7). And this, feminists insist, is itself the masculine cognitive mode of science that subverts women's "situated" or "partial" cognitive style (cf. Barbara Little's [1994:541] excellent synopsis of Evelyn Fox Keller's 1985 argument for a historic relationship between gender ideology and the development of Western science).

The construal of the pedestal story as one about power and gender not only undermines the seamless operation of cognitive autonomy in field practice. It raises questions about whether men and women conduct scientific research differently within the positivist, objectivist, rationalist ideology of science identified as masculinist. It touches on the "hush-hush topic" (*Science* 1993:384) that science is not sexless, and that scientific practice is itself dominated by masculinist arrangements, modes of interaction and putting forth arguments, upheld by a litany of anecdotal accounts of masculinist styles of conducting research: more aggressive, more competitive, and more strongly hierarchical (cf. special issue of *Science* [1993]: "Gender and the Culture of Science," Vol. 260:383 ff.). Tentatively, Franco and Laura's story upholds this assertion.

Dichotomous A/Not-A Logic at Arroyo Seco

The second ethnographic story that I promised, about dichotomous reasoning and credibility, follows from a second foundational epistemic position of "malestream" science. Here we confront the peculiar characteristic of scientific logic that places first observations, and ultimately knowledge, in contradictory dichotomous categories, either A or Not-

A ("true" or "not true"), eliminating intermediary positions as logically impossible. Following Nancy Jay (1991), we immediately note that not all dichotomous distinctions are formulated in this logic: the recognition of A and B as distinct categories (sickness/health or man/woman) allows any degree of continuity between them and may even suppose the two categories to have a good deal in common. In such cases, both A and B have a "limited" positive reality, failing to encompass C (that is, a third possibility: hypochondria, or hermaphrodite) and logically permitting the A-B dichotomy to become A-B-C. Thus mere oppositional distinctions are not eternally tied to dichotomous structure, and *as* dichotomies they are limited in scope (Jay 1991:95).

But the logical formulation of A/Not-A posits only one category as having a positive reality while the other category exists as a privation or absence of A. The structure of A/Not-A is such that a third term is impossible: everything and anything must be either A or Not-A (ibid.). This "all-encompassing" quality of binary logic emerges as a consequence of a quality of Not-A referred to as "the infinitation of the negative"; Not-A is extended infinitely and exists without internal boundaries. Thus, A/Not-A covers every possible case of the category and makes further categories, as well as commonality or continuity between categories, logically impossible. Depending as they do on an empty excluded middle, dichotomous A/Not-A constructs obliterate gradation, indeterminancy, overlap, and ambiguity between categories; they deny qualifiers, context, and degree of intensity, stripping a subject of its specificity or variance. The logic of A/Not-A presumes, requires, and in the end actually creates fixed, ready-made, universal objects of knowledge. And, I will argue, it is precisely this logic that is equated, in archaeology as in science more generally, with cognitive mastery and, in the end, with power.

The archaeology at Arroyo Seco illustrates A/Not-A logic in practice, demonstrated now by paired archaeological crew members who work together to construct a level map. At Arroyo Seco (as in most excavations), all soil stains were mapped at the bottom of each ten-centimeter excavation level, whether or not these could be identified at the time as "natural" disturbances (animal burrows, tree root holes, and so on), modern disturbances (plow marks, recent drainage features, and so on), or archaeological cultural indicators (pits, postmolds, trenches, and so on). Mapping teams, almost always gendered pairs, identified the shapes of soil discolorations, outlining the perimeter of each with a trowel tip to isolate the identified stain and measuring its location from established grid points by plotting points along its perimeter. Typically (here and in many other observations of this arrangement), the woman is seated outside the excavation unit as a recorder and the man is inside the excavation unit, measuring and calling out locational points to be mapped.

The negotiation between the "reality" of the soil stain to be mapped and the representation of that stain as it begins to appear on the map requires constant checking by both parties to assure they agree on what is seen and to keep pace with each other as they work around the perimeter of the stain, calling out and recording specific map coordinates. The irregularity of most shapes of stains and the lack of a shared mental template of what is being represented offers the recorder little guidance in predicting where the next point will fall and seeing how it should connect to previous points; smoothly coordinated practice is often challenged in the absence of shared assumptions and prior knowledge. In one observed sequence at Arroyo Seco, the male measurer regularly resolved misunderstandings by displacing the person doing the recording, taking over the pencil and map to make his own corrections when he couldn't communicate the shape of the stain simply by reading off grid coordinates. At another point following a lunch break, this same mapper found himself needing to rely on the emerging map representation to "see" the stain as it "actually" existed in the dirt. Not surprisingly, again, the final knowledge product resulted from a complex, situated, negotiated set of social practices that are obscured by final accounts.

Mapping stains, of course, involves just the kind of dichotomous reasoning discussed above: A or Not-A, "stain" or "not-stain"; we can now turn to gendered practice by comparing two maps from Arroyo Seco. Figure 9.6 shows a stain mapped in Unit 63, level 5: the perimeter of the stain had been clearly delineated and boldly outlined in the soil, then mapped in the same strong, unambiguous lines. Figure 9.7 shows a stain mapped in Unit 65, level 5: here, the perimeter was not easily distinguished and had to be erased and redrawn several times in the soil until its indeterminate boundaries were most closely approximated; the corresponding map is sketched lightly in fainter lines, with layers of erasures. Figure 9.6 offers a politically powerful, assimilable "feature" whose production is recognized as successfully wresting A from Not-A; this mapper moves up in the informal crew hierarchy in terms of cognitive skills. At the same time, Figure 9.7 slips in importance to an indeterminate soil stain, where the available categories of A and Not-A are evidently not accepted as adequate to represent the internal boundaries of Not-A; this mapper shows little mastery of archaeological skills. It may not surprise readers that the first map was made by a man (Juan), the second by a woman (Liliana).

Several additional comments are needed here. Although my observations focus on a single contrastive situation, they suggest a gendered

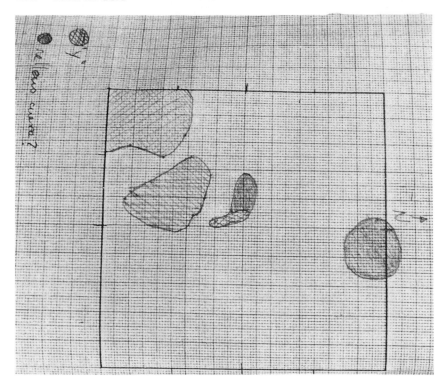

Figure 9.6. Juan's map of stains in Unit 63, level 5. (Courtesy of Joan M. Gero)

pattern of science that many other women have reported felt "right" to them in archaeology and elsewhere. Women, bombarded by a gender ideology of femininity, practice a "feminine" science in which intuition and needing to feel that one has gotten it "right" often overwhelm the politics of advancing one's practice through the hierarchy of practitioners competing to produce useful data (after Keller, quoted in *Science* 1993:392). It is not an insignificant pattern, despite the insignificant "sample size."

In addition, Liliana, whose mapping is discussed here, was new to archaeology while Juan was very experienced. It therefore could be argued that the observed contrast in mapping styles is due more to level of experience than to gender. This may be so, but the contrast still reinforces the point that dichotomous thinking is learned, necessary to the politics of masculinist science, and not always easy. In the "real" world, there is no such entity as "not-stain"; the nonexistent Not-A category requires ignoring or flattening all variation in soil character

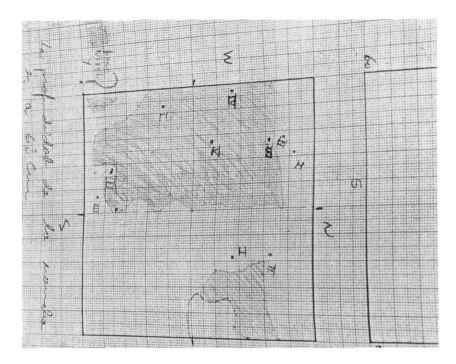

Figure 9.7. Liliana's map of stains in Unit 65, level 5. (Courtesy of Joan M. Gero)

except that which characterizes A. Under other rules of practice, ambiguity and indefiniteness would resolve into finer grained observations, honored as a closer scrutiny by a different eye. Had the woman mapper used the dotted line convention to represent ambiguous stain outlines, preserving A/Not-A, she would have been further along the designated masculinist road to cognitive mastery, but archaeology would not necessarily be any better served: congealing the world in order to clarify it may ultimately cost more than is gained (Jay 1991:101).

Finally, I discussed my observations on gendered mapping with the Arroyo Seco crew at the end of my stay and found considerable disagreement over whether the stains I had watched being mapped were "really" more or less ambiguous in the two instances. Most interestingly, crew members were fiercely divided along gender lines, with men hotly contending that in fact Liliana's stain was less well-defined and difficult to map than Juan's stain, while the women rejected this, insisting that before Juan's stain took on the incontestable status of a trowel-outlined feature, the stain was barely discernible in the ground. Whether this was gender solidarity, or whether women actually saw gradations more acutely—or resisted A/Not-A more actively—I cannot determine.

Concluding Contestations

The two ethnographic stories from Arroyo Seco reveal patterns of encounters with data that are reiterated in other archaeological practices, at this site and elsewhere. The identification, delineation, and highlighting of data are entwined with negotiations of power and gender in a context of rules of practice that assumes and reinforces both scientific and social knowledge. In the end, we find the foundational terms and practices of archaeology coded with values and messages of gender and power, where the most successful styles of practice are undertaken by males, but even more critically where the practices most venerated as "scientific" are symbolically and rhetorically charged as "male." Thus, practices associated with the highly valued (male) attributes of objectivity and autonomy, and free from the disqualifying (female) attributes of subjectivity and interdependence make scientific rationality "masculine" (Keller 1985: chap. 4), and these practices are "re-masculinized" in practice by on-site power hierarchies, where males assert control over such terms and practices.

The point here is not to do away with gendered foundations of science and archaeology but rather to question what is *authorized* by the theoretical and logical positions that establish these foundations, and to note what they exclude or foreclose (Butler 1992:7). If, as Nancy Jay points out, "the rules of logic we choose to inherit are ultimately principles of order" (cited in Harstock 1990:162), then the archaeological practices that lump disorder into a fixed (negative) category, as in the A and Not-A categorizations, and that transform unsettled and doubtful realities into resolved, determinate ones (John Dewey, cited in Jay 1991:101) may also be about social order. That is, where the archaeological rules of practice are categorically closed and oppositional, they are also human-controlling and reinforcing of dichotomy, ideationally and practically. What such practices foreclose may be both rhetorically and at least to some extent contextually gendered as female.

In the account of practice offered here, women archaeologists have attended differently, more closely, to the specificity of the phenomena they encounter, in making pedestals and making maps, and to the extent that they have done so, they have been disqualified from positions of cognitive authority, disadvantaged and disempowered within the male-identified epistemological framework of scientific archaeology. Yet the style of practice identified with women at Arroyo Seco, with its hesitancy to obliterate variance or to homogenize and standardize data presentation, its attention to idiosyncracy, has much to recommend itself. It partakes of a different research tradition, one that Evelyn Fox Keller (1983) describes in her biography of Nobel Prize–winning biogeneticist Barbara McClintock who insisted on an "exceedingly strong feeling" for the oneness of things: "Basically, everything is one. There is no way in which you draw a line between things. What we [normally] do is to make these subdivisions, but they're not real" (McClintock, cited in Keller 1983:198). In preference to imposing a disembodied, external cognitive framework on data, wresting or prying knowledge from nature, the cognitive style that feminists identify with depends on getting in touch with new knowledge, "hear(ing) what the material has to say to you" (ibid.). The women's research style at Arroyo Seco also suggests qualities what Donna Haraway (1988) points to as "situated" and "partial" (feminist) ways of knowing, avoiding the arrogance of overview for the intimacy of what one actually sees. The argument that appears in feminist writings, then, is for a practice that is "close to the ground and honed by the case at hand" (Stacey and Thorne 1985:310, cited in Conkey 1993:9).

By contesting the foundations of this logic, we expose the "silent violence" of the thinking that has operated to marginalize groups who hold to alternative cognitive values: the more particular, more situated, less generalized recording of detailed variance and specificity, the admission of ambiguity and continuity between categories, the experiential accounts. Moreover, a contestation of dichotomous A/Not-A logic forces us to recognize that using unproblematized, nonambiguous categories produces a contingent, internally structured practice of archaeology, which, however, itself remains unproblematized and which itself has a specificity and an experiential accounting that is ignored or rejected in rational accounts of itself. The archaeology that depends on A/Not-A logic and on an ideal of autonomous reason is *one* archaeology, but it is neither the only nor necessarily the most powerful archaeology that could be.

Ironically, of course, gender itself is a dichotomous category, and some feminists have argued that all dualisms have their origin in and relate back to the basic male/female distinction; more importantly, dualisms always involve hierarchies so that dual organization is hierarchical organization (Hekman 1987:79). But there is increasing recognition among scholars of a multiplicity of "feminisms," as gender is seen to crosscut race and class, but also as feminist knowledge increasingly situates and contextualizes the knowledge of specific social groups. In fact, in the end the most productive route through this might be to recognize and embrace a wide range of cognitive styles. We already know that a "masculine" style doesn't map comfortably and with complete correspondence to the male sex, nor does contextualized knowledge converge comfortably with the category of female sex. Defining a more inclusive, feminist archaeological practice, a task that awaits us in the future, will allow distinct cognitive styles to operate. That is not a danger. The danger, instead, is validating only a single research style, a purportedly neutral but ultimately exclusionary and dismissive style.

Acknowledgments

The observations of field practice reported in this study were made possible by the generous invitation and support of Dr. Gustavo Politis, Department of Archaeology at the University of La Plata and director of the Arroyo Seco Archaeological Project in Tres Arroyos, Buenos Aires, Argentina. His enthusiasm for an ethnographic study of his Paleo-Indian project and his extraordinary generosity in allowing us full access to all aspects of fieldwork, record keeping, collections management, and personnel were both rare and exemplary and are hardly repaid by even my most heartfelt admiration and gratitude. Recognizing how distracting it was to have "ethnographers" at the site, an (almost) unprecedented practice in archaeological research, I cannot overstate my appreciation to the entire team of excavators at Arroyo Seco who allowed us to peer continuously over their shoulders, question what was undertaken, video and take slides of all stages of work, and generally position ourselves in awkward and bothersome relations to their important work. With supreme gratitude for being allowed to intrude and for teaching me so much about the organization of archaeological practice, I acknowledge the following (note that crew members' names mentioned in the text are fictitious): Gustavo Politis, Alejandro Acosta, Gustavo Barrientos, Monica Beron, Maria del Carmen Langiano, Maria Luz Endere, Susana Garcia, Anahi Ginarte, Gustavo Gomez, Maria Gutierrez, Cecilia Landini, Marcela Leipus, Patricia Madrid, Sergio Magallanes, Julio Merlo, Victor Monje, Miguel "Chuli" Mugueta, Pablo Ormazabal, Roberto "Charlie" Peretti, Julietta Soncini, Marta Roa, and Fernando Oliva, all of Argentina, as well as the visiting international participants, Zoe Crossland (England), Arturo Jaime (Venezuela), Eileen Johnson (United States), Maribel Martinez (Spain), and Julian Ortiz (Colombia). The excellent companionship itself was a wonderful experience. Financial costs of undertaking this study were partially supported by the Universidad de Buenos Aires en Olavarria, Facultad de Ciencias Sociales, to whom I also extend my gratitude.

Fieldwork observations at Arroyo Seco were undertaken with Charles Goodwin, my colleague at the University of South Carolina, with whom I shared many invigorating discussions about contextualized knowledge and situated practices. Many of his thoughts about interactive practice are by now interwoven with my own and are reflected in this chapter, derived from our common observations, discussions, and readings. Nevertheless, neither Chuck Goodwin nor Gustavo Politis, both crucially involved in this research, should be understood to agree with the interpretations of fieldwork I put forward here.

Earlier drafts of this work have benefited considerably from discussions in different invited anthropology colloquiums: the College of Charleston, Tulane University, University of South Carolina, and the Universities of Tromso and Bergen in Norway. I owe special thanks to Rita Wright for her patience and encouragement, Dolores Root for a helpful critique, and Alison Wylie for her exceptionally generous and insightful comments on this chapter. The many flaws are mine. Finally, I would like to dedicate this piece to my mom who knew my excitement for this work and was eager to hear its outcome.

Note

1. At Arroyo Seco, "level photographs" were taken at the bottom of each excavated level for the area covered by the four contiguous two-by-two-meter excavation units that had been opened simultaneously at the beginning of the field season. A fifth two-by-two-meter excavation unit was opened later, with the arrival of additional field crew, but because this unit was initiated after the others and was therefore always shallower than the units started earlier, "level photographs" only recorded the sixteen-square-meter levels of the original four excavation units.

References

Butler, Judith
  1992 "Contingent Foundations: Feminism and the Question of 'Postmodernism.'" In *Feminists Theorize the Political*, edited by J. Butler and J. Scott, 3–21. New York: Routledge.
Claassen, Cheryl, ed.
  1992 *Exploring Gender through Archaeology: Selected Papers from the 1991 Boone Conference*. Madison, Wis.: Prehistory Press.
  1994 *Women in Archaeology*. Philadelphia: University of Pennsylvania Press.
Code, Lorraine
  1991 *What Can She Know? Feminist Theory and the Construction of Knowledge*. Ithaca, N.Y.: Cornell University Press.
Conkey, Margaret W.
  1993 "Making the Connections: Feminist Theory and Archaeologies of Gender." In *Women in Archaeology: A Feminist Critique*, edited by H. du Cros and L. Smith, 3–15. Canberra: Department of Prehistory, Australian National University.
Conkey, Margaret, and Janet Spector
  1984 "Archaeology and the Study of Gender." In *Advances in Archaeological Method and Theory*, edited by M. Schiffer, 7:1–38. New York: Academic Press.
du Cros, Hilary, and Laurajane Smith, eds.
  1993 *Women in Archaeology: A Feminist Critique*. Canberra: Department of Prehistory, Australian National University.
Edgeworth, Matthew
  1991 "The Act of Discovery: An Ethnography of the Subject-Object Relation in Archaeological Practice." Ph.D. thesis, Department of Anthropology and Archaeology, University of Durham.
Fotiadis, Michael
  1994 "What Is Archaeology's 'Mitigated Objectivism' Mitigated By? Comments on Wylie." *American Antiquity* 59:545–55.
Fowler, Don
  1987 "Uses of the Past: Archaeology in the Service of the State." *American Antiquity* 52:229–48.

Garfinkle, Harold
    1967   *Studies in Ethnomethodology.* Englewood Cliffs, N.J.: Prentice Hall.
Gathercole, Peter, and David Lowenthal, eds.
    1990   *The Politics of the Past.* London: Unwin Hyman.
Gero, Joan M.
    1985   "Socio-politics and the Woman-at-Home Ideology." *American Antiquity* 50:342–50.
    1993   "The Social World of Prehistoric Facts: Gender and Power in Paleo-indian Research." In *Women in Archaeology: A Feminist Critique,* edited by H. du Cros and L. Smith, Occasional Papers in Prehistory No. 23, 31–40. Canberra: Department of Prehistory, Australian National University.
    1994   "Gender Division of Labor in the Construction of Archaeological Knowledge in the U.S.A." In *The Social Construction of the Past: Representation as Power,* edited by George Bond and Angela Gilliam, 144–53. New York: Routledge.
    N.d.   "Archaeology (In)Forms." Paper presented to the Department of Archaeology, University of Cambridge, November 1991.
Gero, Joan M., and Margaret W. Conkey, eds.
    1991   *Engendering Archaeology: Women and Prehistory.* Oxford: Basil Blackwell.
Gero, Joan, David Lacy, and Michael Blakey, eds.
    1983   *The Socio-politics of Archaeology.* Research Report No. 23. Amherst: Department of Anthropology, University of Massachusetts.
Gilbert, G. Nigel, and Michael Mulkay
    1984   *Opening Pandora's Box: A Sociological Analysis of Scientists' Discourse.* Cambridge: Cambridge University.
Goodwin, Charles
    1994   "Professional Vision." *American Anthropologist* 96:606–33.
Goodwin, Charles, and Marjorie Harness Goodwin
    N.d.   "Formulating Planes: Seeing as a Situated Activity." In *Cognition and Communication at Work,* edited by D. Middleton and Yrjo Engestrom. Cambridge: Cambridge University Press.
Handsman, Russell, and Mark Leone
    1989   "Living History and Critical Archaeology in the Reconstruction of the Past." In *Critical Traditions in Contemporary Archaeology,* edited by V. Pinsky and A. Wylie, 117–35. Cambridge: Cambridge University Press.
Haraway, Donna
    1988   "Situated Knowledges: The Science Question in Feminism and the Privilege of Partial Perspective." *Feminist Studies* 14:575–99.
Harstock, Nancy
    1990   "Foucault on Power: A Theory for Women?" In *Feminism/Postmodernism,* edited by L. Nicholson, 157–75. New York: Routledge.
Hekman, Susan
    1987   "The Feminization of Epistemology: Gender and the Social Sciences." *Women and Politics* 7 (3): 65–83.
Heritage, John
    1984   *Garfinkle and Ethnomethodology.* Cambridge: Polity Press.
Jay, Nancy
    1991   "Gender and Dichotomy." In *A Reader in Feminist Knowledge,* edited by Sneja Gunew, 89–106. New York: Routledge.

Keller, Evelyn Fox
   1983   *A Feeling for the Organism: The Life and Work of Barbara McClintock.* New
          York: W. H. Freeman.
   1985   *Reflections on Gender and Science.* New Haven, Conn.: Yale University
          Press.
Latour, Bruno, and Steve Woolgar
   1979   *Laboratory Life.* Beverly Hills: Sage Library of Social Research.
Little, Barbara
   1994   "Consider the Hermaphroditic Mind." *American Antiquity* 59:539–44.
Lynch, Michael
   1985   *Art and Artifact in Laboratory Science: A Study of Shop Work and Shop Talk
          in a Research Laboratory.* London: Routledge.
   1988   "The External Retina: Selection and Mathematization in the Visual
          Documentation of Objects in the Life Sciences." *Human Studies* 11:201–
          34.
Pinsky, Valerie, and Alison Wylie, eds.
   1989   *Critical Traditions in Contemporary Archaeology.* Cambridge: University of
          Cambridge Press.
Politis, Gustavo
   1984   "Investigaciones arqueologicas en el area Interserrana Bonaerense."
          Etnia 32:7–21.
   1986   "Archaeological Investigations at Site 2 of Arroyo Seco, in Tres Arroyos,
          Province of Buenos Aires, Argentina." In *New Evidence for the Pleistocene
          Peopling of the Americas,* edited by A. Bryan, 222–69. Orono, Maine:
          Center for the Study of Early Man.
   1989   "Quien mató al Megaterio?" *Ciencia Hoy* 1 (2): 26–35.
Politis, Gustavo, and Monica Salemme
   1989   "Pre-Hispanic Mammal Exploitation and Hunting Strategies in the
          Eastern Pampa Subregion of Argentina." In *Hunters of the Recent Past,*
          edited by Leslie Davis and Brian Reeves, 352–72. London: Unwin
          Hyman.
Pollner, Melvin
   1974   "Mundane Reasoning." *Philosophy of the Social Sciences* 4:35–54.
Rose, Hilary
   1986   "Beyond Masculine Realities: A Feminist Epistemology for the Sci-
          ences." In *Feminist Approaches to Science,* edited by Ruth Bleier, 57–76.
          London: Pergamon Press.
Science
   1993   "Gender and the Culture of Science." *Science* 260:383 ff.
Walde, Dale, and Noreen Willows, eds.
   1991   *The Archaeology of Gender: Proceedings of the 23rd Annual Chacmool Con-
          ference.* Calgary: Archaeological Association, Department of Archae-
          ology, University of Calgary.
Wilk, Richard
   1985   "The Ancient Maya and the Political Present." *Journal of Anthropologi-
          cal Research* 41:307–26.
Wobst, H. Martin, and Arthur Keene
   1983   "Archaeological Explanation as Political Economy." In *The Socio-politics
          of Archaeology,* edited by J. Gero, D. Lacy, and M. Blakey, 79–89. Am-
          herst: Department of Anthropology Research Report Series No. 23,
          University of Massachusetts.

Wylie, Alison
    1992   "The Interplay of Evidential Constraints and Political Interests: Recent
            Archaeological Research on Gender." *American Antiquity* 57:15–35.
    1994   "On 'Capturing Facts Alive in the Past' (Or Present): Response to Fo-
            tiadis and to Little." *American Antiquity* 59:556–60.

Contributors

Gillian R. Bentley is a Royal Society Research Fellow at the University of Cambridge, England. She has trained both as an archaeologist and as a bioanthropologist, conducting fieldwork primarily in the Middle East and Africa. Her research interests are in reproductive ecology, with the long-term goal of explaining the evolution of human reproductive physiology and behavior.

Elizabeth M. Brumfiel is a professor of anthropology and Chair, Department of Anthropology and Sociology, Albion College. She has directed archaeological investigations at three Aztec hinterland sites in the Basin of Mexico. She focuses on two research questions: how social inequality has been and is constructed along the lines of class, gender, and ethnicity, and how struggles for status within human groups sometimes lead to social change.

Margaret W. Conkey is a professor of anthropology at the University of California, Berkeley, where she also is Director of the Archaeological Research Facility. She is currently carrying out fieldwork in the Midi-Pyrénées of France, focusing on the social geography of the material and visual culture of the peoples of the late Ice Age, which involves regional open air survey and distributional and landscape archaeology. She has worked on the interpretation of Paleolithic art, on issues of style in archaeology, and on issues of gender and feminist archaeology. She is currently President-Elect of the Association for Feminist Anthropology of the American Anthropological Association.

Cathy Lynne Costin is a lecturer in anthropology at California State University, Northridge. She has conducted extensive archaeological fieldwork and ethnohistoric research to document the technology and organization of pottery and textile production in the prehispanic complex societies of Andean South America. Her focus on specialization as social labor forms the framework for her research on the origins and economic, social, and political ramifications of divisions of labor.

Joan M. Gero is an associate professor of anthropology at the University of South Carolina. She conducts her own archaeological excavations in early complex societies of the Andes, in the Callejon de Huaylas area of northcentral Peru and, more recently, in northwestern Argentina. Her ongoing interest in archaeological constructions of knowledge and practical constructions of gender persist in increasingly self-reflexive methodologies, as she promises next to turn her critical eye upon her own organizational framework and decision-making in the field.

Rosemary A. Joyce is an associate professor of anthropology and director of the Phoebe Apperson Hearst Museum of Anthropology at the University of California, Berkeley. Her fieldwork in Honduras is aimed at understanding the dynamics of social relations of an area long considered simply a passive periphery for the Classic Maya. In pursuit of this goal, she has been led to investigations of settlement patterns, analyses of pottery, and interpretations of texts and images from both Maya and non-Maya traditions of Lower Central America.

Judith A. McGaw is an associate professor of the history of technology at the University of Pennsylvania. She is completing a study of American womens' relationship to feminine technologies, such as those discussed in her essay, and masculine technologies, such as the gun. The work also examines how technologies become gendered.

Janet V. Romanowicz is an advanced graduate student in the Department of Anthropology at New York University. Her field experience includes excavations at Upper Paleolithic rock shelters in France, medieval sites in England and Wales, and contact period North America. Her recent research focuses on aspects of social, political, and economic interaction and change in Anglo-Saxon/Early Medieval England (c. A.D. 400–1066), as well as an exploration of the relationship between historical and archaeological sources of evidence.

Ruth E. Tringham is a professor of anthropology at the University of California, Berkeley. She has carried out archaeological fieldwork at many Neolithic sites in Southeast and Central Europe. She focuses on the life histories of villages and people and the construction of prehistoric places through analysis and reconstruction of architecture and landscapes. She has written and is writing conventional linear monographs reporting this research and is currently working on a feminist-oriented, non-linear hypermedia product for CD-ROM publication that interprets the research of her excavations at Opovo, in the former Yugo-slavia.

Rita P. Wright is an associate professor of anthropology at New York University. Her research interests are in the social relations of production and distribution, especially gender and class divisions of labor in early complex societies. She has conducted fieldwork in Afghanistan, Iran, and Pakistan and currently is involved in excavations at the large urban settlement of Harappa in the Indus Valley civilization and directing a settlement survey of sites in its hinterlands.

Author Index

Subject Index

Ache, 28, 31
Aegean, 9
Age: at marriage, 31; at weaning, 31
Agricultural groups, 7, 26, 29, 79
Agriculture: advent of, 36–37; development of, 25, 36; societies, 25–28; surplus, 36; technology, 29
American Anthropological Association, 204, 213
American midwest: Archaic period, 37, Middle and Late Woodland periods, 35–37; Mississipian period, 37
American popular culture, 205–6
Ancient matriarchies, 14
Androcentrism, 4
Animal and plant remains, 205–12
Archaeological research: archaeological record, 38, 201, 205, 218; constructing prehistory, 239; cultural dynamics and "context," 12, 199, 227, 252, 253, 255–58, 264–67, 270; data, 255, 259; "facts," 203, 234; ecofacts, 205–12; evidence, 4–5; "fieldwork," 258–59; hierarchy, 253, 264; interpretation, 206, 208, 225, 230, 232–34, 236, 241; unity of science, 253
Archaeology: and popular culture, 230; and the goddess, 199, 201, 225–26, 229–34, 244; household, 204–5; Inkan, 9, 16, 123–33; material culture, 205, 209–10; Mayan, 167–88; media representation, 201, 206, 217, 232–33, 237; Mediterranean, 199, 230, 233–35, 244–45; Mesoamerican, 148–62; narratives, 232, 236–37; New Archaeology, 200, 212; prehistory of Europe, 199, 226–35, 244; storytelling in, 236; teaching of, 224–26

Architecture: and family size, 24; building technology, 59–60; households, 202, 207–10
Argentina, 12, 251, 258–77
Artifacts, 202, 205; analysis of, 209
Artisanry, 114, 119–20
Ashante, 123
Austen, Jane, 60
Automobiles, 56, 69
Aymara, 180
Azerbaijan, 105
Aztec, 9–10, 14–15, 181–82, 187–88, 190

Bathroom, 52, 67–68
Bathtub, 67
Bioarchaeological evidence, 6, 35
Bioarchaeology, 2, 25, 33, 35–36
Biology and technology, 55, 57, 68–70
Bra burning, 56, 71n.6
Brassiere, 7, 52, 54–58, 68–69
Breastfeeding, 27, 33–34, 39
Brummel, Beau, 64
Bureau, 59

Cabinet, 57–60, 66
Cargo system, 185–86
Carthage, 38–39
Ceramics, 37, 44, 146–62; in ritual, 122, 170, 178, 180, 183, 188; production of, 117
Chachawarmi, 180
Chamula, 174
Childe, V. Gordon, 82
Children: birth intervals, 27, 29; breast feeding, 27, 33–34, 39; childbirth, 2, 38;

Pleistocene, 26
Popular: culture, 201–3; literature, 201;
magazines, 204–6
Population: densities of, 26; increase in,
26–28; levels, 24–25, 29; migration, 25;
prehistoric, 26; pressure, 28. *See also*
Malthusian models
Prehistoric art, 229, 239–45
Prehistoric belief systems, 230, 244

Reindeer Moon, 236
Religion: Aztec, 145, 149, 182; Mesopotamian, 99
Reproduction, 13, 24, 31, 39, 211; abortion, 7, 25, 37–38; aerobic exercise,
36; amenorrhea, 35; and age at marriage, 30; biological parameters, 6, 13;
contraception, 25–26, 30, 37; disease,
25, 27–29, 32, 34; energy output, 29,
36, 37; fertility, 9, 13, 23–32, 35, 39;
energy output, 29, 36, 37; infanticide,
25; interbirth intervals, 27, 33, 35, 39–
40; gestation, 31; menarche, 27, 31–32,
35; menopause, 24, 27, 31–32; nonenvironmental factors, 6; nutritional
stress, 25, 29, 34–37; premenarcheal,
24, 31–32; proximate determinants of
fertility, 30–31; workload stress, 13, 25,
29, 37. *See also* Children; States
Reproductive: ecologists, 3; ecology, 4,
6, 13, 25, 26, 29, 39, 199; patterns, 6,
26–27
Ritual, 10, 15; cargo systems, 185–87; illness and curing, 145–49; imagery, 168–
69, 178, 185, 190. *See also* Household
rituals

Sausa, 210
Science: contextual assumptions, 254;
critique of, 14; hierarchies, 252, 265,
269, 271–72, 274–75; objectivity, 256,
259, 262, 265, 268–69, 274; rationality,
255, 257–58, 266, 269, 274; studies,
251–55; subjectivity, 274. *See* Archaeological research; Feminist critiques of
archaeology
Seals, personal, 86
Second Industrial Revolution, 56
Sites: Arroyo Seco, 12, 251, 258–73; Ashkelon, 39; Chichen Itza, 169, 172;

Copan, 175–76, 183, 202; Huexotla,
149–53, 155, 160; Lepenski Vir, 234–
36, 245; Naranjo, 173, 175–76, 183–84;
Opovo, 235; Palenque, 170, 183–85;
Piedras Negras, 175, 184; Templo
Mayor, 146–47, 156; Teotihuacan, 147;
Tenochtitlan, 10, 153, 154; Texcoco, 151;
Tikal, 170, 173, 183–84; Varna, 244; Xal-
tocan, 149–151, 153, 155; Xico, 149–53,
160; Xultun, 175–77, 183–85; Yaxchilan,
170, 183–84
Skeletal remains, 6, 16, 30, 32, 34–37, 119;
chemical analysis, 32–33; composition,
33–34; dentition, 33–35, 37; lesions on,
31; osteological, 28, 32, 35–39
Software knowledge, 7, 60–62, 66, 69,
83–84
Source readings, 204, 229
Spatial symbolism, 172–76
Spindle whorls, 100, 125–26
Spinning, 125–27, 145
States: and reproduction, 102–3, 114–16,
160, 162n.9, 169, 176, 182, 188–90; conquest, 118; formation of, 103, 146, 168,
188, 201; elites, 79, 168–69; ideological
domination, 144, 146; ideologies, 14, 80,
131, 144, 149; kinship groups, 103, 168,
189–90; land holding, 84, 89–91, 98,
101; non-elites, 79; peasant groups, 10,
148; policies, 14, 80, 102–4; resistance
to, 146; status of women, 80, 144–46,
156–60, 182, 189. *See also* Class; Gender
and class; Weavers
Storage: of food, 58; technology, 59–61,
69
Strontium/calcium ratios, 33–34

Teachers, as mediators, 227, 232, 246–47
Teaching: banking method, 203, 226;
coaching model, 12, 15, 226–27, 245;
evaluations, 246–47; formats, 204, 212,
215, 225, 228; fragments, 246; graduate
level, 11, 200, 212–16; interdisciplinary,
245–46; museum collections, 241;
panels, 227–32, 234–47; performance
model, 12, 225–26; reading assignments,
204, 229; team teaching, 225, 227
Technological: choice, 54, 63, 69; history,
4, 53; knowledge, 53, 62–63, 94–95
Technology: and archaeology, 81–82; and